LIVING SPANISH

LIVING SPANISH

R. P. LITTLEWOOD, B.A., F.I.L., F.I.A.L.

*Head of the Department of Modern Languages and
General Education at the Charles Keene College of
Further Education, Leicester*

UNIVERSITY OF LONDON PRESS LTD

Tape recordings of *Living Spanish* are available
from the Tutor-Tape Company Ltd, 258 Wimbledon
Park Road, London SW19

ISBN 0 340 15630 9

First published 1949
Twelfth impression 1971

University of London Press Ltd
St Paul's House, Warwick Lane, London EC4P 4AH

Printed and bound in Great Britain by
Hazell Watson and Viney Ltd, Aylesbury, Bucks

PREFACE

THIS book is intended primarily for students in commercial and technical institutes, and for private students preparing for such examinations as the elementary stages of the Royal Society of Arts, the Institute of Linguists, etc. The book can hardly be said to be commercial in character, nor is such intended. It has been my experience that students enrolling for language courses usually fall into two broad categories : those who wish to learn " commercial Spanish " for business reasons and who state that they are not otherwise interested in the language, and those who desire to learn the language for cultural reasons or for purposes of travel. The latter either give no opinion at all or state categorically that they desire to avoid " school Spanish " at all costs. What is meant by " commercial Spanish " is usually not at all clear, but it will be agreed that it is essential from the outset to stress the point that a language is something living, with a wide background, and not merely a mechanical means of communicating thought. Once a student becomes interested in the language for its own sake, the rest follows naturally, and he will be able to fit his own specialised requirements into the general scheme later on. As for " school Spanish," there is much to support the student's insistence upon a more intensive course than is usually possible with younger people, for, after all, the average student will be in a position to devote at the most only two hours per week to actual class work, and, unless progress is both rapid and tolerably interesting, his enthusiasm will tend to wane.

The present book is based largely on material that has been used in evening classes over a course of years, and a definite attempt has been made to provide a fairly broad

5

background to the language and a solid foundation on which to build further studies. The average student should have no difficulty in assimilating the material over the period of a year's evening classes. The chapters cover a wide range of topics, which, it is hoped, will prove of interest to the student.

Each chapter is divided into four sections : the reading piece, notes, grammar, and exercises.

The reading pieces are based for the most part on personal impressions and experiences, but in two cases the text was suggested by Spanish writers. For instance, the chapter entitled " Las Moscas " is a version of the anecdote to be found in Julio Camba's *Londres*, and the chapter entitled " Viaje en Tercera Clase " contains the story as suggested by Jacinto Benavente's play *No Fumadores*. The vocabulary of these pieces is fairly wide and varied and, whilst there is intended repetition, it is hoped that this is not too obvious. All the pieces have been tried out in actual class teaching.

The purpose of the notes is fourfold : to afford explanations of difficult or linguistically interesting words and expressions, to expand existing vocabulary, to supplement certain grammatical points, and finally to provide material for discussions in either Spanish or English. It is, in fact, an excellent plan to devote perhaps a quarter of an hour to such discussions or lecturettes, even at the very early stages of learning the language.

The grammar is intended to cover the more elementary points and is introduced, as far as possible, in correlation with the reading pieces. The arrangement is, of necessity, sometimes rather scattered, but it is hoped that the table of contents will prove helpful in enabling students to locate any section for the purpose of reference. Again there is repetition which is intentional.

No list of words is given after the reading pieces, since

it is intended that the teacher should deal orally with the subject before any attempt is made to read or translate. The pieces are designed to this end and generally each piece bears some relation, either from the point of view of subject or vocabulary, to the preceding text. In all cases it should be possible to " get across " the general meaning at any rate by action, gesture, and simple explanation. The private student should endeavour to puzzle out the meaning of words before having recourse to the vocabulary at the end of the book.

Most of the exercises are based on the direct method, but material is provided for translation from English into Spanish, based on the reading pieces. Certain exercises are, by their construction, designed to lead up to the writing of free composition, which, of course, should evolve gradually from the outset.

After each fifth chapter are added recapitulation exercises.

Finally, vocabularies are appended at the end of the book. The Spanish–English vocabulary is comprehensive and illustrated by numerous examples. The meanings given are usually those occurring in the texts.

There are no separate lists of irregular verbs, radical changing verbs, etc., since it has been thought more convenient to include them in the Spanish–English vocabulary in alphabetical order. Thus, in the case of the verb *poner*, for example, the student will find the irregular forms, the idiomatic uses, etc., all under the one heading.

The introduction contains notes and exercises on pronunciation, etc., but it will be realised that to acquire a correct pronunciation it is essential to have access to a fluent Spanish speaker. Alternatively, several tape-recordings and gramophone records of spoken Spanish are now available. Particularly useful for beginners are those dealing with the sounds of Spanish.

CONTENTS

The Spanish alphabet. Pronunciation—vowels,
diphthongs, triphthongs, consonants. Accentua-
tion—stress, the written accent. Diæresis.
Sinalefa. Exercises. Punctuation. Use of capital
letters. Regional differences in pronunciation.

Notes to vocabulary.

Grammar: The singular definite and indefinite
articles—*el*, *la*, *un*, *una*. The gender of nouns
ending in *-o*, *-a*, *-e* or a consonant. Contraction
of the definite article—*del*, *al*. Possession.
Third person singular of the present indicative
tense. Infinitives. Omission of subject pronouns. Questions — inversion, interrogative
words, question marks. Negation—omission of
indefinite article after a negative. Partitive
expressions.

Exercises.

Notes to vocabulary.

Grammar: The plural definite and indefinite
articles—*los*, *las*, *unos*, *unas*. The omission of
the indefinite article in the partitive sense. The
plural of nouns ending in *-o*, *-a*, *-e* or a consonant.
The gender of nouns ending in *-ión*. The agreement and position of adjectives. Nouns used
adjectively. Third person plural of the present
indicative tense. Comparison of *está* and *es*.

Exercises

Notes to vocabulary.

Grammar : Demonstrative adjectives—*este, ese,* etc. Demonstrative pronouns—*éste, ése,* etc. Cardinal numbers 21–100—*cien.* Expressions of time—the hour. Formation of adverbs. Radical changing verbs—*atravesar, costar, volver, preferir.* Irregular verbs of the present indicative—*venir, poner.* Impersonal verb—*llover.*

Exercises.

Notes to vocabulary.

Grammar : Interrogative pronouns—*qué, quién, cuál,* adjectival use of *qué,* exclamatory use of *qué.* Relative pronouns—*que, quien, el cual, cuyo, lo que.* Cardinal numbers 100–1000—*mil.* Radical changing verbs—*pedir.* Verbs of the type *conocer.* Changes of spelling—*vencer, dirigir, distinguir.* Irregular verbs of the present indicative—*oir.*

Exercises.

Notes to vocabulary.

Grammar : Object personal pronouns (conjunctive)—*me, te, le,* etc., position and order of pronouns. Reflexive verbs. Use of reflexive verb to replace English passive form. Reflexive pronouns. Future indicative tense. Irregular verbs of the future indicative—*tener, decir, poder, haber, hacer.* Future perfect tense. Irregular past participle—*dicho.* Comparison of *gustar* and *querer.* Impersonal verb—*habrá. Saber* and *conocer.*

Exercises.

Notes to vocabulary.

Grammar : Object personal pronouns continued (conjunctive)—juxtaposition of third person forms, the question of ambiguity. Personal pronouns preceded by a preposition (disjunctive

INTRODUCTION

THE SPANISH ALPHABET

THE Spanish alphabet has 29 letters. Of these, 25 are common to English and Spanish. *W* does not exist in Spanish. In addition, Spanish counts as separate letters:

ch	China	ñ	niño
ll	calle	rr	perro

The letter *k*, however, is little used, and occurs only in a few words of foreign origin:

kilómetro

PRONUNCIATION

Vowels

In Spanish the pronunciation of the vowels is constant. Wherever Spanish is spoken, the vowels have the same value. Compared with English, the pronunciation of the Spanish vowel is much more tense. English vowels are generally " diphthongised " and very often vary in value according to position. For instance:

a cantata—where each *a* has a different sound.

Remember that Spanish vowels have always the same value, but vary occasionally in length and are pronounced more or less open, according as to whether they occur in open or closed syllables. For example:

In an open syllable (i.e. not closed by a consonant)

me-sa   **co-mo**

the vowels are more closed in pronunciation than in the case of a closed syllable (i.e. a syllable closed by a consonant):

el   **ver-de**

Thus, in the pronunciation of **postre**, the *o* is more open than in the case of **poco**.

A. The Spanish *a* is not like the English *a*, either as in *father* or as in *sat*, but rather resembles the French *chat*. The Spanish *a* is pronounced with the tongue flat and the mouth fairly open.

casa **criar**

Note that in such a word as **patata**, each *a* has precisely the same value : **pa-ta-ta**.

In front of a vowel or consonant which is pronounced at the back of the mouth, and in front of *l*, the vowel *a* is pronounced correspondingly farther back.

causa **paja** **canal**

Exercise

Read the following :

casa mata patata pan la al paja pausa sal

E. The pronunciation of the Spanish *e* in an open syllable almost corresponds to the French *é*, as in *café*, and in a closed syllable to the more open sound, as in *mais*.

Beware of pronouncing the closed sound as in the English *pay*, where the vowel is "diphthongised." It is good practice to prolong the closed sound of *é*, making quite sure that there is no tendency to pronounce a diphthong instead of the pure vowel.

In open syllables and in syllables closed by -*s* or -*n*, the Spanish *e* is closed :

me-sa **es-to** **sen-ta-da**

In closed syllables the Spanish *e* is more open :

sa-ber **el** **ver-de**

Before the consonant *rr* the *e* is very open :

pe-rro

Exercise

Read the following :

este   pelo   enero   ser   saben   le   entrar   madre

I (also *y* at the end of a word). The Spanish *i* is not pronounced as the English *fit*, but rather resembles the French as in *fille*. It is similar to the English *me*, but is more closed, more tense, and never "diphthongised."

ri-ca   mil   pi-la   rey

Exercise

Read the following :

gritar   escribir   ley   casita   sí   sin

O. In the pronunciation of the Spanish *o*, the lips are more rounded than in the case of the English.

In an open syllable the Spanish *o* resembles the French as in *beau*.

co-mo   la-go   can-to   lo

In closed syllables the Spanish *o* is more like the French as in *chose*.

en-can-ta-dor   mon-te   son-ri-sa

Exercise

Read the following :

comestible   contar   cola   cacao   los   cosecha   col

U. The sound resembles the English *pool*, but the lips are more rounded and pushed farther forward than in the case of the English. Compare the French *poule*. The Spanish *u* is generally closed and is never loosely pronounced as in English.

cum-bre   cu-na   cu-ca-ra-cha

Exercise

Read the following :

culebra   legumbre   mudar   museo   música   suma

Diphthongs

When strong vowels (i.e. *a, e, o*) come together, they retain their individual values and are pronounced separately.

> ca-o-ba   co-rre-o   co-rre-a

When a strong vowel is followed by a weak vowel (*i, u*), the strong vowel takes the main stress and the weak vowel loses some of its value.

AI baile	EI rey	OI soy
AU causa	EU Europa	

When a weak vowel precedes a strong vowel and follows a consonant, the strong vowel again takes the stress, and the weak vowel becomes itself semi-consonantal.

> IA, UA   hacia   cuando
>
> IE, UE   bien   cuento
>
> IO, UO   patio   antiguo

When two weak vowels come together, the second takes the main stress and the first becomes semi-consonantal.

> IU   ciudad   UI   cuidado

Triphthongs

When three vowels (two weak and one strong) come together, the strong vowel again takes the stress.

UEI(Y) buey   IAI estudiáis   IEI estudiéis

UAI(Y) Uruguay

Exercise

Read the following :

soy ley cambia Paraguay cielo cual cuenta

Consonants

B, V. In the spoken language no distinction is made between these two letters. There are two pronunciations, according to position :

(*a*) Pronounced as the English *b* at the beginning of a breath group, and after *n* or *m*.

Buenos Aires también vamos al teatro

un buen plato buen vino

(*b*) The other sound is neither the English *b* nor tne English *v*. The Spanish sound is produced if one tries to pronounce the English *b*, but with the lips slightly open, so that the air passes through a narrow slit. This pronunciation occurs whenever the Spanish *b* or *v* are in positions other than those mentioned in (*a*) :

saber lavar estaba una copa de vino esta ventana

The English *v* does not exist at all in Spanish. The uneducated Spaniard has, in fact, great difficulty in distinguishing the written letters, and it is no uncommon thing to see painted on the walls of country inns :

Aquí se bende bino (for Aquí se vende vino—wine sold here).

C. This letter has two pronunciations in Spanish :

(*a*) Pronounced as *k* when followed by *a*, *o*, or *u*, or by a consonant :

calor costar cumbre clase

(*b*) Pronounced as the English *th* (as in *think*), when followed by *i* or *e* :

cielo   **celoso**   **céntimo**   **preciso**

K. The same sound as the *c* followed by *a, o, u.* Is found only in one or two words of foreign origin.

kilómetro   **kilogramo**

Q. The letter *q* is always found in conjunction with *u*. *qu* is always followed either by *i* or *e*. The hard *c, k,* and *qu* have precisely the same sound.

quitar   **que**   **quinta**   **querer**

Z. *z* has the same sound as *c* followed by *i* or *e*, i.e. the sound of *th* as in the English *think*.

zapato   **zorro**   **zumo**

Occasionally *z* is followed by *i* or *e*.

zeta (the name of the letter *z*)   **zinc**

CH. This letter has the same sound as the English *ch* in *chip*. It never has the sound of the French *ch*.

muchacho   **mucho**

D. This letter has three distinct pronunciations, according to position.

(*a*) At the beginning of the breath group or after *l* and *n* the Spanish *d* is similar to the English.

duro   **un día**   **el día**   **Don Alberto iba a la iglesia**

(*b*) In the middle of a word or breath group the Spanish *d* is very much softer and resembles the English *th* as in *though*.

cuidar   padre   nada   le he dado el libro

(*c*) At the end of a word or in the termination -*ado* the Spanish *d* has even a softer pronunciation, and in popular speech tends to disappear altogether.

usted   ciudad   hemos terminado

F. This letter has the same value as the English.

flor   filósofo

Notice that the English *ph* is always replaced by *f* in Spanish.

phonetic—fonético   telephone—teléfono

G. This letter has three distinct pronunciations according to position.

(*a*) At the beginning of a breath group, before *a*, *o*, *u*, and after *n* the *g* has the same sound as the English in *gorse*.

gastar   golondrina   gustar   tengo

(*b*) Within a word or breath group the *g* is pronounced much more softly than the English.

esto me gusta   una golondrina   agua   cargar

(*c*) Before *i*, *e*, the Spanish *g* has a harsh, guttural sound, similar to the *ch* of the Scottish *loch*. It is very much stronger than the English aspirate *h*.

gesto   ágil   gente   gitano

J. The Spanish *j* has the same sound as the *g* when followed by *i* or *e*.

jamón   jurar   joya

The *j* is also found followed by *i* or *e*, and has the same sound.

jinete   extranjero

H. This letter is not sounded in Spanish.

hielo   hermano   hierba

L. The *l* has almost the same sound as the English, but the tongue is farther forward in the Spanish.

limpio   cielo

LL. Considered as a separate letter in Spanish. The sound is that of *l* followed by a "yod." It resembles the English *li* as in *million*, but is actually between the English and French pronunciations of the word.

pitillo   llamar   calle

M. The same sound as the English.

mano   suma

N. The *n* is pronounced in several ways according to position.

(*a*) As in English.

noche   poner   son

(*b*) Before *g*, *j*, or hard *c* (*qu*) the sound is pronounced farther back and resembles the English *n* as in *sink*.

un gato   un jamón   conque

(*c*) Before *f* the *n* has the sound of a nasalised *m*, i.e. the *n* is attracted by the *f* and the tongue no longer touches the ridge behind the teeth, as in the normal pronunciation.

don Fernando   **enfermo**

(*d*) Before *p*, *b*, *v*, the *n* is pronounced as *m*, again by attraction.

enviar   **un vaso**   **un pico**   **un billete**

(*e*) *nm* is pronounced as *mm*.

inmenso

Ñ. This is considered as a separate letter in Spanish. Pronounced almost like the *ni* in the English *onion*, but with more of the "yod" sound.

niño   **caña**   **España**

P. Pronounced as in English.

papá   **pasta**   **soplar**

R. The Spanish *r* is always trilled and is *always* pronounced. According to its position it is more or less trilled.

(*a*) The weakest *r* is that which is at the end of a word.

cantar   **encantador**

(*b*) *r* in the middle of the word is slightly more trilled.

enero   **Carlos**

(*c*) At the beginning of the word or after *n*, *l*, and *s*, the *r* is pronounced with several vibrations of the tongue.

río   **honra**   **alrededor**

Note that after *s*, the *r* is pronounced almost as the double letter (*rr*), and that in rapid speech the *s* is elided.

los reyes católicos

Note also that the " French " (uvular) *r* does not exist in Spanish.

RR. The double letter is very trilled, with four vibrations of the tongue.

ferrocarril

It is very important to distinguish the single and double letters, especially in such cases as :

pero (but)   **perro** (dog)

para (in order to)   **parra** (vine)

S. This letter has two pronunciations according to position.

(*a*) As a sibilant (i.e. as the English *s* in *house*) when final, initial, intervocalic or before unvoiced consonants.

canciones   **saco**   **casa**   **Castilla**

(*b*) As the sound of the English *z* (for instance : *ease*, *cheese*) when followed by a *voiced* consonant such as *m, g, d, n, v, b.*

mismo   **desde**   **los gatos**   **las niñas**   **los baños**

los vinos

We have remarked already how the *s* disappears in rapid speech before the *r.*

los ríos   **muchas ratas**

T. Pronounced as in English, but with the tongue against the teeth.

trenes   **patata**

X. Before a vowel, pronounced as *eks* or *eggs*, and in rapid speech before a consonant as *s.*

Before a vowel : **éxito**

Before a consonant : **extraordinario**
excepto
extranjero

Y. As in English.

yo **ya** **yacer**

Remember, however, that *y* is also a semi-vowel when preceded by a vowel.

rey **ley** **soy**

W. Although, strictly speaking, *w* is not a letter of the Spanish alphabet, remember that the *sound* is produced when *u* precedes a vowel.

hueso **agua**

ACCENTUATION

If a Spanish word ends in a vowel or in the consonants *n* or *s*, the stress falls naturally on the last syllable but one.

canta'mos **can'to** **muchachi'to** **tie'nen** **sombre'ro**
ca'sas

If a word ends in any consonant other than *n* or *s*, the stress falls naturally on the last syllable.

corra'l **canta'r** **acto'r** **relo'j** **ciuda'd**

The *written accent* is used to indicate exceptions to the above rules.

canción **jícara**

Similarly, the written accent is used to stress a weak vowel which otherwise could not bear the accent.

país   río   hacía   me mareé

To distinguish words that have two meanings.

si (if)	sí (yes)
el (the)	él (he)
de (of)	dé (give)
cuando (when)	¿ cuándo ? when ? (interrogative)

THE DIÆRESIS

We have noticed already that when *g* is followed by *i* or *e*, it has the harsh, guttural sound of *j*.

If, however, we wish to harden the *g* before either of these two vowels, *u* must be inserted.

Guerra (the *g* is hard as in *gone*. The *u* is *not* sounded).

Of course if the *g* is followed by *a*, *o*, or *u*, the sound is naturally hard (**gato, gusto, golpe**), and if *u* is inserted, the *u* assumes semi-consonantal value.

guapo (pronounced as *w*)

Sometimes it is necessary to preserve this sound of *w* even when the *g* is followed by *i* or *e*, and it is then that the diæresis is used.

averiguar (to ascertain)

but **averigüé** (I ascertained)

and similarly **pingüino** (penguin)

antigüedad (antiquity)

" SINALEFA "

When, within a breath group, a word ending in a vowel is followed by a word beginning with a vowel, both vowels are linked together in pronunciation, although both retain their full vocalic value. In other words, there can be no pause in Spanish.

For instance, in the following sentence :

El campesino_andaluz/iba_a la_aldea

It is most essential to learn to pronounce in the correct manner in order to be able to follow the flow of Spanish as spoken by a native. It is very important to form this habit from the very beginning, since otherwise it will be difficult to acquire the necessary fluency later on.

Exercises

Read the following :

1. un vaso	buenas tardes	el cabo	sabio	costar	ciento
chino	todo el mundo	doy	padre	fenicio	gorra
algo	agua	gemelo	jícara	girar	alegre
hilar	jota	viaje	caja	hallar	llover
música	alma	nombre	nueve	un casco	infancia
un poco	un billete	inmoral	peña	señal	pastor
que	cuando	quien	queso	rata	enero
enredo	sin razón	perro	pero	criar	el río
mismo	los dedos	sal	piso	ante	tapar
tres	los ríos	extraño	exaltar	excusa	yate
yo	soy	zapato	alzar	cuenta	puente

2. No tengo nada que decirle.

Mañana va a salir para Madrid.

Los numerosos arroyuelos que lo cruzan en todas direcciones.

La fama de aquel hecho llenó al instante toda Andalucía.

Cataluña es la región más oriental de España.

Buenos Aires es una ciudad muy agradable.

Zaragoza está a orillas del río Ebro.

General gusto causó el cuento del cabrero.

El abuelo murió a la edad de ochenta años.

Es un territorio montañés y risueño, bien poblado y cultivado.

PUNCTUATION

Usage is the same in Spanish and English, but notice that inverted question and exclamation marks are placed at the beginning of the sentence.

¿ A qué hora llegó Vd. ?	What time did you arrive ?
¡ Qué niño tan estúpido !	What a stupid child !

Notice that at the beginning of a letter a colon is used in Spanish where a comma is preferred in English.

Dear John,
      I have just received . . .

Querido Juan :
      Acabo de recibir . . .

CAPITAL LETTERS

Capital letters are used in Spanish at the beginning of a sentence or line of poetry and with proper names.

Notice the difference between the English and Spanish :

Carlos y yo.	Charles and I.
Habla inglés.	He speaks English.
El mes de mayo.	The month of May.
Vendrá el sábado que viene.	He will come next Saturday.

DIFFERENCES IN PRONUNCIATION

We have already stated that Spanish vowels are pronounced the same wherever Spanish is spoken. It is not so, however, with the consonants. In Latin America little distinction is made between *s, c,* and *z* (all being pronounced very often as the sibilant *s*), and the *ll* often becomes a yod sound or *j* (like the French *j* in *Jean*). Similarly, the Spanish of Castile (el castellano) often differs from the Spanish of Andalusia or Galicia. Again, each region and each country uses words which have only local value. Of course the same may be said of English as spoken in the various parts of Great Britain and Ireland and throughout the world. In other words, it is no more necessary to learn a special brand of Spanish in order to go to Mexico or Chile than it is to learn North American English in order to go to the United States or Canada.

un campesino
— countryman
la
aldea — village
una cabra — goat
un burro — donkey
un buey — bullock

CHAPTER I

EL CAMPESINO

Un campesino va por el camino. ¿Quién es el campesino? El nombre del campesino es Ramón. Ramón trabaja mucho en el campo. Vuelve a la aldea, donde vive con la familia. Un buey va al lado del hombre.

Conchita es la mujer de Ramón. Cuando Ramón entra en la casa, Conchita prepara la comida. ¿Qué come Ramón? Come pan y un plato de sopa. ¿Qué bebe? Bebe un vaso de vino.

Ramón tiene un hijo y una hija. El nombre del hijo es Manuel y el nombre de la hija es Manolita. Manuel es el hermano y Manolita es la hermana. Ramón es el padre y Conchita es la madre.

El campesino tiene también un burro. No tiene vaca, pero tiene una cabra.

NOTES

El campo

This word has two meanings : (1) *country* as opposed to town. (2) *field*.

El campesino vive en el campo.   The peasant lives in the country.

Ramón trabaja en el campo.   Ramón is working in the field.

El buey

In rural parts of Spain the bullock is still used for ploughing and drawing carts.

Trabaja

The Spanish *j* (jota) often corresponds to the French " yod."   Thus :

trabaja	travaille (he works)
el ojo	œil (eye)
la abeja	abeille (bee)
el ajo	ail (garl'c)
la paja	paille (straw)

La mujer

This word means either " woman " or " wife."   A more polite word for " wife " is, however, la señora or la esposa (spouse).   Señora also corresponds to the English " Mrs."

La señora Rodríguez

Similarly :

El señor Rodríguez   (Mr.)
La señorita Álvarez   (Miss)

Señorito (Master) is often used by servants when addressing the master of the house.

Notice the use of the definite article in the above cases.   If, however, a person is addressed directly and not merely referred to, the article is omitted :

Buenos días, señor Álvarez.
Good morning, Mr. Álvarez.

El hijo

You will have noticed that the feminine form of this word is obtained by changing the -*o* into -*a*. El hijo—the son. La hija—the daughter.

This applies in many other cases :

el hermano	la hermana	brother ; sister
el primo	la prima	cousin ; girl cousin
el abuelo	la abuela	grandfather ; grandmother
el tío	la tía	uncle ; aunt
el nieto	la nieta	grandson ; grand-daughter

La vaca

Many peasants in Spain are too poor to possess cows and the country is often too barren and mountainous to supply adequate fodder. On the other hand, goats thrive and cost little to support. In country towns the animals are often led through the streets and milked on the spot. Use is also made of sheep's milk, from which cheese is made.

GRAMMAR

Definite and Indefinite Articles

Nouns in Spanish are either masculine or feminine.

The definite article EL is used before masculine nouns and the definite article LA before feminine nouns.

el hijo   the son   la hija   the daughter

The indefinite article UN.is used before masculine nouns and the indefinite article UNA before feminine nouns.

un burro   a donkey   una aldea   a village

Gender of Nouns

Most nouns in Spanish end in -o or -a. With very few exceptions nouns ending in -o are masculine and those ending in -a are feminine.

el camino	the road	la comida	the meal
el vaso	the glass	la casa	the house

Other nouns end in -e and are mostly masculine. There are, however, important exceptions to this rule, which will be pointed out as they occur.

el hombre	the man	el nombre	the name

Nouns which end in other letters are of varying genders, and it is advisable to learn all such nouns *together with the article.*

el buey	the bullock, ox	la mujer	the woman

In some cases it is not difficult to remember the correct genders. It is obvious that **buey** is masculine by meaning, and **mujer** feminine for the same reason.

Contraction of Article

When the masculine singular form of the definite article is preceded by the prepositions A (to, at) or DE (of), the following contractions take place:

A plus EL becomes AL	Al lado del campesino.
	At the side of the peasant.
DE plus EL becomes DEL	El nombre del hijo.
	The name of the son.

Possession

Such a form as the English " the son's name " is not possible in Spanish. This must be expressed as :

el nombre del hijo	the name of the son

Verbs

The third person singular of the present indicative practically all verbs in Spanish ends in either -a or -e.

El campesino trabaja. The peasant works (or is working).
La mujer come pan. The woman eats (or is eating) bread.

An exception is ES—is:

El nombre del hijo es Manuel. The son's name is Manuel.

In order to look up a verb in a dictionary, however, it is necessary to know the infinitive. There are three types of infinitive in Spanish, ending respectively in *-ar*, *-er*, and *-ir*. Thus the following verbs:

trabaja, entra, prepara

belong to the first conjugation or *-ar* type, the infinitives being:

trabajar (to work), entrar (to enter), preparar (to prepare).

Verbs of which the third person singular ends in *-e* may belong to either of the remaining conjugations. Thus:

vuelve, come, bebe, tiene

belong to the second conjugation or *-er* type, the infinitives being:

volver (to return), comer (to eat), beber (to drink),
tener (to have).

One verb is of the third conjugation or *-ir* type:

vive

the infinitive being: vivir (to live).

The two forms **es** and **va** are irregular.

es comes from the verb ser (to be)
and **va** comes from the verb ir (to go, walk).

Omission of Personal Pronouns

You will have noticed that it is not always necessary in Spanish to express the subject pronouns. If it is clear what the subject is, the pronoun may be left out, unless special emphasis is required.

Ramón es el nombre del campesino. Vive en el campo. Tiene una cabra.

Ramón is the name of the peasant. He lives in the country. He has a goat.

Questions

The simplest way to make an affirmative sentence interrogative is to invert the order of subject and verb.

El campesino tiene una casa.	The peasant has a house.
¿ Tiene el campesino una casa ?	Has the peasant a house ?

And where the subject is understood but not expressed :

Tiene una cabra.	He has a goat.
¿ Tiene una cabra ?	Has he a goat ?

In the written question the interrogation marks are the only indication in such a case that the interrogative is intended. In the spoken question this would, of course, be indicated by the interrogative pitch of the voice. You will now understand why the inverted question marks are written at the beginning of a question in Spanish.

As in English a question may also begin with an interrogative word.

¿ Quién es Ramón ?	Who is Ramón ?
¿ Dónde vive ?	Where does he live ?

Notice that all such interrogative words bear the written accent.

Be careful to note that such forms as " does he eat ? " are peculiar to English.

Does Ramón eat ?	¿ Come Ramón ?

Negation

This is expressed by placing NO immediately in front of the verb.

El campesino trabaja.	The peasant is working.
El campesino no trabaja.	The peasant isn't working.

¿ Come Conchita?   Is Conchita eating?
¿ No come Conchita?   Isn't Conchita eating?

Ramón tiene una cabra.   Ramón has a goat.
Ramón no tiene cabra.   Ramón hasn't a goat.

Notice that the *indefinite* article is usually omitted after the negative.

Similarly, when the noun is used in a partitive sense, the article is omitted.

Ramón come pan.   Ramón is eating (some) bread.

EXERCISES

(1) Answer the following questions in Spanish:

1. ¿ Quién va por el camino? 2. ¿ Qué es Ramón?
3. ¿ Dónde trabaja Ramón? 4. ¿ Trabaja Ramón mucho?
5. ¿ Qué va al lado del hombre? 6. ¿ Qué prepara Conchita? 7. ¿ Qué come Ramón? 8. ¿ Qué bebe?
9. ¿ Quién es Manuel? 10. ¿ Qué nombre tiene la hija?
11. ¿ Tiene Ramón una vaca? 12. ¿ Qué es un campesino?
13. ¿ Dónde vive la familia? 14. ¿ Quién es la madre?
15. ¿ Quién tiene una cabra?

(2) Insert appropriate words in the blank spaces.

(Example: La cabra es un ——.   La cabra es un animal.)

1. El hombre va por el ——. 2. El burro es un ——.
3. Manuel es el ——. 4. El nombre de la mujer es ——.
5. Ramón —— en el campo. 6. Ramón vive en la ——.
7. Conchita prepara la ——. 8. El campesino vuelve a la ——. 9. Ramón bebe —— y come ——. 10. Manolita es el —— de la hija.

(3) Write the appropriate definite and indefinite articles.

(Example: camino.   el camino, un camino.)

buey   sopa   hombre   mujer   burro   plato   vaca
                hijo   campesino   cabra

(4) Re-write the following sentences, making the contraction of preposition and article where necessary.

(Example: El nombre de (el hijo). El nombre del hijo.)

1. La casa de (el hombre). 2. La cabra de (la mujer). 3. El buey va a (el lado) de (el hombre). 4. El campesino vuelve a (la aldea). 5. El nombre de (la hija) es Manolita. 6. El nombre de (el campesino) es Ramón. 7. La casa de (un campesino). 8. El pan de (el hermano). 9. El hijo de (el padre). 10. La casa de (la familia).

(5) Insert appropriate verbs in the blank spaces.

(Example: Manuel —— el hijo. Manuel es el hijo.)

1. Ramón —— la sopa. 2. La mujer —— la comida. 3. El buey —— al lado del hombre. 4. El campesino —— en la casa. 5. El campesino no —— vaca. 6. La hermana de Manuel —— Manolita. 7. Ramón —— a la aldea. 8. Conchita —— un hijo y una hija. 9. Manuel —— mucho pan. 10. El burro no —— vino.

(6) Make the following statements interrogative.

(Example: Ramón bebe vino. ¿Bebe Ramón vino?)

1. Ramón va por el camino. 2. El campesino vuelve a la aldea. 3. Manuel es el hijo. 4. El padre tiene una cabra. 5. Manolita no bebe vino.

(7) Make the following sentences negative.

(Example: El campesino va por el camino. El campesino no va por el camino.)

1. El nombre del padre es Manuel. 2. Ramón tiene un burro. 3. ¿Tiene Manuel un plato de sopa? 4. El buey va al lado del hombre. 5. ¿Entra el campesino en la casa?

(8) Put into Spanish:

Ramón lives with Conchita in a house in the country. Ramón has a son and a daughter. The daughter's name is Manolita. Ramón works hard in the field, and when he returns to the village, Conchita prepares a meal of soup, bread, and wine. A bullock works with Ramón in the field. The peasant has also a donkey and a goat, but he has no cow.

CHAPTER II

LA ESCUELA DEL CAMPO

En el centro de la aldea está la escuela, blanca y pequeña.

El maestro, don Alfonso, enseña en la escuela. Es un hombre viejo pero es muy simpático, tiene mucha paciencia y contesta siempre a las preguntas que hacen los discípulos.

Don Alfonso está sentado en una silla detrás de la mesa. Da una lección de geografía. Habla de las provincias de España. Escribe con tiza en la pizarra los nombres de las provincias. Es una lección interesante y útil. Los niños escuchan con atención.

Durante la semana los niños aprenden muchas cosas—hacen cálculos sencillos, copian letras y palotes en los cuadernos con pluma y tinta o con lápiz, cantan canciones, leen libros y dibujan. Cuando el maestro cuenta un cuento o describe episodios históricos los discípulos escuchan con alegría.

Detrás de la escuela está el patio. Aquí en el patio juegan los niños durante las horas de recreo.

NOTES

El niño

El niño—little boy. **La niña**—little girl. **Los niños**—children, girls and boys.

The masculine plural denotes both sexes. Thus: " El hombre tiene cuatro hijos " might mean that the man has four sons, or that he has four sons and daughters. If he has four daughters it is, of course, " cuatro hijas."

Similarly :

el padre, la madre, los padres (parents).

el rey—the king, **la reina**—the queen, **los reyes**—the sovereigns.

el tío—la tía—los tíos (uncle and aunt).

los hermanos—brothers and sisters.

El maestro

El maestro is usually the village schoolmaster. A secondary school teacher is **el profesor,** and a university professor is **el catedrático.**

El discípulo usually refers to a child at school ; **el alumno** to a pupil in a secondary school or college ; **el estudiante** to a university student.

La escuela is the ordinary word for school ; **el instituto** is usually a state secondary school ; **la universidad** is the university. There is also **el colegio,** which is generally a private or Church-controlled secondary institution, often for girls.

Enseña

From **enseñar**—to teach. **La enseñanza** is teaching or education.

Simpático

This word is difficult to translate. It means *kind, affable, good to get on with,* and has often the vague sense of *nice.* The word is very much used in Spanish.

Contesta

The " answer " is la contestación.

La letra

This is a letter of the alphabet—las letras del alfabeto.   A
letter in the sense of epistle is la carta.

Aprender

School subjects in Spanish are called las asignaturas.   The
principal ones are :

la lectura	reading
la aritmética	arithmetic (los cálculos—sums)
la geografía	geography
la historia	history
el dibujo	drawing
el canto	singing (la canción—song)

Con atención

Notice the adverbial use of nouns.

con atención—attentively (with attention)
con alegría—merrily, joyfully (with merriment)

Juegan

The noun corresponding to this verb is el juego—game,
play.   This word also has the meaning of *gambling*, but the
context will always indicate the sense.

En

You will have noticed that EN means " in," " into," and
also " on."   E.g. Entra en la casa—" he comes into the house."
Está en la escuela—" he is in the school."   Está sentado en
la silla—" he is seated on the chair."

There is another word in Spanish, SOBRE, which is often
interchangeable in the sense of " on."   E.g. La tiza está sobre
la mesa—" the chalk is on the table."

Don

A title used in Spanish, but only before a Christian name. For instance : Don Juan Rodríguez or simply Don Juan.   It is usual to use this title even after señor, if the Christian name is also given.

Señor don Juan Rodríguez

There is no equivalent in English.

Similarly :

(Señora) doña Emilia

GRAMMAR

Definite and Indefinite Articles

The plural form of EL is LOS, and the plural form of UN is UNOS.

Similarly for the feminine articles : LA becomes LAS, UNA becomes UNAS.

el niño	the child	los niños	the children
un libro	a book	unos libros	some books
la casa	the house	las casas	the houses
una mujer	a woman	unas mujeres	some women

The plural indefinite article is not always expressed however.

No tengo libros.	I have no books.
Tengo lápices.	I have some pencils.

But

Tengo unos lápices rojos.   I have $\left\{ \begin{array}{l} \text{some} \\ \text{several} \end{array} \right\}$ red pencils.

Plural of Nouns

Nouns ending in *-o*, *-a*, or *-e* form the plural by adding *-s*.

el vino	the wine	los vinos	the wines
la casa	the house	las casas	the houses
el nombre	the name	los nombres	the names

Nouns ending in a consonant or the semi-consonant *-y* take *-es* in the plural.

la mujer	the woman	las mujeres	the women
el buey	the bullock	los bueyes	the bullocks

Nouns which end in -*z* regularly form their plural by adding -*es*, but the -*z* followed by -*e* becomes -*c*.

> el lápiz   the pencil   los lápices   the pencils

You will notice that some nouns such as **la canción** bear a written accent on the last syllable.   In the plural such nouns lose their written accent since, as the stress falls naturally on the last syllable but one in Spanish, the written accent is no longer required.

> la canción   the song   las canciones   the songs

Gender of Nouns

Most nouns in Spanish ending in -*ión* are feminine.

> la canción   the song   la ambición   ambition
> la atención   attention

Adjectives

Adjectives agree in gender and number with the noun they qualify.   They usually follow the noun.

una casa blanca a white house   casas blancas white houses

Adjectives in the masculine singular end in -*o*, -*e*, or a consonant, as in the case of nouns.

> simpático   interesante   útil

In the case of adjectives ending in -*o*, four forms exist, corresponding to the masculine and feminine, singular and plural.

> un lápiz blanco   lápices blancos
> la casa blanca   las casas blancas

Adjectives ending in -*e* have two forms only, one for the singular and one for the plural.

> un libro interesante   libros interesantes
> una lección interesante   lecciones interesantes

Adjectives ending in a consonant normally form the plural

by the addition of *-es*. There are, however, some exceptions to this rule, which will be discussed later.

una lección útil	lecciones útiles
un libro útil	libros útiles

Nouns used as Adjectives

A noun cannot be used as an adjective in Spanish, as is often the case in English.

a geography lesson   una lección de geografía

This use of the noun is, of course, very common in English. Very often Spanish expresses the idea by the use of a different word.

a book	un libro
an exercise book	un cuaderno

Verbs

The third person plural of the present indicative is formed by adding *-n* to the singular.

el campesino trabaja	los campesinos trabajan
la mujer come	las mujeres comen

The plural of ES is SON.

Manuel es el hijo.   Manuel y Manolita son los hijos.

You will have noticed that there are two verbs in Spanish to express the English " is," " are."

Don Alfonso es un maestro viejo.	Don Alfonso is an old teacher.
Don Alfonso está en la clase.	Don Alfonso is in the classroom.
Los niños son inteligentes.	The children are intelligent.
Los niños están en el patio.	The children are in the playground.

Whenever the English " is " can be replaced by " is situated " the verb **está** must be used.

Remember that whenever *situation* is indicated, **está**, **están** are to be used.

Madrid **es** la capital de España.   Madrid **está** en España.
Madrid is the capital of Spain.   Madrid is in Spain.

EXERCISES

(1) Answer in Spanish :

1. ¿ Dónde está la escuela? 2. ¿ De qué color es la escuela? 3. ¿ Dónde enseña don Alfonso? 4. ¿ Es don Alfonso un hombre muy viejo? 5. ¿ Tiene el maestro mucha paciencia? 6. ¿ Qué hacen los discípulos? 7. ¿ Dónde está sentado don Alfonso? 8. ¿ Dónde está la silla? 9. ¿ De qué habla el maestro? 10. ¿ Cómo [how] escuchan los niños? 11. ¿ Qué aprenden los niños? 12. ¿ De qué color es la tiza? 13. ¿ Con qué escribe don Alfonso los nombres en la pizarra? 14. ¿ Cuándo escuchan los niños con alegría? 15. ¿ Qué hacen los niños durante las horas de recreo?

(2) Put the following sentences into the plural.

(Example: El niño tiene un libro. Los niños tienen libros.)

1. La lección es interesante. 2. El niño juega. 3. La mujer prepara la comida. 4. La escuela es pequeña. 5. El discípulo está sentado en la silla. 6. Una lección de geografía. 7. El libro es útil. 8. El buey va al lado del hombre. 9. ¿ De qué color es el lápiz? 10. El maestro escribe en la pizarra.

(3) Make the adjectives agree where necessary.

(Example : La casa **blanco**. La casa blanca.)

1. Un cálculo **sencillo**. 2. Una lección **útil**. 3. Un libro **útil**. 4. Las canciones son **interesantes** 5. El patio es **pequeño**. 6. La mujer es muy **vieja** 7. La mujer está **sentado** en una silla. 8. Las preguntas son **útil** 9. El maestro describe unos episodios **histórico** 10. Los niños cantan canciones **sencillo**

(4) Replace the blanks by **es**, **está**, **son**, **están**, whichever form is appropriate.

(Example: Don Alfonso —— el maestro. Don Alfonso es el maestro.)

1. Manuel *es* el hijo, Manolita *es* la hija. 2. Las escuelas *son* pequeñas. 3. Los niños *están* en el patio. 4. La silla *está* detrás de la mesa. 5. El niño *está* sentado en la silla. 6. La lección de geografía *es* muy interesante. 7. La tiza *está* sobre la mesa. 8. Los libros *son* útiles. 9. Los discípulos *están* en la sala de clase. 10. La pizarra *es* negra.

(5) Replace the blanks by an appropriate word, or words.

(Example: Don Alfonso da una ——. Don Alfonso da una lección.)

1. Los niños —— en el patio. 2. El maestro cuenta un ——. 3. Don Alfonso es viejo pero es muy ——. 4. Los discípulos hacen ——. 5. El maestro escribe con —— en la pizarra. 6. La lección es ——. 7. Detrás de la mesa está la ——. 8. Los niños juegan ——. 9. Los discípulos escuchan ——. 10. El maestro da una lección de ——.

(6) Make up sentences using the following words or expressions.

(Example : mucho   Tiene mucha paciencia.)

detrás de   al lado de   sobre   con alegría   por

(7) The following are answers to questions. What are the original questions?

1. Ramón tiene una cabra. 2. Los niños juegan en el patio. 3. Los niños juegan durante las horas de recreo. 4. El maestro da una lección de geografía. 5. Don Alfonso escribe con tiza. 6. La escuela está en el centro de la aldea. 7. La escuela es blanca. 8. Es una lección interesante. 9. Los niños escuchan con atención. 10. Conchita prepara la comida.

(8) Put into Spanish :

The children are playing in the yard behind the school. The teacher is an old man, but he is very patient. The children learn many things at school. They write, read, draw, and do simple sums. But they always listen very attentively when don Alfonso tells a story or describes historical episodes.

CHAPTER III

LA CASA DE MANUEL

Un día en la escuela Manuel hace una descripción de la casa donde habita.

— Vivimos en la casa blanca en la calle de Atocha al otro lado del río. Es una casa bonita. Por encima de la puerta crece una parra que da uvas sabrosas. Las

ventanas del piso bajo tienen rejas y las de arriba balcones de hierro, donde por la tarde tomamos el fresco. En el piso bajo hay una cocina muy grande que da al corral detrás de la casa y otro cuarto que llamamos la sala. Arriba hay dos dormitorios con una alcoba. En la alcoba no hay mucha luz.

En el corral hay una fuente de agua cristalina y un gallinero. También tenemos una huerta donde cultivamos hortalizas y legumbres.

El maestro interrumpe a Manuel y pregunta :
— ¿ Tienes tú ganas de vivir en la ciudad ?

El niño contesta : — Sí, señor maestro, deseo mucho ir a Barcelona como mi hermano. Él tiene una casa moderna con comedor, sala, cuarto de baño y muchos dormitorios. Y Vd. señor ¿ tiene Vd. también ganas de vivir en la ciudad ?

— No, Manuel, yo soy demasiado viejo para dejar la aldea.

NOTES

Una parra

This is the climbing vine. An ordinary vine is **la vid.**

El piso bajo

El piso is a floor or storey. " La casa tiene cinco pisos." —The house has five floors. **El piso bajo** is the ground floor ; **el piso principal** is usually the first floor, whilst **el primer piso** would correspond to our second floor. **El piso** is also used in the sense of *flat*.

Reja

The ground floor windows of Spanish houses are generally protected by a grille, whilst upstairs windows usually open out on to balconies.

Tomar el fresco

It is the custom in Spain to sit on the balcony and enjoy the cool of the evening when the sun has lost its power.

Dormitorio

Bedroom. Also **el cuarto de dormir, la alcoba, la habitación. Alcoba** is of Moorish origin ; an alcove built into the corner of the bedroom. Such an alcove has no windows and often little ventilation. By extension **alcoba** often means the bedroom itself.

La habitación has also the meaning of bedroom. For instance : El hotel tiene cien habitaciones. The hotel has a hundred bedrooms.

El **cuarto** is also used in the general sense of room. Other rooms are :

la cocina   —kitchen
el comedor   —dining-room (we have already met with
                       the verb **comer**—to eat)
la sala   —drawing-room. Note also **la sala de clase**
                       —classroom
el cuarto de baño—bathroom
el sótano   —basement, cellar

El corral
A yard, usually at the back of a building. Sometimes, as for instance in South America, an enclosure for cattle.

El patio
El patio is a courtyard surrounded by buildings and usually possessing a well or fountain. They are very often planted with shrubs or covered with the climbing vine. The patios of some buildings, particularly in Moorish Spain, are very elaborate. The old inn-yards of Shakespearean England are perhaps the nearest approach to the Spanish patio.

We have already met with **el patio de recreo**—playground.

El gallinero
La gallina is the hen, and the place where hens are kept **el gallinero**. **Gallinero** is also used in a slang sense, meaning the upper gallery of a theatre. **El gallo** is the cock. A pullet is **el pollo** and a small chicken **el pollito**.

La huerta
La huerta is the kitchen garden. A flower garden is **el jardín**. Notice also **el huerto**—orchard.

Huerta is the name given to land which is irrigated and cultivated. This applies particularly to the Valencian district. Many of the early novels of Blasco Ibáñez deal with life in the " huerta valenciana."

Por encima de
Above, over. The simple preposition is **encima de.** For instance : **el reloj está encima de la puerta**—the clock is over the door.

Por encima de suggests motion, i.e. the vine climbs up and over the doorway. This distinction will be discussed later.

GRAMMAR

Conjugation of Verbs. Present Indicative

As stated before, there are three conjugations in Spanish. The infinitives end respectively in *-ar*, *-er*, or *-ir*.

	HABLAR—to speak		COMER—to eat
(yo)	hablo	I speak	como—I eat, etc.
(tú)	hablas	thou speakest	comes
(él)	habla	he speaks	come
(ella)	habla	she speaks	come
(Vd.)	habla	you speak	come
(Nosotros)	hablamos	we speak	comemos
(Vosotros)	habláis	you speak	coméis
(ellos)	hablan	they speak	comen
(ellas)	hablan	they speak	comen
(Vds.)	hablan	you speak	comen

	VIVIR—to live
(yo)	vivo—I live, etc.
(tú)	vives
(él)	vive
(ella)	vive
(Vd.)	vive
(Nosotros)	vivimos
(Vosotros)	vivís
(ellos)	viven
(ellas)	viven
(Vds.)	viven

The endings of the three conjugations are therefore :

-ar :   -o, -as, -a, -amos, -áis, -an
-er :   -o, -es, -e, -emos, -éis, -en
-ir :   -o, -es, -e, -imos, -ís, -en

Notice that the endings of the second and third conjugations are identical with the exception of the first and second

persons plural. It will be noticed that there are two forms
for " you " in Spanish :

   tú hablas ; Vd. habla   vosotros habláis ; Vds. hablan

The first form is known as the *familiar* and is used only
within the family or when addressing personal friends,
children, or animals. The mother speaking to her child would
say : **tú hablas,** or to her children : **vosotros habláis.**

The second form is known as the *polite* form and is a relic
of the old days when an inferior would address one of superior
rank as " Your Honour," " Your Worship." Instead of
saying, for instance, " you are speaking," one would say :
" Your Worship is speaking "—hence the form used in
Spanish, which is equivalent to the *third person*.

" Your Worship " was, in Spanish, " Vuestra Merced,"
which has been contracted to usted. In the written form it is
further contracted to **Vd.** The plural of these forms is
ustedes, Vds.

The polite form must always be used when addressing
strangers. Unless on very intimate terms, a foreigner would
never address a Spaniard in the familiar form.

Naturally it is essential to be able to recognise both forms
but, remember, always use the polite form when writing to or
addressing Spaniards.

As has been pointed out before, the personal subject pronouns are not normally expressed in Spanish, unless special
emphasis is desired, or in order to avoid ambiguity.

Yo leo y él escribe.   *I* read and *he* writes.
¿ Cuántos lápices tiene usted? How many pencils have you?

Usted, ustedes (Vd., Vds.), having been expressed once in a
sentence, may afterwards be omitted in the same sentence,
unless there is any likelihood of confusion.

In such a sentence as **nosotros comemos** (we eat), it is
assumed that the speakers are of masculine or mixed genders.
If they were all feminine, one would say **nosotras comemos.**
Similarly : vosotros, vosotras ; ellos, ellas.

" It " is not normally expressed.

El burro bebe. Bebe el agua de la fuente.
The donkey is drinking. It is drinking the water of the well.

Irregular Verbs

TENER—to have, possess. This verb is irregular. The present indicative is :

      tengo, tienes, tiene, tenemos, tenéis, tienen

Personal " a "

NB

A peculiarity of Spanish is that all verbs (with the important exception of **tener**—to possess) must be followed by " a " when the direct object of the verb is a proper noun or a noun indicating a definite or particular person.

Amo a mi padre.	I love my father.
Visito a Alfonso.	I am visiting Alfonso.

But

Tengo dos hermanos.	I have two brothers.
Escribo la carta.	I write the letter.

This use is extended sometimes to things or animals for which one has a particular affection and which are, so to speak, personified.

Deseo ver a Madrid.	I wish to see Madrid.
Los niños quieren al borrico.	The children love the donkey.

If, however, the direct object (although a person) is not definite or particular in character, the personal " a " is omitted.

      Mi hermano ama los niños.   My brother loves children.

In this case no definite children are referred to, only children in general.

Impersonal Verb

HAY is an impersonal verb, used only in the third person. It corresponds to *il y a* in French and means " there is " or " there are."

Hay tinta en el tintero.	There is ink in the inkwell.
Hay muchos niños en el patio.	There are many children in the yard.

Questions

Notice the order of the words in such a sentence as :

¿ Tiene reja la ventana de arriba?   Has the upstairs window a grille?

This is simply a question of balance.   Similarly :

Las preguntas que hacen los niños.   The questions that the children ask.

Gender of Nouns

We have stated that nouns ending in -*o* are usually masculine.   One very important exception is :

la mano   the hand

Nouns ending in -*a* are usually feminine.   One very important exception is :

el día   the day

Most nouns ending in -*z* or -*d* are feminine.

la luz	light	la ciudad	city
la cruz	cross	la edad	age

Notice, however, the important exception :

el lápiz   the pencil

Nouns ending in -*e* and denoting things are usually masculine, but notice two exceptions met with in the present chapter :

la legumbre   vegetable   **la** fuente   fountain, well

El agua (feminine) is not really an exception.   When a word begins with an accented " a " or " ha," the definite article " la " or the indefinite article " una " cannot stand, although the word is feminine.   For the sake of euphony the masculine forms are used instead.

el agua	the water	un ala	a wing
el haba	the bean	el águila	the eagle

But

las aguas   the waters

This change does not take place, of course, when the first syllable does not bear the stress:

la harina   the flour

EXERCISES

(1) Answer the following questions in Spanish:

1. ¿Dónde vive Manuel? 2. ¿Dónde está la casa de Manuel? 3. ¿Cómo es la casa? 4. ¿Qué crece por encima de la puerta? 5. ¿Qué da la parra? 6. ¿Qué tienen las ventanas de arriba? 7. ¿Qué hace la familia de Manuel por la tarde? 8. ¿Qué hay detrás de la casa? 9. ¿Hay mucha luz en la alcoba? 10. ¿Dónde cultiva el padre las hortalizas? 11. ¿Qué pregunta el maestro? 12. ¿Vive Vd. en la ciudad o en el campo? 13. ¿A dónde desea ir Manuel? 14. ¿Cómo es la casa que tiene el hermano de Manuel? 15. ¿Por qué [why] no desea don Alfonso dejar la aldea?

(2) Put the appropriate definite and indefinite articles before the following nouns.

(Example: casa   la casa, una casa, las casas, unas casas.)

buey   discípulo   día   agua   legumbre   comedor
balcón   luz   hombre   puerta   ciudad   descripción

(3) Put the following sentences into the plural:

1. Es demasiado viejo para vivir en la ciudad. 2. ¿Tienes ganas de vivir aquí? 3. La casa tiene un balcón. 4. El niño interrumpe. 5. Tengo una casa muy bonita. 6. El discípulo hace una descripción de la casa. 7. ¿No tiene Vd. ganas de dejar la aldea? 8. ¿Dónde vives? 9. Como mucho pan. 10. La niña cultiva hortalizas. 11. Deseo mucho ir a Barcelona. 12. ¿Tiene Vd. una gallina? 13. El balcón da al corral. 14. Por la tarde el padre toma el fresco. 15. Hay una casa muy hermosa en la aldea.

(4) Replace the infinitives in brackets by the appropriate form.

(Example: Los niños (cantar). Los niños cantan.)

1. Vds. (trabajar). 2. Tú no (vivir) aquí. 3. Yo (tener) muchas gallinas. 4. Nosotros (desear) dejar la aldea. 5. El viejo (vivir) en el piso bajo. 6. Vosotros (tomar) el fresco. 7. Manolita (cultivar) legumbres. 8. Nosotros (interrumpir) al maestro. 9. Tú (preparar) la comida. 10. ¿ Cómo (llamar) Vd. al burro?

(5) Conjugate in full the following verbs in the present indicative:

tener   tomar   interrumpir   desear   comer

(6) Put into the negative:

1. ¿ Tienes tú ganas de dejar la aldea? 2. Hay una fuente en el corral. 3. La cocina es muy grande. 4. ¿ Tienen rejas las ventanas de arriba? 5. La casa está al otro lado del río.

(7) The following statements are inaccurate. Correct them in Spanish.

1. Manuel hace una descripción de la escuela. 2. La parra crece por encima de la ventana. 3. En el piso bajo hay dos cuartos de dormir. 4. Manuel tiene ganas de vivir en el campo. 5. Hay mucha luz en la alcoba.

(8) Make up sentences using the following words or expressions:

hay   dar a   tener ganas de   demasiado   encima de

(9) Put into Spanish:

It is a pretty house. The upstairs windows have balconies which overlook the river. Here the family enjoys the cool of the evening. Grapes grow over the door, and behind the house are a yard and a kitchen garden where Manuel's father grows vegetables. He has also a few hens. But the house is not modern. There is no dining-room and the family eats in the large kitchen. The daughter wants to go to Barcelona like her sister,* who lives in a very modern house. Manolita's mother also wishes to go into the city, but she says she's too old to leave the village.

* her sister—su hermana.

CHAPTER IV

LAS MOSCAS

Seis hombres están sentados en un café. Hay un inglés, un francés, un español, un alemán, un ruso y un chino— seis nacionalidades.

Hace mucho calor, hace mucho sol y todos tienen sed. Cada persona tiene delante un vaso de cerveza.

Hay también seis moscas en el café y las moscas tienen también sed. Una mosca cae en el vaso del inglés, otra mosca cae en el vaso del francés, otra mosca en... etc. Las seis moscas caen en los seis vasos de cerveza.

El inglés va a beber y... ¡ve la mosca! Llama al camarero, que trae otro vaso de cerveza.

El francés ve también la mosca que está nadando en la cerveza. Está furioso, jura, da gritos....

El español mira la mosca, hace un gesto desdeñoso y sale orgullosamente del café.

El alemán retira la mosca del vaso y bebe la cerveza.

El ruso bebe la cerveza... y la mosca.

El chino toma la mosca con los dedos, contempla al pobre insecto, come la mosca y bebe la cerveza.

NOTES

One version of this story of the six men drinking in a café is to be found in the humorous book *Londres* (London), by Julio Camba, the Spanish writer and journalist.

El café

Although a good deal of wine is drunk in Spain, drunkenness is rare. A Spaniard will normally take wine with his meal and finish with coffee and perhaps a liqueur. There are Spaniards, however, who take little alcoholic refreshment, and water, though scarce in some parts at certain times of the year, is, on the whole, good.

The Spaniard uses the café as a rendezvous rather than a drinking place, and will often talk all evening or play games (cards, dominoes, and chess are very popular) over one or two glasses. All cafés have their habitués and many are, in fact, clubs, where business men, artists, and literary people meet to hold discussions. There is a large variety of beverages. Some of the more common are:

el vino—wine.

el café—coffee.

la gaseosa—mineral water, lemonade.

la horchata—a drink usually made from almonds.

la cerveza—the beer is generally very light.

el chocolate—Spanish chocolate is usually very thick and is served in special cups called **jícaras**.

los licores—liqueurs, of which **el anís** (aniseed) is very popular, and also **el aguardiente** (brandy).

el helado—ice-cream is served in infinite varieties and colours.

El vaso

El vaso is a drinking glass or tumbler. **El vidrio** is the substance, glass.

A wine-glass is **la copa**.

Extensive use is also made of the **botijo**, usually a fat-bellied earthenware vessel with a handle and a very broad spout. To drink from such a vessel it is necessary to hold it in the air and allow the water or diluted wine to pour in a fine stream into the open mouth. Considerable skill is required, since the vessel does not touch the mouth. A similar vessel made of glass is the **porrón (el)**, which is found particularly in Catalonia.

El camarero

Another word used with the meaning of "waiter" is **el mozo**. **Mozo** also means a lad in general, a railway porter, an hotel boy, etc.

El grito

The verb is **gritar**—to shout.

Desdeñoso

The noun is **el desdén**—scorn, disdain.

La mosca

Note also : **el mosquito**—midge or mosquito.

Los dedos

There is no separate word in Spanish for " toe." **Los dedos de la mano** are " fingers," and **los dedos del pie** " toes." The context usually indicates clearly which meaning is intended.

GRAMMAR

Adjectives

It has been stated before that adjectives ending in a consonant have normally one form only for masculine and feminine.

un libro útil   una lección fácil   libros, lecciones útiles

Adjectives which denote nationality or locality and adjectives ending in -*or* form the feminine by the addition of -*a*.

un campesino inglés	campesinos ingleses
una ciudad inglesa	ciudades inglesas
un niño encantador (charming)	una niña encantadora
un amigo alemán	una amiga alemana
un español	una española

There are one or two adjectives ending in -*ón* and -*án* which also form the feminine by the addition of -*a*.

un muchacho holgazán (lazy)	una muchacha holgazana
un viejo socarrón (cunning)	una vieja socarrona

Note that comparatives ending in -*or* have the same form for both masculine and feminine. These will be discussed later.

este pan es mejor   la mejor calidad
this bread is better   the best quality

Numerals

The cardinal numbers from 1 to 10 are:

1 uno	2 dos	3 tres	4 cuatro	5 cinco
6 seis	7 siete	8 ocho	9 nueve	10 diez

With the exception of **uno** which is variable (**uno, una, unos, unas**), these numerals never change in form.

nueve casas   nine houses   cuatro lápices   four pencils

Note: un amigo   a friend (or) one friend,
but   uno de mis amigos   one of my friends (i.e. when not immediately preceding a masculine singular noun).

Adjectives—cada (each), otro (other)

Cada. This adjective has one form only:

cada día   each day   cada casa   each house

Otro. Be very careful with this word. It is never used with the *indefinite* article.

Aquí tengo otro libro.   Here I have *another* book.
But El otro libro está aquí.   The other book is here.

Verbs

The **present participle** is regularly formed by adding *-ando* to the stem of the -AR verb, and *-iendo* to the stem of the -ER or -IR verbs:

cantar (to sing)   cantando (singing)
comer (to eat)   comiendo (eating)
vivir (to live)   viviendo (living)

Used in conjunction with the verb **estar,** the present participle forms the " continuous " tenses.
For instance:

Estoy cantando.   I am singing.
Vd. está escribiendo.   You are writing.

The use is similar to that in English. It indicates an action which is going on at the time of speaking or writing.

Compare:

> José canta en la iglesia cada domingo.
> José sings in church every Sunday.

> José está cantando en el cuarto de baño.
> José is singing in the bathroom.

Estar and ser

The present indicative of these two verbs is as follows:

Estar estoy, estás, está, estamos, estáis, están

Ser soy, eres, es, somos, sois, son

Estar is irregular only in the first person singular. **Ser** is irregular throughout the tense.

We have already seen that *is* can be translated by two different verbs in Spanish:

El maestro está en la clase.	The teacher is in the class.
El maestro es muy viejo.	The teacher is very old.

The understanding of the differences between **estar** and **ser** is very important. Study the following cases:

Estar	**Ser**
1. El vaso está sobre la mesa.	¿Qué es esto? Es un vaso.
The glass is on the table.	What is this? It is a glass.
2. El francés está furioso.	Es un hombre muy viejo.
The Frenchman is furious.	He is a very old man.
3. La ventana está cerrada.	El balcón es de hierro.
The window is closed.	The balcony is (made) of iron.
4. Estoy comiendo.	El libro es de Juan.
I am eating.	The book is John's.

You will see that, broadly speaking, **estar** is used to express that which is of a *temporary* character, and **ser** to express that which is of a *permanent* character. There are cases where it is at first more difficult to decide. For instance, one can argue that to be rich or poor is a temporary condition, but the Spanish always uses **ser**:

Es muy rico.   He is very rich.
La vieja es muy pobre.   The old woman is very poor.

Remember, however, that **estar** is always used whenever
place is indicated, whenever the condition is purely *temporary*,
and always with the " continuous " form of the verb.

Ser is always used to denote *possession, age, permanent*
characteristics, and *inherent* qualities.

According to the choice of verb a fine shade of meaning can
often be indicated.   For instance :

está loco	he is furious	es loco	he is mad (insane)
está enfermo	he is ill	es un enfermo	he is an invalid

Other uses of these two verbs will be pointed out later.
Make a note of all unusual cases, for observation alone will
teach the more idiomatic uses.

Irregular verbs of the present indicative.

Notice that the following verbs are irregular only in the
first person singular.

VER	to see	**veo,** ves, ve, vemos, veis, ven
DAR	to give	**doy,** das, da, damos, dais, dan
HACER	to make, do	**hago,** haces, hace, hacemos, hacéis, hacen
TRAER	to bring	**traigo,** traes, trae, traemos, traéis, traen
CAER	to fall	**caigo,** caes, cae, caemos, caéis, caen
SALIR	to go out	**salgo,** sales, sale, salimos, salís, salen

IR, to go, is wholly irregular :

voy, vas, va, vamos, vais, van

This verb is used before the infinitive with the preposition
" a " in the sense of " to be going to."

Voy a hablar.   I am going to speak.
Vamos a ver.   We are going to see, let's see.

Idiomatic Uses of hacer and tener

Note the following impersonal expressions :

hace calor	it is warm
hace frío	it is cold
tengo frío	I am cold
tengo calor	I am warm

Such expressions can be compared directly with the French : *il fait chaud*, *j'ai chaud*, etc.

Similarly :

tengo sed	I am thirsty
tengo hambre	I am hungry
tengo razón	I am right
no tengo razón	I am wrong

It is important to remember that in such an expression as " I am *very* thirsty," the Spanish is : Tengo mucha sed (literally, " I have much thirst "). **Muy (very), an** adverb, cannot, of course, qualify a noun.

Finally, compare the following :

I am cold.	Tengo frío
It is cold (weather).	Hace frío
The soup is cold.	La sopa está fría

EXERCISES

(1) Answer the following questions in Spanish :

1. ¿ Qué es una mosca?   2. ¿ Cuántos hombres están en el café?   3. ¿ Hace frío en el café?   4. ¿ Tiene Vd. sed? 5. ¿ Por qué tienen los seis hombres sed?   6. ¿ Qué hace el inglés cuando ve la mosca?   7. ¿ Qué trae el camarero? 8. ¿ Por qué está furioso el francés?   9. ¿ Qué hace el francés?   10. ¿ Bebe el español la cerveza?   11. ¿ Qué hace el alemán antes de beber la cerveza?   12. ¿ Hace el chino un gesto desdeñoso?   13. ¿ Qué bebe Vd. cuando tiene sed? ¿ Agua, vino o cerveza?   14. ¿ Dónde trabaja el camarero? 15. ¿ Qué está nadando en la cerveza?

(2) Make the following adjectives agree where necessary:

1. ¿ Desea Vd. **otro** pluma? 2. Las provincias **español**.
3. Una lección **interesante** y **útil**. 4. La cerveza **alemán**.
5. Tengo muchos libros **inglés**. 6. La mosca es **negro**.
7. La abeja es un insecto muy **útil**. 8. Una casa **chino**.
9. La mujer es **pobre**. 10. Una canción **francés**.

(3) Replace the blanks by appropriate forms of **estar** or **ser**.

1. Un vaso de cerveza _está_ sobre la mesa. 2. Madrid _es_
en España. 3. Madrid _es_ la capital de España. 4. Las
abejas _son_ insectos muy útiles. 5. El hombre _está_ nadando
en el río. 6. Don Alfonso _es_ maestro de escuela. 7. Nosotros _estamos_ en la sala de clase. 8. Vds. _están_ escribiendo una
carta. 9. La mujer _está_ furiosa. 10. Don Alfonso no _es_
rico. 11. Los balcones _son_ de hierro. 12. La parra _está_
encima de la puerta. 13. Yo _soy_ inglés. 14. Tú _estás_
comiendo pan. 15. La escuela _es_ blanca y pequeña.

(4) Replace the blanks by appropriate words:

1. Hace calor y tengo mucha _sed_. 2. La mosca _cae_ en
la cerveza. 3. El maestro _tiene_ la tiza y escribe en la ——.
4. El niño está _nadando_ en el río. 5. Cuando _cae_ la mosca en
la cerveza el español sale del café. 6. Hay _seis_ hombres en
el café. 7. Los ingleses hablan _inglés_ pero los españoles hablan
español. 8. El _mozo_ trae dos vasos de cerveza. 9. El
inglés desea otro vaso y _llama_ al camarero. 10. El alemán
retira la mosca del vaso.

(5) Give the opposites of the following words:

entrar   blanco   delante   tomar   contestar   jugar

(6) Give the Spanish for the following numbers:

1 ; 3 ; 10 ; 8 ; 9 ; 6 ; 4 ; 7 ; 5 ; 3 ; 9 ; 2 ; 4 ; 7 ; 6 ; 9 ; 8 ; 10 ; 5 ; 7.

(7) Give the 1st person present indicative of the following
verbs:

(Example : tomar   tomo.)

ir   salir   ver   traer   comer   dar   interrumpir   hacer
desear   caer

(8) Put into Spanish:

When he is thirsty Ramón goes to a little café in the village. One day he is seated in the café when two men come in. They call the waiter, who brings two glasses of wine. There are a lot of flies in the room and one falls into one of the glasses. What does the man do when he sees the fly swimming in the glass? He calls the waiter, who takes the insect out of the glass. But the man is furious, tells the waiter that he does not wish to drink the wine, and goes out of the café. The other man drinks the two glasses of wine.

CHAPTER V

CARTA DESDE SEVILLA

SEVILLA.

12 de abril.

QUERIDO PAPÁ : Muchas veces has descrito las bellezas de Sevilla y tengo que admitir que estoy completamente de acuerdo con los que dicen : Quien no ha visto Sevilla, no ha visto maravilla.

La casa de mi tío está situada en las afueras de la ciudad. Es una casa muy hermosa, rodeada de fincas y propiedades muy extensas a orillas del río.

Como sabes, mi primo Ignacio trabaja en una casa de comercio cerca del muelle. Algunas veces voy con mi primo por la mañana hasta la oficina y después doy un paseo por las calles y avenidas de la ciudad.

He subido una vez a la Giralda. La vista de la ciudad desde lo alto del campanario es verdaderamente estupenda. ¡ Y hay que ver también el Alcázar, joya de la arquitectura morisca !

Dice mi tío que aquí hace un calor tremendo durante el verano pero ahora, en el mes de abril, es muy agradable. Nunca hace frío.

Ya he dado unos paseos en bicicleta. Ignacio tiene también una bicicleta pero la suya es muy vieja. Sin embargo tenemos intención de hacer muchas excursiones por toda la región. Sobre todo deseo visitar las ruinas romanas que abundan en la vecindad.

Ya es tarde y ahora vamos a cenar. Estoy cansado y tengo mucho sueño.

Recuerdos a toda la familia.

Tu hijo que te quiere y que no te olvida,

PEPITO.

NOTES

Querido

From the verb **querer**—to love.

Caro is generally used in the sense of dear, expensive. "Este traje es demasiado caro." This dress is too dear. Another word meaning " to love " is **amar.**

Querer, besides meaning "to love," also means "to wish, want." ¿ Quiere Vd. tomar un vaso de cerveza? Will you have a glass of beer?

Papá

Daddy.   Note also **mamá.**

La belleza

The adjective is **bello**—beautiful.

Another common word is **hermoso,** from which the noun **la hermosura**—beauty.

Fincas y propiedades

La hacienda and **la finca** both mean farm, estate. **La hacienda** is used extensively in Latin America to indicate a large farm, plantation, etc.

Another common word is **la granja**—farm.   Compare the French *la grange* with its change of meaning.

El muelle

This word has two meanings : (1) a quay or wharf, (2) the spring, for instance of a watch.   The one word is connected with the English " mole " in the sense of breakwater.

Por la mañana

Note : POR la mañana.   IN the morning.
           POR la tarde.   IN the afternoon.
           POR la noche.   AT night.

Dar un paseo

El paseo is also used in the sense of avenue, promenade.
El Paseo de Colón—Columbus Avenue.

Other words of similar meaning are : **la avenida, la alameda** and, in Barcelona, **la Rambla.**

La Giralda

The bell tower of the old Moorish mosque (now replaced by the Gothic cathedral) in Seville. El Alcázar is the ancient Moorish fortress and palace. The whole of Andalusia abounds in relics of the Moorish occupation. The Arabs first crossed the straits about the year 711, and were not ultimately driven from Spain until 1492 when Granada, their last stronghold, fell to the Spaniards.

El campanario

Bell tower. **La campana** is a bell. **La campanilla** is a small hand bell, table bell, door bell.

Estupendo

This word is used a great deal in Spanish in the sense of " terrific, stupendous, marvellous."

Ruinas romanas

Andalusia was the centre of successive civilisations. Iberians, Celtiberians, Phœnicians, Greeks, Romans, Carthaginians, and Arabs have all left their traces in Spain.

Cenar

The noun is **la cena**—supper.

Recuerdos

Memory or souvenir.
* Recuerdos a don Antonio—remember me to Antonio.
Un recuerdo muy grato—a very happy memory.
Un recuerdo de Sevilla—a souvenir from Seville.

Carta

La carta—letter.
La tarjeta postal—post card.
El cartero—postman.

An envelope is **el sobre** (that which goes over), and a postage stamp **el sello** (or seal).

The post office is **la casa de correos,** and the post-box is **el buzón.**

Desde lo alto

From the top. **Lo alto** means literally " that which is high." This use of adjectives preceded by the neuter article **lo** is common in Spanish and will be discussed more fully later.

Similarly :

lo importante—the importance, what is important.

GRAMMAR

Possessive Adjectives

The following table gives the possessive adjectives corresponding to the subject personal pronouns.

yo	mi, mis (my)
tú	tu, tus (thy)
él	su, sus (his)
ella	su, sus (her)
Vd.	su, sus (your)
nosotros (as)	nuestro, a, os, as (our)
vosotros (as)	vuestro, a, os, as (your)
ellos	su, sus (their)
ellas	su, sus (their)
Vds.	su, sus (your)

Notice that those adjectives ending in -*o* vary for number and gender, those ending in -*i* or -*u* for number only.

mi casa	my house	mis lápices	my pencils
nuestra casa	our house	nuestros lápices	our pencils

Su casa may mean, of course : his, her, your, or their house. In cases of ambiguity, the following forms are used :

su casa de él	his house.
sus libros de Vd.	your books.

Corresponding to the above possessive adjectives are others which *follow* the noun.

mi	mío, mía, míos, mías	(my)
tu	tuyo, tuya, tuyos, tuyas	(thy)
su	suyo, suya, suyos, suyas	(his, her, your, their)

| nuestro | nuestro, a, os, as | (our) |
| vuestro | vuestro, a, os, as | (your) |

The use of these adjectives is fairly rare. Compare the following:

| mi madre | my mother | ¡ Madre mía ! | Mother of mine ! |

su amigo está aquí	your friend is here.
un amigo suyo	a friend of yours.
(or) uno de sus amigos	one of your friends.

Possessive Pronouns

Possessive pronouns have the same form as the second class of possessive adjectives (i.e. those which follow the noun), with the addition of the definite article.

mi (my)	el mío, la mía, los míos, las mías (mine)
tu	el tuyo, la tuya, los tuyos, las tuyas (thine)
su	el suyo, la suya, los suyos, las suyas (his, hers, yours)
nuestro	el nuestro, la nuestra, los nuestros, las nuestras (ours)
vuestro	el vuestro, la vuestra, los vuestros, las vuestras (yours)
su	el suyo, la suya, los suyos, las suyas (theirs, yours)

Aquí está su libro. ¿ Dónde está el mío ?
Here is your book. Where is mine ?

After the verb **ser,** the definite article is often **omitted,** however, unless special emphasis is desired.

¿ De quién es este libro ? Es mío.
Whose is this book ? It is mine.

¿ Por qué toma Vd. ese libro? Es el mío. No es el suyo.
Why are you taking that book? It is mine. It is not
yours.

As in the case of the possessive adjective the forms " de él,"
" de Vd.," etc., are often used to avoid ambiguity.

> Mi pluma y la de ella.   My pen and hers.

In all cases remember that the adjective or pronoun agrees
in number and gender *with the thing possessed* and not with the
possessor. Thus:

> Manuel tiene su cuaderno y Manolita tiene el suyo.
> Manuel has his copy-book and Manolita has hers.

Numerals

The cardinal numbers in Spanish from 11 to 20 are:

11 once ; 12 doce ; 13 trece ; 14 catorce ; 15 quince ; 16 diez
y seis ; 17 diez y siete ; 18 diez y ocho ; 19 diez y nueve ;
20 veinte.

Notice that from 16 to 19 compounds are employed. They
may also be written as one word:

16 dieciséis   17 diecisiete   18 dieciocho   19 diecinueve

All these numbers are invariable:

> once días   eleven days
> diez y nueve casas   nineteen houses

The Perfect Tense. Past Participles

The past participle is regularly formed by adding *-ado* to
the stem of the infinitive in the case of -AR verbs, and *-ido* to
the stem of the infinitive in the case of -ER or -IR verbs.

> cant-ar   cantado (sung)
> com-er   comido (eaten)
> viv-ir   vivido (lived)

In conjunction with the auxiliary verb **haber** (to have) the perfect tense is formed:

he vivido   I have lived.

he caído   I have fallen (notice the written accent on the weak vowel).

Haber is an irregular verb, the present indicative of which is as follows:

he, has, ha, hemos, habéis, han

The perfect tense is used to indicate an action which is *completed*, usually fairly recently. One should bear in mind that this tense in Spanish is not used to the same extent as the French. Its use corresponds rather to that of the English.

I have written the letter.	He escrito la carta.
¿ Ha visto Vd. la Giralda ?	Have you seen the Giralda ?

Notice that the auxiliary and the past participle must not be separated in Spanish:

I *have* never *seen* her.   No la **he visto** nunca.

There are a few irregular past participles in Spanish. We have already met with two cases:

ver (to see)   visto (seen)

escribir (to write)   escrito (written)

In Spanish, the past participle, when conjugated with **haber**, does not agree either with the subject or object of the verb.

La carta que ella ha **escrito.**
The letter that she has written.

Irregular Verbs of the Present Indicative

saber (to know)	sé, sabes, sabe, sabemos, sabéis, saben
decir (to say, tell)	digo, dices, dice, decimos, decís, dicen
querer (to love, want)	quiero, quieres, quiere, queremos, queréis, quieren.

Negatives Nunca. Jamás.

" Ever " is rendered in Spanish by **jamás**.

¿ Ha visto Vd. jamás la Giralda?   Have you ever seen the Giralda?

" Never " is rendered by **nunca**.

Nunca he visto la Giralda.   I have never seen the Giralda.
              (or) No he visto nunca la Giralda.

Notice that when **nunca** follows the verb, **no** must precede. Spanish does not object to the double negative.

Note also:

¿ Ha visto Vd. la Giralda?

¡ Nunca !—Never !

Idiomatic Use of tener and hay

The verb **tener** is idiomatically used with **que**:

Tengo que escribir la carta.   I have to write the letter.

Note also:

Tengo una carta que escribir.   I have a letter to write.

Similarly:

Hay que ver la Giralda.   One must see the Giralda.
                                  You should see the Giralda.

Hay mucho trabajo que hacer.   There is a lot of work to do.

¿ Por qué ? and Porque

Be careful to distinguish between these two words.

¿ Por qué sale el francés del café?
Why does the Frenchman go out of the café?

Porque está furioso.
Because he is furious.

EXERCISES

(1) Answer the following questions in Spanish:

1. ¿ A quién escribe Pepito? 2. ¿ Dónde vive el primo de Pepito? 3. ¿ Dónde está su casa de usted, en la ciudad o en el campo? 4. ¿ Vive el tío de Pepito en el centro de la ciudad? 5. ¿ Cuál es el nombre del río? 6. ¿ Dónde trabaja Ignacio? 7. ¿ Trabaja usted en una casa de comercio? 8. ¿ Dónde está la oficina de Ignacio? 9. ¿ Cuándo da Pepito un paseo por la ciudad? 10. ¿ Cómo es la vista desde lo alto de la Giralda? 11. ¿ Hace mucho frío en Sevilla? 12. ¿ Tiene usted una bicicleta? 13. ¿ Tiene usted sueño? 14. ¿ Escribe Vd. muchas cartas? 15. ¿ Hay antigüedades romanas en la vecindad de su casa de Vd.?

(2) Replace the English words in brackets by the appropriate forms of the possessive adjectives or pronouns.

(Example: Ramón ha perdido (his) bicicleta. Ramón ha perdido su bicicleta.)

1. La casa de (his) tío. 2. Estoy escribiendo una carta a (my) tío. 3. Esta bicicleta es (hers). 4. (our) casa está situada a orillas del río. 5. ¿ Cuántos libros tiene (thy) hermano? 6. La pluma roja es (mine). 7. El alemán retira la mosca de (his) vaso. 8. (our) ciudad es muy hermosa. 9. Los niños escriben en (their) cuadernos. 10. Han terminado (their) trabajo. 11. Aquí tengo (my) libros. ¿ Dónde están (yours)? 12. Manolita escribe a (her) padre. 13. Aquí está (our) oficina. 14. ¿ Quiere Vd. dar un paseo con (your) primo? 15. (my) padres han visto la ciudad.

(3) Write the following in Spanish:

(a) 3; 15; 11; 20; 18; 14; 13; 17; 12; 16; 19; 20; 12; 17; 4; 19; 17; 15.

(b) (Example: 2 plus 2 is four—dos y dos son cuatro.
4 minus 2 is 2—cuatro menos dos son dos.)

4 plus 10 is 14; 20 minus 11 is 9; 17 plus 2 is 19; 7 plus 11 is 18; 19 minus 12 is 7.

(4) Replace the infinitives in heavy type by the past participle.

(Example : ¿ Ha tomar Vd. el libro? ¿ Ha tomado Vd. el libro ?)

1. He **hablar** con el campesino. 2. ¿ Ha **ver** Vd. la Giralda? 3. Hemos **trabajar** mucho. 4. Ramón ha **beber** dos vasos de cerveza. 5. Pepito ha **escribir** a su padre. 6. Tú no has **vivir** en Madrid. 7. He **tener** que admitir el error. 8. Hemos **preparar** la comida. 9. El maestro ha **describir** las provincias de España. 10. Los niños han **jugar** en el patio.

(5) Replace the infinitives in brackets by the appropriate form of the verb (present indicative).

(Example : yo (escribir)—yo escribo.)

yo (hacer) ; él (traer) ; nosotros (saber) ; Vd. (ir) ; yo (saber) ; ¿ Qué (decir) yo? ; Alfonso (decir) un cuento ; nosotros (ir) al café ; los niños (hacer) cálculos ; vosotros (salir) del comedor.

(6) Make up sentences in Spanish using the following words or expressions :

tener que   tener sueño   ir a   dar un paseo   sin embargo
   a orillas de   también   hasta   cada   cerca de

(7) Put into Spanish :

1. I am thirsty. 2. We are sleepy. 3. It's terribly hot. 4. Are you cold? 5. I have to write a letter. 6. She has never seen the Giralda. 7. I know that your brother is here. 8. We are not going to write the letter. 9. Have you seen your uncle? 10. He says he lives near the wharf.

(8) Put into Spanish :

Pepito is writing a letter from Seville to his father in Bilbao. He describes the city, his walks along the beautiful avenues, his uncle's house on the banks of the Guadalquivir, where he is spending his holidays. Pepito also tells his father that he intends to make cycling trips with his cousin Ignacio. Ignacio works in a business house near the river. Pepito sometimes accompanies him as far as the office.

RECAPITULATION I

EXERCISES

(1) Put into Spanish:

1. The houses of the village are small and white. 2. He has no goats. 3. It is cold and I am very hungry. 4. Have you written your letter yet? 5. She never knows what to do. 6. Has he had to leave the town? 7. There are many charming villages in the provinces. 8. I am not going to eat all the bread. 9. Will you bring another glass? (use " querer "). 10. Do you want a cup of coffee? 11. He is writing a letter to his brother. 12. Where do your parents live? 13. Here is your pen, but where is mine? 14. We spent nineteen days in Barcelona. 15. The water is too cold. 16. They say he is a doctor, but I know they are wrong. 17. Have you seen the school? 18. His uncle and aunt are at present in Madrid. 19. Spanish peasants eat a great deal of soup. 20. Do you want to go for a walk?

(2) Write the appropriate definite article (EL or LA) before the following nouns:

canción   lápiz   libro   luz   calor   fuente   calle   mano
                         agua   muchacha

(3) Give the first person singular (present indicative) of the following verbs:

tener   interrumpir   ser   dar   caer   escribir   ir   saber
                        decir   hacer

(4) Give the first person plural (present indicative) of the following verbs:

caer   ver   estar   haber   decir   saber   querer   dar
                         ir   hacer

(5) Give the present and past participles of the following verbs:

tener　　ver　　interrumpir　　escribir　　gritar

(6) Replace the blanks by appropriate words:

1. Sevilla es una —— muy hermosa.
2. Los niños aprenden a —— en la escuela.
3. Comemos en el ——.
4. La Giralda es un ——.
5. He dado un —— por la calle.
6. Para escribir una carta necesitamos—— —— ——.
7. El burro bebe el agua de la ——.
8. Cultivamos —— en la huerta.
9. La semana tiene —— días.
10. Ya es muy tarde y tengo ——.

(7) The following sentences are answers to questions. Give the original questions.

1. Sí, el río pasa por la aldea.
2. He escrito tres o cuatro cartas.
3. El maestro de escuela es muy simpático.
4. El burro bebe porque tiene sed.
5. Los niños escuchan con atención.

CHAPTER VI

EL ESTANCO

SIEMPRE a las ocho de la mañana sale don José de casa para ir a su trabajo.   Generalmente va a pie pero cuando llueve toma el tranvía.

Esta mañana hace mucho sol y don José va a pie.

Atraviesa la calle, pasa por delante de la Casa de

Correos, toma la primera calle de la derecha, la segunda de la izquierda, y llega a la Plaza de Aragón.   En el centro de la plaza un guardia municipal dirige la circulación— automóviles, tranvías, autobuses, carros y bicicletas.

Al otro lado de la plaza hay un café que lleva el nombre algo pretencioso de " Iberia."   Aquí toma don José una jícara de chocolate o una taza de café con leche.   Después de este desayuno sencillo va directamente a la calle del Conde de Mantua en el barrio comercial.

En esta calle estrecha hay muchas casas comerciales, cafés, establecimientos de limpiabotas y tiendas de todas clases. Aquí también está el estanco a donde va cada día. El tendero sabe exactamente lo que quiere don José. Éste dice solamente :— ¡ Muy buenos días, don Enrique ! — y pone su dinero en el mostrador. Compra un periódico ilustrado, un paquete de cigarrillos y una cajita de cerillas. Además de tabaco don Enrique vende sellos de correo y billetes para la lotería nacional.

Cuando vuelve a casa por la tarde don José puede tomar el tranvía o el autobús. Prefiere el autobús pero cuesta más dinero.

Sus gastos diarios son :

		Pesetas
Desayuno	. .	10.00
Periódico	. .	03.00
Cerillas	. .	01.00
Cigarrillos	. .	11.00
Almuerzo	. .	60.00
Tranvía	. .	02.50
Total	.	87.50 (ochenta y siete pesetas, cincuenta céntimos)

NOTES

Va a pie

Similarly :

ir a caballo —to go on horseback.
But ir en bicicleta —to cycle
ir en automóvil —to go by car

Delante de

El hombre está **delante de** la casa—the man is in front of the house.

El hombre pasa **por delante de** la casa—the man passes (in front of) the house.

Note that in the one case no motion is implied, whilst in the second case the man actually walks past.

De la izquierda

The adjective is **izquierdo**—left.

Note:

a la izquierda—on the left (hand).

a la derecha —on the right (hand).

El guardia municipal

The town policeman, the traffic policeman, employed by the municipality. On the other hand, **el guardia civil** is employed by the state. The " guardia civil " corresponds to the French " gendarme," is often mounted on horseback, and carries rifle and sabre. The distinctive feature of the " guardia civil " is the hat which he wears.

El automóvil

The word **el coche**, formerly carriage, has come to mean motor-car in modern times.

ir en coche—to go by car.

Tiene un hermoso coche. He has a beautiful car.

La jícara

The special cup for drinking chocolate. The ordinary word for " cup " is **la taza.** Compare the French *la tasse.*

Café con leche

White coffee, coffee with milk. Black coffee is called in Spanish **café solo** (i.e. coffee alone).

El limpiabotas

This is a compound of **limpiar** (to clean) and **botas** (boots). Bootblacks abound in Spain. Few Spaniards clean their shoes at home, and it is no uncommon sight to see a man having his boots cleaned whilst he sits drinking in a café. To avoid the too persistent attentions of the bootblacks it is often advisable to wear non-leather footwear, as many Spaniards do. Canvas shoes with rope or hempen soles, so typical of Spain, are called **las alpargatas.**

El estanco

The estanco is really the shop where Government-controlled goods such as tobacco, matches, stamps, etc., are sold. Another Government monopoly is the **lotería nacional**, run on the same lines as a sweepstake. Lottery tickets are sold in the estancos, in cafés, and by street vendors.

El mostrador

Counter. This word derives from **mostrar** (to show). Another derivative is **la muestra** (a sample, i.e. something shown).

El periódico

Newspaper. Also **el diario**—dail**y.**
A magazine is **la revista**

Las cerillas

La cera is wax. **Cerilla** is a diminutive form, meaning " wax vesta." Wooden matches tipped with phosphorus are **los fósforos**, but the latter are generally of poor quality.

La cajita

Another diminutive. **La caja** is a box; **la cajita** a little box. Spanish is very fond of diminutive suffixes.

Los gastos

Expenses. The verb is **gastar** (to spend), from which the noun is derived

GRAMMAR

Demonstrative Adjectives

There are three demonstrative adjectives in Spanish : **este** (this), **ese** (that, near to the person addressed), **aquel** (that, over there, yonder). These adjectives agree in number and gender with the noun they qualify.

este libro	this book	esta pluma	this pen
estos libros	these books	estas plumas	these pens

And similarly:

ese	esa	esos	esas
aquel	aquella	aquellos	aquellas

Demonstrative Pronouns

Corresponding to the adjectives are the pronouns, which are identical in form, except that they bear the accent.

este	(this)	éste	(this one)
ese	(that)	ése	(that one)
aquel	(that)	aquél	(that one over there)

These pronouns agree with the noun they replace in number and gender, just as do the adjectives.

Este lápiz es blanco, ése es rojo y aquél es negro.
This pencil is white, that one is red, and that one over there black.

¿Dónde están mis libros? Éstos son los suyos (or: los de Vd.).
Where are my books? These are yours.

In addition there are three corresponding neuter forms:

esto (this)   eso (that)   aquello (that, yonder)

If, for example, we ask: " What is this? " it is obvious that the gender cannot be ascertained until it is known what the object referred to is.

¿Qué es esto? What is this?
Esto es un lápiz. This is a pencil.

Numerals

The cardinal numbers from 21 to 100 are:

21 veinte y uno	22 veinte y dos	23 veinte y tres, etc.	
30 treinta	40 cuarenta	50 cincuenta	60 sesenta
70 setenta	80 ochenta	90 noventa	100 ciento

Note: 21—veinte y uno, *but* 21 books—veinte y un libros (i.e. twenty books and one book).

Veinte y uno, etc., may also be written as: veintiuno, veintidós, veintitrés, veinticuatro, veinticinco, veintiséis, veintisiete, veintiocho, veintinueve. Note the accents in those cases ending in -s.

100 is **ciento**, but when followed *immediately* by a noun a shortened form is employed.

A hundred houses   cien casas.   (Notice that the indefinite article is NOT used as in English.)

With the exception of those compounds containing **uno**, all these numbers are invariable.

cuarenta y seis días	forty-six days.
ciento treinta y dos sellos	a hundred and thirty-two stamps.
but	
ochenta y una casas	eighty-one houses.

Expressions of Time

¿ Qué hora es ?	What time is it ?
Es la una.	It is one o'clock.
Son las tres de la tarde.	It is three o'clock *in* the afternoon.
A las doce.	At twelve o'clock.

In these cases the word " hora " is understood.

Son las cuatro (horas).
It is four o'clock (hours).

Adverbs

An adverb is regularly formed by adding *-mente* to the feminine singular of the adjective.

hermosa	hermosamente	beautifully
útil	útilmente	usefully
atenta	atentamente	attentively

Adverbial expressions may also be formed by using **con** (with) before the noun.

atentamente (or) con atención
alegremente (or) con alegría

Radical Changing Verbs

There are certain verbs in Spanish which modify their root vowels whenever the stress falls on them.

In such cases E becomes IE and O becomes UE.

atravesar—to cross	costar—to cost
atravieso	cuesto
atraviesas	cuestas
atraviesa	cuesta
atravesamos	costamos
atravesáis	costáis
atraviesan	cuestan

Note that in the case of the *first* and *second* persons *plural* the stress does NOT fall on the root vowel and there is, therefore, no modification of the root vowel.

These changes may affect all conjugations:

poder —to be able	puedo —I am able
volver —to return	vuelvo —I return
preferir—to prefer	prefiero—I prefer
querer —to love, want	quiero —I love
podemos —we are able	
volvemos —we return	
preferimos—we prefer	
queremos —we love	

It is a good plan to take a note of all such radical changing verbs in Spanish, since they can be assimilated only by experience. In many cases there also exist derivatives of these verbs which give useful clues. For instance, **el cuento** (story, tale) is connected with **contar** (to relate, count), which is radical changing.

Present Indicative.   Irregular Verbs

venir—to come   vengo, vienes, viene, venimos, venís, vienen
poner—to put   pongo, pones, pone, ponemos, ponéis, ponen

Impersonal Verb

Note the impersonal verb **llover**, which is also radical changing.

llueve—it rains, it is raining,

but está lloviendo (i.e. no modification of the root vowel when the stress does not fall on it).

EXERCISES

(1) Answer the following questions in Spanish:

1. ¿A qué hora sale don José de casa? 2. ¿Cuándo toma don José el tranvía? 3. ¿Qué hace antes de pasar por delante de la Casa de Correos? 4. ¿Quién está en el centro de la plaza? 5. ¿Qué hace el guardia? 6. ¿Qué hay al otro lado de la plaza? 7. ¿Qué nombre lleva el café? 8. ¿Toma Vd. té, chocolate o café por la mañana? 9. ¿Toma Vd. café solo o con leche? 10. ¿Dónde está situada la oficina de don José? 11. ¿Qué quiere comprar don José? 12. ¿Dice don José al tendero lo que quiere comprar? 13. ¿Qué vende don Enrique además de periódicos, tabaco y cerillas? 14. ¿Prefiere Vd. el autobús o el tranvía? 15. ¿Cuánto cuesta el almuerzo de don José?

(2) Give the Spanish for the following numbers:

(a) 20 ; 40 ; 70 ; 50; 30; 80 ; 90 ; 100 ; 21 ; 44 ; 99 ; 28 ; 56 ; 84.

Write in full:

(b) 21 houses. 33 donkeys. 23 and 46 are 69. 100 minus 55 is 45. 100 letters. It is 10 o'clock. At 1 o'clock. It is 7 o'clock.

(3) Translate the English words in brackets.

1. (This) casa es muy vieja. 2. (Those) cartas sobre la mesa son (mine). 3. (That) edificio es la Giralda. 4. ¿De quién son (those) lápices? (This one) es (mine) y (that one) es (yours). 5. He visto (that) libro pero prefiero (this one). 6. ¿Quiere Vd. darme (that) pluma. No es (yours). 7. Es una casa muy hermosa, pero hay que ver (that) de don José. 8. ¿Qué es (this)? Es (my) cuaderno. 9. ¿Cuántas pesetas cuestan (those) cigarrillos? 10. Cuestan dos pesetas cincuenta, pero (these) cuestan más.

(4) Replace the blanks by the correct forms of **este, ese, aquel.**

(Example : —— tiza.   Esta tiza, esa tiza, aquella tiza.)
—— lápiz.   —— casas.   —— día.   —— descripción.
—— profesor.   —— periódico.   —— mujer.   —— bueyes.
—— canciones.   —— agua.

(5) Form adverbs from the following adjectives :

general   pretencioso   final   útil   diario

What other method is there of expressing : alegremente ; atentamente ?

(6) Replace the infinitives in heavy type by the appropriate form of the present indicative.

(Example : Don José **ir** a la oficina.   Don José va a la oficina.)

1. Don José **querer** comprar tabaco.   2. Nosotros **atravesar** la calle.   3. Yo **preferir** el autobús.   4. Estos cigarrillos **costar** dos pesetas.   5. **Llover** mucho en Inglaterra.   6. Conchita **volver** a casa y **preparar** la comida.   7. Yo **poner** el dinero en el mostrador.   8. ¿ A qué hora **venir** su amigo ? 9. Generalmente ella **ir** a pie.   10. ¿ Cuántas cerillas **comprar** Vd. ?

(7) Put into Spanish :

1. Do you prefer the tram-car ?   2. At what time does he generally arrive ?   3. I intend to go on foot.   4. There are a lot of shops in this town.   5. These cigarettes are yours. Where are mine ?   6. I always say good morning to the policeman.

(8) Put into Spanish :

Don José usually arrives at the office at nine o'clock in the morning.   When it is fine he walks, but when it rains he goes on the tram.   He always goes to the tobacconist's in the street near his office in the commercial quarter of the town, says good morning to don Enrique, and buys cigarettes and matches.   He has breakfast and lunch in a restaurant on the other side of the square.

CHAPTER VII

LOS BURROS

En España hay miles de burros. Los hay de todas clases
—pequeños y grandes, buenos y malos, perezosos y
trabajadores, inocentes y astutos, bonitos y feos, inteligentes y estúpidos. Los hay que trabajan y los que no

trabajan. Con respecto a esto la raza humana no es muy
diferente.

Casi cada familia en el campo tiene su burro. El
animal pasa el día en el prado y la noche en la cuadra.
Algunas veces quiere trabajar, otras veces no—¡lo que
indica su inteligencia! El borrico es amigo de los niños,
pertenece a la familia y conoce a cada miembro de ella.
A veces trata de entrar en la casa.

¿De quién es este burro cargado de mercancías que
anda tan despacio por el camino polvoriento? Es uno

de los muy numerosos que recorren las carreteras de toda España. No está cansado, pero no quiere andar más de prisa.

Dos o tres veces por semana van los campesinos al mercado con sus mercancías. Innumerables burros siguen cada vez el mismo camino como una caravana en el desierto. Y durante todo el día permanecen los burros en la plaza del mercado, dóciles y pacientes, aguardando el regreso al campo.

Los grupos de gitanos que van de pueblo en pueblo tienen también sus burros, los cuales parecen aceptar filosóficamente esta vida errante.

Hay personas en España (como en todos los países) que maltratan a los burros pero por regla general los españoles tienen mucho cariño a estos animales tan simpáticos.

NOTES

Los burros

Perhaps the most delightful book in Spanish dealing with donkeys is *Platero y yo*, by Juan Ramón Jiménez. It is the life story of a little donkey named Platero.

El prado

We have already met the word **el campo**—the field.

El prado is a meadow. **La pradera**—meadow land.

El Museo del Prado in Madrid is the famous art gallery in Madrid, the National Gallery of Spain.

El miembro

For example: Los miembros de la Academia Española— members of the Spanish Academy.

El socio is the member of a society (la sociedad) and also has the meaning of a partner in a business house.

Polvoriento

Dusty.

Do not confuse **el polvo** (dust) with **la pólvora** (gunpowder). El camino está lleno de polvo. The road is very dusty. The word used in the plural (**los polvos**) means face-powder.

La carretera

El camino is the ordinary word for road, way. Cf. the French *le chemin*.

La carretera is a modern, metalled road.

El mercado

Connected words are: las mercancías—merchandise, and el mercader—merchant.

Undoubtedly one of the most picturesque scenes of Spanish life is that of market day in a small country town. Setting out from villages and farms in the surrounding districts the country people flock to the local centre with their wares. From very early morning the roads leading to the market are crowded with every imaginable means of transport—donkeys, horses, mules, bullock carts, buses, and motor-cars.

Los gitanos

There are still many gypsies in Spain. Some continue to live nomadic lives; others have settled down, particularly in Andalusia and the south, and follow some fixed trade or business.

On market days their stalls and booths are often to be found in the dried-up bed of the river. It is in this way that they avoid paying dues to the local authorities.

La cuadra

Another word for stable is la caballeriza (connected with el caballo—the horse).

Be careful to use the word establo in its correct sense.

El establo is for cattle only. Cf. the French: *l'étable*, in this respect.

Do not confuse la cuadra (stable) with el cuadro (picture).

Despacio

An adverb normally ends in *-mente*, as for example:

> desdeñosamente   disdainfully
> orgullosamente   proudly

Despacio is the usual word meaning " slowly." **Lentamente** (from **lento**—slow) is less colloquial.

Andar

This verb means " to walk," " to go," and enters into a large number of idiomatic expressions.

" To walk " is usually rendered by **ir, ir a pie** (to go on foot).

Notice also: **caminar**—to walk, go, travel.

Compare:

Siempre va a pie.	He always walks.
El tren anda despacio.	The train is travelling slowly.
Este reloj no anda bien.	This watch doesn't go well.
Está caminando por España.	He is walking, wandering, travelling through Spain.

GRAMMAR

Interrogative Pronouns

Qué. This word is invariable. It refers to things only. It may be the subject or object (direct or indirect) of a sentence.

¿ Qué es esto ?	What is this ?
¿ Qué dice Vd. ?	What do you say ?
¿ De qué habla Vd. ?	What are you talking about ?
¿ Por qué no viene don Carlos ?	Why doesn't don Carlos come ?

Notice also that this word is used adjectively.

¿ Qué día es hoy ?	What day is it today ?

As an adjective it may also refer to persons.

¿ Qué señor es éste ?	What gentleman is this ?

It is also used in exclamatory sentences.

¡ Qué día !	What a day !

Quién. This word refers to persons only. It is variable—forming a plural **quiénes**—and may be the subject or object (direct or indirect) of a sentence.

¿ Quién viene hoy ?	Who is coming today ?
¿ Quiénes son ?	Who are they ?
¿ A quién ha visto Vd. ?	Whom have you seen ?
¿ Con quién quiere Vd. ir ?	With whom do you wish to go ?

Note particularly :

> ¿ De quién es este libro ?
> Whose (of whom) is this book ?

Cuál. This word refers to both persons and things. It is variable—forming a plural **cuáles**—and may be the subject or object (direct or indirect) of a sentence.

¿ Cuál prefiere Vd. ?	Which (one) do you prefer ?
¿ Cuáles son para vender ?	Which are for sale ?

Relative Pronouns

Que. As a relative the word refers to both persons and things. It is invariable.

When referring to persons it may be the subject or direct object of a sentence.

El hombre que está aquí.	The man who is here.
Las mujeres que están en el campo.	The women who are in the field.
El señor que he visto.	The gentleman I have seen.
Los niños que vemos.	The children we see.

When referring to things it may be the subject or object (both direct and indirect) of a sentence.

Los lápices que están sobre la mesa.	The pencils that are on the table.
Los cuadernos que Vd. ha tomado.	The copy-books you have taken.
La cajita en que Vd. ha metido las cerillas.	The box into which you have put the matches.

Notice that the relative cannot be omitted in Spanish :

> The book I bought.   El libro **que** he comprado.

Quien. Plural: **quienes.** This word refers to persons only. It must be used after a preposition (i.e. as indirect object).

El hombre a quien he escrito.	The man to whom I have written.
Los obreros con quienes trabaja.	The workmen with whom he works.

Quien may be used instead of **que** in such cases as:

El señor quien ha venido, (or) El señor que ha venido.
· La niña a quien he visto, (or) La niña que he visto.

El cual. This word is variable: el cual, la cual, los cuales, las cuales. It refers to persons or things and may be used as the subject or object (direct or indirect) of a sentence. This form is used for emphasis and to avoid ambiguity.

Es el dueño de la casa, de la cual Vd. hablaba ayer.
He is the owner of the house you were talking about yesterday.

There can be no doubt that **la cual** refers to **la casa**.

Cuyo. This word is variable: cuyo, cuya, cuyos, cuyas. It refers to persons or things and agrees in gender and number with the noun it qualifies.

El señor, cuya madre está aquí.	The gentleman whose mother is here.
El pueblo, cuyo nombre he olvidado.	The village the name of which I have forgotten.

Cuyo may also be governed itself by a preposition.

Es don Anselmo, de cuyos padres Vd. hablaba.
It is don Anselmo, about whose parents you were talking.

Lo que. This refers to a clause, a sentence, or an idea.

No comprendo lo que dice.	I don't understand what he says.
Lo que dice es ridículo.	What he says is ridiculous.

Note also:
Los hay que trabajan y los que no trabajan.
There are those who work and those who don't work.

Numerals

The cardinal numbers from 100 to 1000 are:

100 ciento	200 doscientos	300 trescientos
400 cuatrocientos	500 QUINIENTOS	600 seiscientos
700 SETECIENTOS	800 ochocientos	900 NOVECIENTOS
	1000 mil	

The numbers 200 to 900 are variable:

200 men	doscientos hombres
300 houses	trescientAS casas

Note particularly the irregular forms: 500, 700, and 900.

Mil (1000) is invariable. Mil soldados—a thousand soldiers (note that, as in the case of **cien**, the indefinite article is NOT used in Spanish). **Mil** may also be used as a noun, as: miles de burros—thousands of donkeys.

Compare the English system with the Spanish:

seven hundred and sixty-four   setecientos sesenta y cuatro

In dates later than the year one thousand **mil** is employed in the Spanish system.

In the year 1856.   En el año mil ochocientos cincuenta y seis.

Radical Changing Verbs

There is a third type of radical changing verb (of the third conjugation) which changes the root vowel E into I whenever the stress falls on it.

pedir (to ask for)	**seguir** (to follow)
pido	sigo
pides	sigues
pide	sigue
pedimos	seguimos
pedís	seguís
piden	siguen

Notice again that the vowel is not modified in the first and second persons plural, since the stress does not fall on the root vowel.

Changes of Spelling

With regard to the present indicative, there are a number of verbs of the second and third conjugations which modify their spelling in the first person singular. Such are, for example:

vencer—to conquer	VENZO, vences, vence, vencemos, vencéis, vencen
dirigir—to direct	DIRIJO, diriges, dirige, etc.
distinguir—to distinguish	DISTINGO, distingues, distingue, etc.

The reason for this change is obvious, since, were the original letter retained before the -o of the first person singular, a different sound would be produced. The sound that occurs before the infinitive ending must be preserved throughout the whole verb.

There are a few verbs in -CER, -CIR immediately preceded by a vowel which insert z before the -o of the first person singular of the present indicative. Such are:

conocer—to know, be acquainted with.

CONOZCO, conoces, conoce, conocemos, conocéis, conocen

conducir—to lead, conduct.

CONDUZCO, conduces, conduce, conducimos, conducís, conducen.

As in the case of the radical changing verbs, form the habit of noting all verbs which have this peculiarity.

Irregular Verbs of the Present Indicative

oir—to hear.

oigo, oyes, oye, oímos, oís, oyen

EXERCISES

(1) Answer the following questions in Spanish:

1. ¿ Hay muchos burros en Inglaterra? 2. ¿ Dónde pasa el burro el día? ¿ la noche? 3. ¿ Cuándo trabajan los burros? 4. ¿ Cómo andan los burros? 5. ¿ Anda el buey despacio o de prisa? 6. ¿ Está Vd. cansado? 7. ¿ Cuántas veces por semana vienen los campesinos al mercado? 8. ¿ Dónde permanecen los burros durante el día? 9. ¿ Cómo aguardan el regreso al campo? 10. ¿ Qué venden los gitanos? 11. ¿ Son los burros animales inteligentes o estúpidos? 12. ¿ Cómo sabemos que los burros son inteligentes? 13. ¿ Cómo aceptan los burros su vida errante? 14. ¿ Quieren los españoles a los burros? 15. ¿ Hay mercado en la ciudad donde Vd. vive?

(2) Complete the following sentences:

1. El hombre que trabaja mucho es ——. 2. El hombre que no trabaja nunca es ——. 3. El pobre animal está cargado de ——. 4. Los gitanos —— de ciudad en ciudad. 5. El burro pasa la noche en la ——.

(3) The following two lines contain words which have opposite meanings. Pair off these words.

pequeño bueno perezoso bonito inteligente diferente noche

día mismo estúpido malo grande trabajador feo

(4) Replace the English word in brackets by the correct Spanish equivalent.

1. ¿ (What) tiene Vd.? 2. Los burros (that) están en el prado. 3. El aldeano (who) trabaja en el campo. 4. ¿ (Who) ha venido? 5. ¿ (Whose) es este lápiz? 6. ¿ (Which) de estos lápices es el mío? 7. La mujer (who) está preparando la comida. 8. El libro (that) Vd. ha leído. 9. ¿ (Whom) ha visto Vd.? 10. El amigo (to whom) ha dado el libro. 11. ¿ (What) libro tiene Vd. en la mano? 12. ¿ (Who) ha

comido las frutas? 13. ¿ (With whom) tiene Vd. intención de visitar la ciudad? 14. ¿ (Whom) quiere Vd. ver? 15. Los niños (who) aprenden la lección.

(5) Give alternative expressions in Spanish for the following:

rápidamente   lentamente   a veces   atentamente

generalmente

(6) Give the Spanish for the following numbers:

220; 530; 740; 1000; 900; 800; 475; 364; 687; 598.

(7) Give the first person singular and plural (present indicative) of the following verbs:

poner volver venir decir conocer hacer dirigir saber

seguir oir

(8) Put into Spanish:

1. I have a thousand books. 2. Do you know Anita? 3. I know what he wants. 4. The old man goes from town to town along the dusty roads. 5. Whose is this donkey? 6. The animal won't go more quickly. 7. The caravan is crossing the desert. 8. The gipsies are waiting in the market place. 9. There are those who play and those who work. 10. Of whom is he speaking?

(9) Put into Spanish:

Have you ever seen a market in the square of a little Spanish town? The country people come there once or twice a week with their donkeys, laden with fruit and vegetables. And these patient animals stay all day in the square, awaiting the return to the country in the evening. The men and women are buying and selling their merchandise and the children are playing in the street.

CHAPTER VIII

DIALOGO

(Don Jaime y doña Luisa están en la sala. Son las once
de la noche.)

Don Jaime : — Ya es tarde. Voy a acostarme.

Doña Luisa : — ¿ Estarás libre mañana ? ¿ Habrás
terminado ese trabajo ?

Don Jaime : — Sí, alma mía, mañana estaré completamente libre. No tendré nada que hacer.

Doña Luisa : — ¿ Qué haremos pues ?

Don Jaime : — Si no tienes inconveniente iremos a los
toros.

Doña Luisa : — ¡ A los toros ! Ya sabes que no me
gustan los toros....¡ tanta sangre !...¡ qué asco !

Don Jaime : — Pero, queridita, es una corrida algo
especial. Manolete....

Doña Luisa : — ¡ Manolete !

DON JAIME : — ...es un matador muy famoso. ¿ No le conoces ? ¿ No te acuerdas de aquella corrida en Madrid ?...pero, si lo prefieres, iremos a un partido de fútbol o de pelota.

DOÑA LUISA : — Tampoco me interesan esos juegos infantiles.

DON JAIME : — ¡ Juegos infantiles ! Son deportes. Pero...¿ qué quieres tú hacer ? ¿ Quieres pasar la tarde en casa escuchando la radio ? Mañana van a radiar un concierto sinfónico....

DOÑA LUISA : — Te diré lo que haremos. Daremos un paseo hasta la playa. Con el calor que hace pasaremos una tarde deliciosa. Tú podrás bañarte.

DON JAIME : — ¿ Y después ?

DOÑA LUISA : — Después comeremos en ese restaurant. ... ¿ Cómo se llama ese restaurant de la esquina cerca del Museo de Pinturas ?

DON JAIME : — Restaurant de París.

DOÑA LUISA : — Eso es. Y después de cenar iremos al teatro. Echan una comedia de Benavente.

DON JAIME : — Yo prefiero ir al cine. Se estrena una película : Luces de Buenos Aires. Me han dicho que vale la pena de verla. Es una película muy...artística.

DOÑA LUISA : — ¡ Eso dices tú !

DON JAIME : — Bueno. Iremos al teatro. (Don Jaime sale del cuarto y vuelve al cabo de cinco minutos.) He telefoneado al teatro y han reservado dos butacas para mañana.

NOTES

Tarde

Ya es tarde—it is already late.

llegar tarde—to arrive late.

Do not confuse with **la tarde**—the afternoon, the evening.

Note : A las seis de la tarde—at six o'clock IN the evening.

Buenas tardes—good evening, good afternoon. Remember that the plural form is used.

Similarly:

| Buenos días | good day, good morning |
| Buenas noches | good night |

Alma mía

A term of endearment.   Note: el alma (*f.*).

Los toros

Ir a los toros—to go to a bull fight.

Bullfighting is still popular in most parts of Spain, although in Catalonia football and pelota are preferred.   Whilst bull-fighting is undoubtedly a cruel sport, it must be realised that it is primarily the astounding courage, skill, and precision of the matador which attracts the crowds.   A bull fight is **una corrida de toros.**   The bull ring is **la plaza de toros.**   The word **matador** literally means " killer," from the verb **matar**—to kill.   The matador is sometimes called **el espada. La espada** means " sword," and **el espada** the one who wields the sword.

Qué asco !

An expression of repugnance equivalent to the English " It makes me sick ! "

El juego de pelota

Pelota is a ball game of Basque origin, not unlike fives, but played in a much longer court called **el frontón,** and is very popular in North-eastern Spain and some parts of Latin America.   **La pelota** is also the usual word for a ball. The notice: " Se prohibe jugar a la pelota," is commonly seen pasted up on walls and buildings throughout Spain.

La radio

This word is feminine, although ending in -*o*, since it is short for **la radiotelefonía.**

It is also called **la T.S.H.** or **telegrafía sin hilos** (telegraphy without wires).

Bañarse

To bathe, have a bath.
The bath is **el baño.**
A swimming pool is **la piscina.**
To swim is **nadar,** and swimming **la natación.**

Echar una comedia

Echar means literally " to throw." In this respect the English " cast " may be compared.

Estrenar

Estrenar una comedia is to show for the first time.
El estreno is the " first night " of a play or film.

El teatro

A second performance is usually given at Spanish theatres after the evening meal and commencing at ten, ten-thirty, or even later.

Las localidades—seats.

Las butacas—stall seats (literally " arm-chair seats ").

El patio in theatrical language is the pit.

An actor is **un actor** and an actress **una actriz.**

Generally speaking, **ir a la comedia** means " to go to the theatre."

A general word for play is **una pieza de teatro.**

La tragedia is self-explanatory, and **la zarzuela** is a typically Spanish performance in some ways resembling musical comedy.

Telefonear

The noun is **el teléfono.** To ring up is **llamar por teléfono.**

GRAMMAR

Personal Pronouns (Conjunctive)

The following table gives the personal pronouns (direct and indirect objects), corresponding to the subject pronouns.

Subject		Direct Object		Indirect Object	
yo	I	me	me	me	to me
tú	thou	te	thee	te	to thee
él	he ; it	le ; lo	him ; it	le	to him ; to it
ella	she ; it	la	her ; it	le	to her ; to it
Vd.	you	le ; la	you	le	to you
nosotros	we	nos	us	nos	to us
vosotros	you	os	you	os	to you
ellos	they	los	them	les	to them
ellas	they	las	them	les	to them
Vds.	you	los ; las	you	les	to you

Examples :

Jaime me escribe dos veces por semana.
Jaime writes to me twice a week.

Pone el libro sobre la mesa.   Lo pone sobre la mesa.
He puts the book on the table.   He puts it on the table.

La señora ha escrito dos cartas.   Las ha escrito.
The lady has written two letters.   She has written them.

¿ La ha visto Vd. ?
Have you seen her ?

Consider the following case where ambiguity is possible :

Le escribe una carta.   This could mean : " He (or she) writes a letter to him, to her, to you."   If the context were not to make the meaning clear, it would be necessary to write the sentence as follows :

Le escribe una carta a él.	He writes a letter to him.
Le escribe una carta a ella.	He writes a letter to her.
Le escribe una carta a Vd.	He writes a letter to you.

These pronouns normally *precede* the verb.

No lo ha dicho.   He hasn't said so.
¿ No la ha visto Vd. ?   Haven't you seen her (or it) ?

In the case of the infinitive, however, the pronoun follows and is added to the infinitive.

No quiero hacerlo.   I don't wish to do it.
Para verle.   In order to see him.

Similarly in the case of the " continuous " form of the verb.

Le está escribiendo (or) Está escribiéndole.   He is writing to him.

When the latter form is used, notice that it is necessary to write the accent on the present participle in order to preserve the original stress.

When two pronouns come together, the dative always precedes the accusative.

Enrique da el libro a nosotros—Enrique nos lo da.
Enrique gives the book to us —Enrique gives it to us.

Reflexive Verbs

In the present chapter we have met the verb **llamarse.** The simple infinitive **llamar** means " to call." The reflexive verb **llamarse** means " to call oneself " or " to be called."

The verb is conjugated as follows :

(yo)	me llamo
(tú)	te llamas
(él)	se llama
(ella)	se llama
(Vd.)	se llama
(nosotros)	nos llamamos
(vosotros)	os llamáis
(ellos)	se llaman
(ellas)	se llaman
(Vds.)	se llaman

Notice that in the reflexive verb the third person pronoun, both singular and plural, is **se** (oneself, himself, herself, yourself, themselves, yourselves).

A verb may be reflexive both in English and Spanish. For instance, **lavarse** means " to wash oneself," " to have a wash."

Reflexive verbs are much more numerous, however, in Spanish than in English. In the present chapter occurs the word **acordarse**—" to remember." The English verb is not reflexive, but it is easy to see the reflexive sense of the Spanish verb if we substitute " to recall to oneself."

The reflexive construction is often used in Spanish where the English would prefer the passive voice. For instance, note such expressions as :

Aquí se habla español.   Spanish spoken here.

This use corresponds to the French *Ici on parle français.*

Similarly :

Se abre a las tres.	They open at three.
Se prohíbe fumar.	Smoking prohibited.
¿ Cómo se llama este pueblo ?	What is the name of this village ? What is this village called ?

Future Indicative

This tense is formed by adding the present indicative of **haber** (with slight modifications) to the infinitive.

hablar—hablaré	I shall speak, etc.	(h)e
hablarás		(h)as
hablará		(h)a
hablaremos		(h)emos
hablaréis		(hab)éis
hablarán		(h)an

comer—comeré, comerás, comerá, comeremos, comeréis, comerán

vivir—viviré, vivirás, vivirá, viviremos, viviréis, vivirán

There are a few irregular forms. Some have occurred in the present chapter:

tener—tendré, etc.   poder—podré   haber—habré

decir—diré   hacer—haré

Future Perfect

This tense is formed with the future of **haber** and the past participle.

Yo habré terminado.	I shall have finished.
Habremos escrito la carta.	We shall have written the letter.

Notice another irregular past participle: **dicho** (from " decir ").

¿ Qué le habrá dicho ?	What will he have told him ? I wonder what he has told him ?

Gustar

This verb is very important, since it is used to render such forms as " I like," " I am fond of."

The real meaning of the verb is " to please."   For example:

Me gusta el pan.	I like bread (i.e. bread pleases me).
A ella le gusta el vino.	She likes wine.
Nos gustan los libros.	We like books.
Me gusta leer.	I like reading (i.e. it pleases me to read).

Remember that **querer** means " to like, to love," or " to want, wish."

El niño quiere a su padre.	The child loves his father.
¿ Qué quiere Vd. ?	What do you want ?
No quiero hacer eso.	I don't want to do that.
¿ Quiere Vd. venir también ?	Will you come as well ?

Habrá

This is the future indicative form of **hay,** the impersonal verb meaning " there is, there are."

> No habrá concierto mañana.
> There will be no concert tomorrow.

Saber ; conocer

Be careful to distinguish these two verbs.

Saber means " to know a fact," whereas **conocer** has the meaning of " to be acquainted with."

¿ Conoce Vd. a mi hermano?	Do you know my brother?
¿ Sabe Vd. lo que he visto?	Do you know what I have seen?

Remember also:

¿ Sabe Vd. nadar?	Can you swim? (i.e. do you know how to swim?)

EXERCISES

(1) Answer the following questions in Spanish :

1. ¿ Quiénes están en la sala? 2. ¿ A qué hora quiere acostarse don Jaime? 3. ¿ A qué hora se acuesta Vd.? 4. ¿ Qué tendrá don Jaime que hacer al día siguiente? 5. ¿ Ha visto Vd. una corrida de toros? 6. ¿ Quién es Manolete? 7. ¿ Por qué no le gustan a doña Luisa los toros? 8. ¿ Sabe Vd. jugar a la pelota? 9. ¿ Es el fútbol un juego infantil o un deporte? 10. ¿ Le gustan a Vd. los conciertos sinfónicos? 11. ¿ Sabe Vd. nadar? 12. ¿ Dónde está el restaurant de París? 13. ¿ Prefiere Vd. el teatro al cine? 14. ¿ Por qué sale don Jaime del cuarto? 15. ¿ Se acuerda Vd. del nombre de alguna comedia española?

(2) Replace the words in brackets by pronouns, placing them in their correct position in the sentence.

(Example: ¿ Conoce Vd. (a don Jaime) ?—¿ Le conoce Vd. ?)

Don Jaime me da (el libro). Me dará también (los lápices). Me escribirá (la carta). El maestro nos describe (las provincias de España). Luisa escribe una carta (a su hermana). Quiero telefonear (a mi tía). Estoy escribiendo una carta (a mis amigos). Doña Emilia escribe una carta todas las semanas (a sus amigas). ¿ Ha visto Vd. (a su hermano)? Ella tiene mucho cariño (a sus hermanas). Hemos perdido (nuestras plumas). ¿ Ha comprado Vd. (el billete)?

(3) Give the Spanish equivalents of the following:

1. I am going to bed. 2. I shall have to do it. 3. I don't like writing letters to him. 4. Will you give it to me? 5. I will tell you what we will do. 6. He has written two letters to her. 7. He doesn't know us. 8. Has he answered you? 9. I shall go and see him after supper. 10. Do you remember the play?

(4) Conjugate in full the present indicative of the following verbs:

  acostarse   sentarse   llamarse   irse (to go away)
                    acordarse

(5) Put the following verbs into the future indicative.

(Example: Vd. come—Vd. comerá.)

1. Yo hablo. 2. Nosotros comemos. 3. Ella tiene. 4. Manuel dice. 5. Vd. no puede. 6. ¿ Qué hace su hermano? 7. Hay muchas personas. 8. Tú vuelves. 9. Cuesta poco. 10. Vosotros vais. 11. Ellos me dan cinco pesetas.

(6) (a) Form sentences in Spanish using the following words or expressions:

  tener que   hasta   cerca de   al cabo de

(b) By means of short sentences show the difference in meaning between the following pairs of words:

saber—conocer   cuarto—cuatro   mañana—la mañana
                    tarde—la tarde

(7) Put into Spanish:

1. What time shall we go to the theatre? 2. I don't like her sister. 3. What is your name? 4. Have you seen that film? 5. They are putting on one of Benavente's comedies. 6. He tells me that he likes pelota. 7. What is the price of this book? 8. I shall ring him up tomorrow. 9. The children like to play on the beach. 10. Do you remember his name?

(8) Put into Spanish:

My husband is very fond of sports. When it is fine we often go to a football or pelota match. Sometimes we take a walk as far as the beach. I like bathing but cannot swim. Afterwards we have dinner in town and go to the theatre or cinema. My husband likes to see a good film, but I must admit that I prefer the theatre, especially when there is a comedy.

CHAPTER IX

LA TERTULIA

Anita consulta el calendario cada día. El primero de febrero se acerca. Es el cumpleaños de Anita. Tendrá veinte años de edad.

Habrá una reunión. Vendrán todos sus amigos,

Carmen, Andrés, Eulalia, Pilar y...¡ don Antonio ! Anita se pondrá el traje azul porque sabe cuánto le gusta a Antonio este color.

Todo el mundo sabe que Anita y Antonio están enamorados. Siempre se hace la misma pregunta : — ¿ Cuándo se casarán ? ¿ Cuándo se verificará la boda ?

Y todo el mundo sabe también que el papá de Anita consentirá en el matrimonio porque Antonio es un chico muy guapo, muy simpático y — ¡ lo que tiene mucha importancia !—no le falta dinero tampoco.

El papá de Anita ha comprado un maravilloso abanico de marfil y se lo dará a su hija el día de su cumpleaños. Y se sabe también que Antonio va a regalarle un collar de perlas. (El pueblo es muy pequeño y el joyero a quien Antonio ha comprado el regalo se lo ha dicho a todos los vecinos.)

A las siete de la tarde llegan los convidados, amigos de papá y mamá, amigas de Anita y...naturalmente... Antonio. Un poco más tarde llegan los músicos con sus instrumentos.

Primero se sientan todos a la mesa. Es un verdadero banquete; hay por lo menos ocho platos diferentes. Despúes todos beben a la salud de los novios, dándoles la enhorabuena.

Al son de la música empiezan los convidados a bailar. Todos admiran a Anita, que es muy hermosa y muy feliz.

El baile dura hasta medianoche y todos vuelven a casa. Anita acompaña a Antonio hasta la puerta para despedirse de él. Antonio se aleja muy despacio y Anita se queda en la puerta mirando tristemente en la oscuridad.

NOTES

La tertulia

This is a party or a gathering together of friends for purposes of conversation and discussion. The traditional Spanish tertulia used to take place in the parlour of the village chemist, to whose house were invited the village priest and schoolmaster. These friends met to talk about current events, local topics, and to play cards. By extension, any meeting of friends and acquaintances may be called tertulia.

Acercarse   alejarse

From cerca de—near to. The contrary is alejarse, from lejos de—far from, and meaning " to go away from."

El cumpleaños

Birthday. Literally the day when a certain number of years are " fulfilled." **Cumplir**—to fulfil.

Ha cumplido veinte años. He has reached the age of twenty.

Ponerse un traje

El traje means both a man's suit and a woman's dress. Another word for dress is **el vestido.**

Note : **ponerse un traje**—to put on a dress. To take off a dress is **quitarse un traje.**

Guapo

One of the several words for describing a beautiful woman or a handsome man.

Hermoso and **lindo** are other adjectives meaning beautiful, whilst **bonito** suggests prettiness.

Note also the somewhat colloquial : **Una muchacha muy mona**—a very beautiful girl. It appears strange that **el mono** is the Spanish for monkey !

El abanico

Fans are used in Spain by men and women alike. For purposes of advertising, firms often distribute cardboard fans to members of the audience at local theatres.

Regalar

To present, give. **El regalo** is a gift.

El collar

Do not confuse **el collar** (the necklace) with **el cuello** (the neck or collar).

Comprar

Notice that " to buy something from a person " is **comprar algo a una persona.** Similarly with other verbs having the sense of " to take away from."

Thus : El padre le quitó el dinero. The father took the money away from him.

El convidado

Convidar is the verb meaning " to invite."

El músico

The musician.   Music is la música.

El plato

This word means either plate or dish (in the sense of " course ").

La salud

A common toast in Spain is: " ¡ Salud y muchas pesetas ! " being the equivalent of " good health and wealth."

Quedarse

We have already met with the verb permanecer, also meaning " to remain."

Cada día

The days of the week, in Spanish, are:

domingo	lunes	martes	miércoles	jueves
Sunday	Monday	Tuesday	Wednesday	Thursday

viernes	sábado
Friday	Saturday

They are all masculine.   They are not written with capital letters as in English.

Note, however, the use of the article: Viene el domingo. He is coming on Sunday.

Febrero

February.

The months of the year are, in Spanish:

enero January	febrero February	marzo March
abril April	mayo May	junio June
julio July	agosto August	setiembre September
octubre October	noviembre November	diciembre December

Note that they are not written with capital letters in Spanish. All these words are masculine.

The seasons, in Spanish, are:

la primavera   spring (also " primrose ")   el verano   summer
el otoño   autumn   el invierno   winter

GRAMMAR

Personal Pronouns (Conjunctive)—*continued.*

Let us consider the following sentences:

José me da el libro.	José gives me the book.
José lo da a su amigo.	José gives it to his friend.
José me lo da.	José gives it to me.

You will notice that the dative always precedes the accusative.

Now consider the following case:

Le da el libro.	He gives the book to him.
Lo da.	He gives it.

If we were to combine these two sentences we should have **le lo da,** which is considered impossible in Spanish.   In all such cases (where two *third* person pronouns come together) the dative form is replaced by SE.   Thus:

Se lo da.   He gives it to him.

Of course, this sentence without the context could mean:

He gives it to him, to her, to you (singular), to them, to you (plural).

In order to avoid ambiguity, **a él, a ella,** etc., may also be expressed:

Se lo da a él, or a ella, or a Vd., or a ellos, or a ellas, or a Vds.

Notice that SE must be expressed in all such cases, since Spanish does not object to redundancy.   One often finds such forms as:

Le da un abanico a su hija.   He gives a fan to his daughter.

Personal Pronouns (Disjunctive)

These are used after prepositions. They have the same forms as the subject personal pronouns, with two exceptions.

para él, ella, Vd.	for him, her, you
sin nosotros, vosotros	without us, you
de ellos, ellas, Vds.	of them, you

The two exceptions are: **mí** and **ti**.

Este libro es para mí.	This book is for me.
No iré sin ti.	I shall not go without you.

These forms are used after all prepositions with the exception of **con**—" with." This latter exception will be explained in the next chapter.

In addition to these forms there is another disjunctive pronoun **sí**, which corresponds to the reflexive pronoun SE (himself, herself, etc.). Compare the following sentences:

Ha comprado este libro para él.
He has bought this book for him (i.e. another person).

Ha comprado el libro para sí.
He has bought the book for himself.

¿ Ha comprado Vd. este libro para sí?
Have you bought this book for yourself?

In other words, **sí** can refer only to the *subject* of the sentence.

Ordinal Numbers

The ordinal numbers from one to ten are:

first	primero	second	segundo	third	tercero
fourth	cuarto	fifth	quinto	sixth	sexto
seventh	séptimo	eighth	octavo	ninth	nono or
tenth	décimo				noveno

Unlike the cardinal numbers, the ordinals agree with the noun they qualify.

Las primeras calles de la ciudad.	The first streets of the town.
la quinta página	the fifth page
la cuarta vez	the fourth time (occasion)

Primero and **tercero** are alike in that before the *masculine singular* noun they are shortened to **primer** and **tercer.**

el primer día	the first day
el tercer piso	the third floor

It is not absolutely necessary to learn the ordinal numbers beyond 10, as they are rarely used.

The ordinal number is used for the *first* day of the month. but for the rest the cardinal numbers are employed:

el primero de abril	the first of April
el dos de mayo	the second of May

Ordinals are used for kings, sovereigns, etc., up to 10, but not usually beyond:

Carlos quinto	Charles the Fifth
but Alfonso trece	Alfonso the Thirteenth

Future Indicative (Irregular Forms)

SABER (to know)   sabré, sabrás, sabrá, etc.
PONER (to put)   pondré, pondrás, pondrá, etc.
VENIR (to come)   vendré, vendrás, vendrá, etc.

Reciprocal Verbs

A verb such as **lavarse** (to wash oneself) is reflexive. A verb such as **quererse** (to love one another) is said to be reciprocal. The same form is used in Spanish for both.

Anita y Carlos se aman.
Anita and Carlos love each other.

Similarly:

Nos comprendemos perfectamente.
We understand each other perfectly.

Commands

The polite imperative (i.e. the form corresponding to **Vd.**) is formed from the present subjunctive. It can generally be obtained by taking the third persons singular or plural of the present indicative and changing the A of the ending into E, or the E into A.

Thus:

habla	he speaks	hable Vd.	speak !
hablan	they speak	hablen Vds.	speak !
come	he eats	coma Vd.	eat !
comen	they eat	coman Vds.	eat !
escribe	he writes	escriba Vd.	write !
escriben	they write	escriban Vds.	write !

And similarly in the case of radical changing verbs :

muestra	he shows	muestre Vd.	show !
piden	they ask	pidan Vds.	ask !
vuelve	he returns	vuelva Vd.	return !

Sometimes it is necessary to change the consonant :

busca	he seeks	busque Vd.	seek !
distingue	he distinguishes	distinga Vd.	distinguish !

In the case of the irregular verbs, the imperative form *usually* corresponds to the first person singular of the present indicative (with, of course, the change of ending) :

hago	I do, make	haga Vd.	do !
digo	I say	digan Vds.	say !
pongo	I place	ponga Vd.	place !

There are exceptions to this rule, which will be pointed out later. Unless there is any ambiguity it is not necessary to repeat **Vd.** or **Vds.** in the same sentence. For instance :

Tome Vd. la pluma y escriba la carta.
Take the pen and write the letter.

In positive sentences the pronoun is added to the *end* of the verb.

Tómelo Vd.	Take it.
Escríbannos Vds.	Write to us.

Notice the accent which must be added in order to preserve the original stress.

In negative sentences, however, the pronoun precedes the verb:

No lo tome Vd.	Don't take it.
No nos escriban Vds.	Don't write to us.

The imperative may be less forcibly expressed by using such a form as:

¿ Quiere Vd. darme el libro?	Please give me the book. Will you give me the book?

or

Hágame Vd. el favor de darme el libro.	Do me the favour of giving me the book.

EXERCISES

(1) Answer the following questions in Spanish:

1. ¿ Qué edad tiene Anita? 2. ¿ Cuántos años tiene Vd.? 3. ¿ Por qué se pondrá Anita su traje azul? 4. ¿ Qué pregunta se hace siempre en el pueblo? 5. ¿ Es pobre don Antonio? 6. ¿ Qué ha comprado el papá de Anita? 7. ¿ Cómo sabe todo el mundo que don Antonio va a regalarle a Anita un collar de perlas? 8. ¿ A qué hora llegan los convidados? 9. ¿ Cuándo llegan los músicos? 10. ¿ Sabe Vd. bailar? 11. ¿ Hasta qué hora dura el baile? 12. ¿ Por qué acompaña Anita a don Antonio hasta la puerta? 13. ¿ Cómo se aleja don Antonio? 14. ¿ Qué hace Anita cuando Antonio se va? 15 ¿ Cómo se llama un hombre que vende joyas?

(2) Replace the words in heavy type by pronouns, and re-write the sentences, placing the pronouns in their correct position.

1. Dice adios **a su novia.** 2. Le da **el cuaderno.** 3. ¿ No ha comprado Vd. **el reloj a su amigo?** 4. Me ha regalado **este libro.** 5. Pondrá **los lápices** sobre la mesa. 6. Le diré **que Vd. ha llegado.** 7. ¿ Cuándo le venderá Vd. **su bicicleta?** 8. ¿ Quiere Vd. prestarme **su reloj?** 9. Escriba Vd. **la carta** en seguida. 10. ¿ Ha terminado Vd. **el trabajo?**

(3) Replace the English words in brackets by the correct Spanish equivalents.

(Example : No quiero ir con (him).   No quiero ir con él.)

1. Esta carta es para (me).   2. No iré sin (you). 3. ¿ Quiere Vd. venir con (us) ?   4. Estas rosas son para (thee).   5. ¿ Se acuerda Vd. de (him) ?   6. He comprado una caja de cerillas para (you—plural).   7. No queremos hacerlo sin (them).   8. El viejo está hablando con (her). 9. ¿ Quién irá con (them—feminine) ?   10. Lo haré después de (you).

(4) Put into Spanish :

1. The fifth day.   2. The second of May.   3. He is coming on the first of July.   4. Alfonso X and Alfonso XIII. 5. Don't eat it.   6. Write the letter to your son.   7. The 30th of December.   8. The first time.   9. This is the third volume (el tomo).   10. Answer me.

(5) Put the following sentences into the future indicative :

1. Tengo diez años.   2. No le doy nada.   3. ¿ A qué hora viene su amigo ?   4. No lo hacemos.   5. ¿ Cuándo vuelve a casa ?   6. ¿ Puede Vd. venir con nosotros ?   7. Vd. se lo dice.   8. No le interrumpo a Vd.   9. Se pone el traje azul. 10. ¿ A qué hora se acuesta Vd. ?

(6) Give the opposites of the following words or expressions :
acercarse   comprar   el calor   preguntar   hermoso   tristemente

(7) Give the English equivalents of the following :

1. Carlos y María se quieren mucho.   2. Aquí se prohíbe fumar.   3. Se dice que Antonio se ha casado con la chica. 4. No me falta dinero.   5. Se lo diré a Vd. mañana.

(8) Put into Spanish :

In the little town everybody knows that Anita is in love with Antonio, and that they are going to get married. It is her birthday today and all her friends are coming to have dinner with the family. Of course, Antonio is coming too, and Anita will put on her blue dress, because she knows that Antonio is fond of this colour. All the guests arrive in the afternoon, and after dinner they dance until midnight.

CHAPTER X

EL NEGOCIANTE

EL señor Álvarez es negociante. Es el dueño de una casa comercial en Barcelona. Vive en una casa particular en las afueras de la ciudad. Es un hombre de unos cuarenta años, ni grande ni pequeño, enérgico y trabajador. Siempre va vestido de negro y lleva un bastón.

Suele levantarse a las siete de la mañana, se desayuna y sale en seguida para la ciudad.

Cuando llega al despacho el señor Álvarez empieza el trabajo del día. Habla con el gerente y visita las oficinas y la fábrica, donde hay empleados más de cien obreros. A veces llama por teléfono a sus socios en Madrid y Zaragoza, donde la casa tiene importantes sucursales. Casi todos los días va también al Banco de España y a la Bolsa.

A eso de las doce y media vuelve a casa para comer, juega después con los niños y duerme la siesta en el jardín o en la biblioteca.

A las cuatro de la tarde le encontramos otra vez en la oficina, donde se queda hasta la hora de cenar. Algunas veces vuelve a casa, otras veces suele cenar en la ciudad con algunos de sus amigos.

En el restaurant consulta la lista de platos y escoge. Toma sopa, entremeses, algún pescado (le gusta mucho el bacalao), una chuleta de ternera o carne asada, legumbres o ensalada. Como postres hay frutas, queso o galletas. Termina la comida con una taza de café solo y a veces toma una copita de coñac y fuma un puro.

Luego vuelve a casa, pasa algún tiempo con su familia y se acuesta.

NOTES

El negociante

A related word is **los negocios**—business.

Levantarse

Llevar

Be careful not to confuse these two words.

Levantar means " to lift," and **levantarse** " to lift oneself up, or to get up."

Llevar means " to carry, or to wear."

Desayunarse

The noun is **el desayuno**—light breakfast.

This meal is followed by **el almuerzo** (lunch) and **la cena** (supper, normally taken about eight or nine o'clock in the evening). In the country, however, it is the custom to take a heavier breakfast (also called **el almuerzo**), followed by **la comida** (dinner) and **la cena** (supper).

The verbs corresponding are: **almorzar** (to have breakfast or lunch), **comer** (to dine or eat) and **cenar** (to have supper).

Tea is not usual, although sometimes a light snack is taken about four o'clock. This is called **la merienda.**

En seguida

Immediately, at once. Also: **inmediatamente.**

El despacho

Office. Another word for office is **la oficina.**

An employee in an office or shop is, in Spanish, **el dependiente.**

El banco

This word has two distinct meanings: (1) bank. El banco de España—the Bank of Spain. (2) seat. Sentarse sobre un banco—to sit on a seat.

Dormir la siesta

This after-lunch rest is almost universal throughout Spain and Latin America, and is indeed very necessary where the climate is hot. Most shops and business houses close from about midday to three o'clock for this purpose but, of course, work until a correspondingly later hour. The Spanish say that only Englishmen and dogs are to be seen abroad at this hour!

La biblioteca

Library. Do not confuse this word with **la librería** which is a book shop.

Lista de platos

The classic Spanish dish is **el puchero** or **el cocido**, a stew containing meat, sausage, vegetables. In peasant families, whilst the various members are at work, such a dish can be left to cook slowly over a charcoal fire with little attention. It is an economical and highly nutritious dish. The meats, vegetables, and flavourings naturally vary according to individual tastes.

Postres

Fruits such as one might normally expect for dessert are:

la naranja	orange
las uvas	grapes
el melocotón	peach
las cerezas	cherries
la manzana	apple
la pera	pear
el plátano	banana

Nuts are also very often served as dessert. Nut in Spanish is **la nuez** (plural—nueces).

GRAMMAR

Disjunctive Pronouns (mí, ti, and sí)

When the proposition **con** (with) precedes these pronouns, a special form is used:

conmigo (with me)   contigo (with thee)   consigo (with him, her, you, etc.)

For example:

Iré contigo.	I will go with you.
¿ Quiere Vd. venir conmigo?	Will you come with me?
¿ Por qué lleva la maleta consigo?	Why is he taking the suit-case with him?

Negatives

Study the following carefully:

alguno   ninguno

Tengo algunos lápices.	I have a few pencils.
¿ Tiene Vd. algún azúcar?	Have you any sugar?
No tengo ningún lápiz.	I have no pencil.

algo   nada

¿ Tiene Vd. algo que darme?	Have you anything to give me?
No tengo nada que darle.	I have nothing to give you.

también   tampoco

Iré también con él.	I shall go with him also.
No iré tampoco.	I shall not go either.

y   ni... ni...

Tengo pluma y tinta.	I have pen and ink.
No tengo ni pluma ni tinta.	I have neither pen nor ink.

You will notice that in all these cases **no** is used before the verb to complete the negation. As has been pointed out before, Spanish does not object to the double negative.

If the negative pronoun or adverb precedes the verb, however, **no** is omitted, as, for instance:

Nada tengo.	Tampoco iré yo.	Nunca viene a verme.
I have nothing.	I shan't go either.	He never comes to see me.

It is usual for **no** to precede the verb in ordinary language, unless the negative pronoun is the subject of the sentence, as, for instance:

Ninguno de mis amigos ha venido. Not one of my friends has come.

Even in the latter case one can say: No ha venido ninguno de mis amigos. The important thing to remember is that when such words follow the verb, **no** must not be omitted.

You will notice also that **alguno** and **ninguno** are shortened to **algún, ningún** before a masculine singular noun.

No tengo ningún dinero.	I have no money at all.
Vendrá algún día.	He will come some day.
But No tengo ninguna tiza.	I have no chalk at all.

Expressions of Time

Es la una y media.	It is half-past one.
Son las tres y media.	It is half-past three.

In these cases **media** is an adjective and agrees with **hora**. i.e. media hora.

Es la una y cuarto.	It is a quarter past one.
Son las diez menos cuarto.	It is a quarter to ten.

In such cases **cuarto** is a noun meaning " a quarter." **i.e.** menos un cuarto de hora—less a quarter of an hour.

Son las cuatro y veinte.	It is twenty past four.
Son las once menos cinco.	It is five to eleven.

This is a short form of: y veinte minutos... menos cinco minutos.

Future Indicative (Irregular Verbs)

Salir (to go out)　　saldré, saldrás, saldrá, saldremos, saldréis, saldrán.

Querer (to love, want)　　querré, querrás, querrá, querremos, querréis, querrán.

Note also :

soler—to be wont to.

This verb is radical changing (suelo, sueles, etc.), and is also defective, since it is used only in the present and imperfect indicative.

¿ A qué hora suele venir ?　　What time does he usually come ?

It is an extremely useful verb for rendering such English expressions containing " generally " or " usually."

volver a—to do something again.

In addition to the usual meaning of " return," this verb, when followed by " a " and another infinitive, has the sense of " to do something again " or, literally, " to return to do something."

Vuelvo a escribir la carta.　　I write the letter again.

Of course one could also say :

Escribo la carta otra vez.

EXERCISES

(1) Answer in Spanish the following questions :

1. ¿ Qué es el señor Álvarez ?　2. ¿ Dónde vive ?　3. ¿ Qué edad tiene ?　4. ¿ A qué hora se levanta Vd. ?　5. ¿ Con quién habla el señor Álvarez cuando llega a la oficina ?　6. ¿ Dónde tiene sucursales la casa de comercio ?　7. ¿ Cuántos obreros se emplean en la fábrica ?　8. ¿ Dónde pasa las horas de la siesta el señor Álvarez ?　9. ¿ Cuántas horas por día trabaja ?　10. ¿ Come el señor Álvarez en la ciudad o en

casa? 11. ¿ Qué prefiere Vd. como postres? ¿ Queso o
frutas ? 12. ¿ Qué toma el señor Álvarez después de la
comida? 13. ¿ Le gusta a Vd. el pescado? 14. ¿ Cómo se
llaman los que trabajan en una oficina? 15. ¿ Cuáles son las
tres comidas principales del día?

(2) Give the 1st person singular of (a) present indicative,
(b) future indicative, (c) perfect, of the following verbs.

(Example: hablar.   hablo ; hablaré ; he hablado.)

saber acabar vestirse empezar decir venir salir encontrar
seguir permanecer

(3) Write short sentences in Spanish, making use of the
following words or expressions:

desayunarse   en seguida   a veces   otra vez   por fin

(4) The following two lines contain words which have
similar meanings.   Pair these words.

quedarse   despacho   en seguida   volver   acabar
terminar   permanecer   oficina   regresar   inmediatamente

(5) Give the opposites of the following words:

levantarse   trabajador   salir   blanco   algo

(6) Put into Spanish:

Señor Álvarez is a business man.   He lives in the suburbs
and has to go into the city by tram or bus.   He usually gets
up about seven o'clock, spends the morning in the office or in
the factory, has his lunch at home, takes his siesta, and then
returns to his work.   Sometimes he has dinner in town with
friends, sometimes he comes back home, has supper with the
family, and goes to bed at ten or eleven o'clock.   Once a
month Señor Álvarez has to go to Madrid or Saragossa to visit
the firm's branches.

RECAPITULATION II

EXERCISES

(1) Put into Spanish:

1. Do they sell stamps in that shop? 2. What time is it? It is half-past eleven. 3. Do you know how to count in Spanish? Count up to a thousand. 4. It is beginning to rain. Have you got an umbrella? 5. Write the letter again. 6. What is the date today? It is March 10th. 7. What have you been doing today? Nothing. 8. Whose is this book? It is yours. 9. Which of the two magazines do you prefer? 10. Ask him for his pencil. 11. I know that man very well. He has neither money nor friends. 12. What time do you get up? Late or early? 13. He will give it to you tomorrow. 14. For whom is this wine? 15. Will you come with me? 16. She usually comes after supper. 17. I shall ring him up before noon. 18. My brother says he can't come either. 19. Don't ask too many questions. 20. Do you like onions?

(2) Give the first person singular (present indicative) of the following verbs:

querer   venir   poner   oir   saber

(3) Give the first person plural (future indicative) of the following verbs:

querer   salir   poner   venir   saber

(4) Write in Spanish a few words on each of the following, so as to illustrate their meanings:

el guardia municipal	la tertulia	un burro
el estanco	el mercado	postres
el torero	el teatro	el músico
el negociante		

(5) Give the polite imperative (singular and plural) of the following verbs:

volver   no caer   empezar   pedir   buscar

(6) Expand in Spanish the following outline:

El señor González—dependiente—casa de comercio—levantarse—lavarse—desayunarse—ir a la ciudad—trabajar—almorzar—la siesta—la comida—el restaurant—el cine—volver a casa—acostarse.

CHAPTER XI

LA VIEJA CRIADA

CUANDO yo visitaba el pueblo de Fuente Calderón la vieja Carmencita tenía más de setenta años de edad. Todo el mundo la conocía, desde el hijito del zapatero hasta el señor cura. Trabajaba de criada en la familia de don Anselmo, abogado retirado.

Yo la veía cada día. A eso de las nueve de la mañana después del desayuno salía la vieja criada de la casa, cerrando con mucho cuidado la puerta del jardín. Siempre iba vestida de negro. Nunca llevaba sombrero pero cuando hacía mucho sol o cuando entraba en la iglesia se ponía un pañuelo de color. Por regla general iba sola pero a veces la acompañaba Alberto, hijo de don Anselmo. Al pasar por la calle siempre saludaba a todos los transeuntes. Su itinerario era fijo—siempre seguía la

calle Mayor, atravesaba la plaza de Cervantes y volvía
después por la calle del Obispo cerca de la iglesia.

Carmencita iba de compras todos los días. Pero las
tiendas no eran muy numerosas. Había la panadería,
donde compraba pan cada día y panecillos los sábados;
la carnicería, donde compraba carne, jamón y salchichas;
la zapatería a donde llevaba los zapatos de toda la
familia; y la tienda de comestibles. Aquí le vendían
café, azúcar y arroz, leche, mantequilla, queso y huevos,
aceite y vino, legumbres y frutas. No era posible obtener
pescado en Fuente Calderón pero de vez en cuando la
vieja criada compraba una lata de sardinas para don
Anselmo.

Y no hay que olvidar la farmacia. ¡ El boticario, don
Joaquín, era sin duda una de las personas más importantes del pueblo ! Pero a decir verdad Carmencita
tenía un poco de miedo al señor boticario por sus conocimientos científicos.

A Carmencita le gustaba charlar con todos; era casi su
única diversión.

NOTES

Zapato

el zapato —the shoe
el zapatero —the shoemaker
la zapatería—the shoemaker's (shop)

Similarly:

la fruta	el frutero	la frutería
la carne	el carnicero	la carnicería
el pan	el panadero	la panadería
la leche	el lechero	la lechería

Hijito

Little son. This is another example of the diminutive
suffix. Sometimes, however, the diminutive ending does not

always suggest " smallness " as in the case of " hijito," but may have acquired an independent meaning.   For instance :

el paño—cloth   el pañuelo—handkerchief

Desde... hasta...

Desde el hijito del zapatero hasta el señor cura—from the shoemaker's little son to the village priest.

These two words are also used in connection with time and place :

Desde el año 711 hasta 1492.
Desde Madrid hasta Zaragoza.

El abogado

Lawyer.   Law as a subject studied is **el derecho.**

El abogado estudia el derecho.   The lawyer studies law.

The laws of a country are, however : **Las leyes** de un país.
A similar distinction exists in French :

el derecho—*le droit*
la ley   —*la loi*

Cuidado

Care, trouble, worry.   Note the expression : ¡ Cuidado ! as an exclamation equivalent to the English : " Look out ! Take care ! "

Saludar

To greet.   " How do you do ? " is, in Spanish : " ¿ **Cómo está Vd. ?** " or, more colloquially, " ¿ **Qué tal ?** " (" How goes it ? ")

Ir de compras

To go shopping.   Also **ir de tiendas** with the same meaning.

Tienda de comestibles

Another word meaning " grocery, food store " is **la tienda de ultramarinos,** indicating a shop where are sold goods such as coffee, sugar, spices, etc., which have been brought from overseas (i.e. ultramar).

Posesiones de ultramar—overseas possessions

La diversión

Diversion, amusement. Also note the word **el divertimiento** with a similar meaning and the verb **divertirse(ie)**—to amuse oneself, to be amused.

Se divierte mucho en Madrid.   He's having a good time in Madrid.

El pescado

Fish as a commodity. Literally " that which has been fished."
A fish in the water is **el pez** (plural **peces**).

¿ Le gusta a Vd. el pescado ?   Do you like fish ?
La sardina es un pez muy pequeño.   The sardine is a very small fish.

pescar—to fish, go fishing
el pescador—fisherman

GRAMMAR

Nouns in Apposition

When two nouns are in apposition the article is omitted :

Don Anselmo, abogado retirado.   Don Anselmo, *a* retired lawyer.
Madrid, capital de España.   Madrid, *the* capital of Spain.

But notice :

Madrid, la capital más alta de Europa.
Madrid, the highest capital in Europe.

In the latter case, the noun in apposition is qualified by a superlative and the article is retained.

Al with the Infinitive

This construction corresponds to the English " on " + the present participle.

Al entrar en la casa siempre saludaba a la criada.
On entering (as he went into) the house, he always greeted the servant.

A similar usage is that of " el " + the infinitive:

El viajar es interesante. To travel (or) travelling is interesting.

One could also say:
Es interesante viajar. It is interesting to travel.

Comparison of Adjectives

The comparative of adjectives is formed by placing **más** (more) in front of the positive form.

grande—big   más grande—bigger

Notice also:

menos grande—less big, not so big

The comparison of inequality is:

más... que...   menos... que...

Su casa es más grande que la mía. Your house is larger than mine.

Esta ciudad es menos hermosa que ésa.
This town is less beautiful than that one.

The comparison of equality is:

tan... como...

Soy tan rico como él. I am as rich as he is.

Such forms can, of course, be negative.

No es tan viejo como mi abuelo.
He is not so old as my grandfather.

Imperfect Indicative

The imperfect indicative tense is used to express habitual or repeated action or actions, subsidiary to the narrative, and which do not carry the story forward. It is usually descriptive.

Carmencita **era** vieja pero **iba** de compras cada día.
Carmencita was old but she used to go shopping every day.

Entré en el comedor. Mi hermano **estaba** sentado en un sillón y **leía** el diario. Le di la carta que había recibido.
I went into the dining-room. My brother was seated in an arm-chair and was reading the paper. I gave him the letter which I had received.

Be very careful to render correctly the English " would " in the sense of " used to."

Durante las vacaciones leía una novela cada día.
During the holidays he would read a novel every day.

This meaning is often best expressed however by the use of " soler " (see page 124). Thus :

Durante las vacaciones solía leer una novela cada día.

The imperfect tense is formed very simply. To the stem of the -AR verbs are added the endings : aba, abas, aba, ábamos, abais, aban, and to the stem of the -ER and -IR verbs the endings : ía, ías, ía, íamos, íais, ían.

FUMAR (to smoke)	COMER (to eat)	VIVIR (to live)
(yo) fumaba	(yo) comía	(yo) vivía
fumabas	comías	vivías
(él) fumaba	(él) comía	(él) vivía
fumábamos	comíamos	vivíamos
fumabais	comíais	vivíais
fumaban	comían	vivían

You will notice that the first and third persons singular are identical in form. In cases of ambiguity the subject (or subject pronoun) must be expressed.

Yo escribía y él leía. I was writing and he was reading.

There are only three irregular forms of the imperfect :

IR (to go)	iba	ibas	iba	íbamos	ibais	iban
SER (to be)	era	eras	era	éramos	erais	eran
VER (to see)	veía	veías	veía	veíamos	veíais	veían

Just as we saw that HAY (corresponding to the French *il y a*) meant " there is " or " there are," so the imperfect of **haber** means " there was " or " there were."

Había dos mercados en la ciudad.   There were two markets in the town.

No había pescado.   There was no fish.

As in the case of the present indicative, the imperfect of **estar** with the present participle forms the " continuous imperfect."

> La niña estaba cantando en el jardín.
> The little girl was singing in the garden.

Conditional Indicative

If we add to the infinitive of any conjugation the endings : ía, ías, ía, íamos, íais, ían, we form the conditional.

FUMAR (to smoke)   (yo) fumaría (I would, should smoke), etc.
fumarías
(él) fumaría
fumaríamos
fumaríais
fumarían

Similarly :

COMER (to eat)   comería, comerías, comería, comeríamos, comeríais, comerían

VIVIR (to live)   viviría, vivirías, viviría, viviríamos, viviríais, vivirían

Irregularities in this tense correspond to those of the future indicative, since the two tenses are formed from the infinitive.

Thus :

PONER   pondré—I shall put   pondría—I should put
QUERER   querré—I shall wish   querría—I should wish

In other words, all verbs that are irregular in the future, are also irregular in the conditional.

For the use of the conditional, consider the following sentences :

A mí me gustaría hacer eso.   I should like to do that.
Querían saber si yo vendría.   They wanted to know whether
                                  I would come.

EXERCISES

(1) Answer the following questions in Spanish:

1. ¿Dónde vivía la vieja criada? 2. ¿Dónde trabajaba ella? 3. ¿Qué era don Anselmo? 4. ¿A qué hora salía Carmencita? 5. ¿Cómo iba vestida? 6. ¿Qué se ponía en la cabeza cuando iba a la iglesia? 7. ¿Iba Carmencita siempre sola? 8. ¿Había muchas tiendas en Fuente Calderón? 9. ¿Qué se puede comprar en casa del panadero? 10. ¿Dónde se puede comprar carne? 11. ¿Toma Vd. té sin o con azúcar? 12. ¿Prefiere Vd. sardinas frescas o en lata? 13. ¿Cómo se llama en español el dueño de una farmacia? 14. ¿Por qué tenía Carmencita miedo al boticario? 15. ¿Qué es un transeunte?

(2) Put the following sentences into the imperfect indicative.

(Example: Yo no tengo nada. Yo no tenía nada.)

1. Escribo una carta cada día. 2. No me gusta la leche. 3. La criada va de compras por la mañana. 4. ¿Conoce Vd. al boticario? 5. ¿A qué hora se acuesta el niño? 6. ¿Cuándo volvemos a casa? 7. Hay muchas personas en la playa. 8. ¿Preparas tú la comida? 9. ¿Toma ella el autobús o el tranvía? 10. Se viste siempre de negro.

(3) Give the first person singular and third person plural of the conditional tense of the following verbs:

(Example: comer   yo comería   ellos comerían.)

tener volver poner recibir saber conocer querer salir venir
decir

(4) Put into Spanish:

1. Anita is more beautiful than María. 2. Bilbao is not so large as Barcelona. 3. I am less intelligent than he is. 4. He has more than ten pesetas. 5. They walk more slowly

than we do. 6. Señor Álvarez is not as wealthy as the other partners of the firm. 7. He is uglier than his brother. 8. The old woman was more frightened of the chemist.

(5) Complete the following sentences:

1. El hombre que hace zapatos se llama el ——. 2. El hombre que vende carne se llama el ——. 3. El frutero es el hombre que vende ——. 4. La tienda donde se vende pan se llama la ——. 5. En la huerta se cultivan ——. 6. La gallina da ——. 7. Hay sardinas frescas y sardinas en ——. 8. La última comida del día se llama la ——. 9. La vaca da ——. 10. Con leche se hace ——.

(6) Give the verbs corresponding to the following nouns:

(Example: el trabajo   trabajar.)

la visita   el desayuno   el almuerzo   la compra
el conocimiento

(7) Put into Spanish:

I used to know Carmencita very well. She was an old servant who worked at don Anselmo's and everybody liked her. I have visited Fuente Calderón on many occasions and I always used to see her in the street when she was going shopping. She was always dressed in black, but wore a coloured handkerchief on her head when it was sunny. She always said good morning to me. About eleven o'clock she would return along Bishop Street, her basket full of meat, butter, eggs, and vegetables. She carried the basket on her head and usually had a bottle of oil or wine in her hand. There was no fish in the village, but sometimes she would buy a tin of sardines. But I am sure *she* didn't like them; they were for don Anselmo.

CHAPTER XII

LA AMÉRICA LATINA

La América latina se extiende desde la frontera de los Estados Unidos de Norteamérica hasta el estrecho de Magallanes. Este territorio comprende 19 repúblicas independientes—Méjico, las islas de Cuba y de Santo Domingo, 6 repúblicas de la América central y 10 de la

América del Sur. Fuera del Brasil, donde se habla portugués, el idioma oficial de todas estas repúblicas es el español.

En el año 1492 Cristóbal Colón hizo su primer viaje al Nuevo Mundo y descubrió la isla de Santo Domingo. Durante la época que siguió al primer descubrimiento salieron los exploradores españoles de Andalucía en busca de tierras desconocidas y, por espacio de unos cincuenta años, conquistaron casi todo el territorio que se extiende desde San Francisco hasta Chile.

Fué Núñez de Balboa quien tuvo la gloria de descubrir el Pacífico, Hernán Cortés quien llevó a cabo la conquista de Méjico, Francisco Pizarro quien venció a los incas del Perú. El portugués Cabral descubrió el Brasil en el año 1500.

Es muy fácil criticar las crueldades de estos conquistadores, los abusos de los primeros gobernadores, la administración de las primeras colonias de ultramar, pero no hay que olvidar los peligros, las dificultades físicas, económicas y políticas que confrontaron a estos aventureros intrépidos quienes llevaron a los territorios conquistados la civilización española, la fe católica y la cultura europea.

La historia de la América latina desde la época de la colonización hasta el nacimiento de las repúblicas independientes del siglo XIX es la historia de una gran obra civilizadora.

En el año 1898 la madre patria perdió sus últimas colonias, pero el imperio español no ha desaparecido. Su lengua, su cultura, su arquitectura y muchas de sus tradiciones viven todavía entre los pueblos de este vasto territorio que ahora llamamos la América española.

NOTES

La América latina

When the name of a country is qualified by an adjective notice that the article is used. Similarly: **la América central, la América del Sur.**

One may say either **la América del Sur** or **Sud-América.** Notice the two words **sud** and **sur,** both meaning " south." Compare : **Sud-África** (or) **África del Sur.**

The cardinal points in Spanish are :

el norte	north
el sur	south
el este	east
el oeste	west

El Perú

Some names of countries are masculine in Spanish and are used generally with the article, whether qualified by an adjective or not. For instance:

el Brasil   Brazil
el Paraguay   Paraguay

Here is a list of the republics of Latin America:

Méjico, Cuba, Santo Domingo (la República Dominicana), Costa Rica, Guatemala, Honduras, Nicaragua, el Salvador, Panamá, Venezuela, Bolivia, Colombia, el Perú, el Ecuador, Chile, la (república) Argentina, el Uruguay, el Paraguay, el Brasil.

The countries indicated with the definite article are normally used with the article, e.g.:

ir a Bolivia   to go to Bolivia
but ir al Perú   to go to Peru

On the other hand, other masculine countries such as Méjico, Portugal, Panamá are not used with the article.

El idioma

EL idioma—the language
Note also la lengua—tongue, language.

San Francisco

Reference to a map of the United States will show that many place names in the area stretching from San Francisco to the Mexican border are Spanish. The famous Colorado canyon was discovered by Spanish explorers, as well as all the Mississippi area. Up to the beginning of the nineteenth century Florida still belonged to Spain.

El nacimiento

The verb is nacer—to be born.

El pueblo

This word corresponds to the French *peuple* and to the English " people " in the sense of " race."

Another meaning is, of course, " small town, village."

Be very careful to render correctly the English " people " in such sentences as:

> There were many people there.
> Había mucha gente allí.
> (or) Había muchas personas.

El estrecho

As a noun the word means " strait, narrows." As an adjective:

> una calle estrecha   a narrow street

Comprender

Like the French *comprendre* this word has the two meanings of (1) to understand, (2) to comprise.

GRAMMAR

The Preterite Tense

The preterite (or past definite) tense expresses an action in the past, a definite, single action. It can be said to describe " what happens next." It is employed both in written and spoken Spanish. In Spanish it is used to a far greater extent than the preterite in French. Where the French would use the perfect (or past indefinite) in, shall we say, conversation or a letter, the Spanish would often use the past definite.

We must distinguish carefully between the three tenses: perfect, imperfect, and preterite. Study the following examples:

Bajé al salón, leí el periódico y escribí una carta.
I came down to the drawing-room, read the paper, and wrote a letter.

The verb in each case illustrates a definite action, an accomplished action. Each action carries the story one step forward.

Cuando entré, mi hermano escribía una carta.
When I came in, my brother was writing a letter.

" I came in " describes the principal action of the sentence. " He was writing " is incidental and describes what was happening when the main action took place.

Yo compraba pan cada día. I used to buy bread every day.

The verb here describes an action that was habitual, that was repeated. Hence the imperfect.

Mi hermano entró en el comedor y me vio.—¿Qué has hecho esta mañana?—preguntó. Contesté:—Fui a casa de Ramón. Dimos un paseo hasta la playa, e hicimos algunas compras en la ciudad. Cuando volví, escribí una carta.
My brother entered the dining-room and saw me. " What have you been doing this morning? " he asked. I replied : " I went to Ramon's. We went for a walk as far as the beach, and made a few purchases in town. When I returned, I wrote a letter."

Even in conversation you will notice that the preterite is normally used.

The following table illustrates the regular formation of the preterite tense :

HABLAR (to speak)	COMER (to eat)	VIVIR (to live)
(yo) hablé	comí	viví
hablaste	comiste	viviste
habló	comió	vivió
hablamos	comimos	vivimos
hablasteis	comisteis	vivisteis
hablaron	comieron	vivieron

It will be noticed that the endings of the second and third conjugations are identical.

The only accents occur in the first and third persons singular.

In the case of the first and third conjugations, the first person plural has the same form as the present indicative. For example:

> hablamos   we speak or we spoke
> vivimos   we live or we lived

The context will indicate the meaning required.

There are a number of irregular forms in the preterite. Here are a few of them:

SER (to be)	fui, fuiste, fue, fuimos, fuisteis, fueron
ESTAR (to be)	estuve, estuviste, estuvo, estuvimos, estuvisteis, estuvieron
TENER (to have)	tuve, tuviste, tuvo, tuvimos, tuvisteis, tuvieron
HACER (to do)	hice, hiciste, hizo, hicimos, hicisteis, hicieron

In the case of **hacer** note the change of c into z when followed by o.

Shortened Forms

We have already met with a number of words (e.g. uno, alguno, primero, etc.), which are shortened before the masculine singular.

Similar cases are:

bueno—good	una buena comida	a good meal
	buenos días	good morning
	but hace buen tiempo	it's fine weather
malo—bad	de mala gana	unwillingly
	but un mal negocio	a bad piece of business
santo—saint	Santa Teresa	Saint Theresa
	but San Pedro, San Juan	

This loss of letters takes place only before the *name* of the saint. One says, for instance: un santo mártir—a holy martyr. There are, however, one or two exceptions such as: Santo Domingo and Santo Tomás. E.g. La isla de Santo Domingo.

grande—big

This word usually shortens to **gran** before either a masculine or feminine singular noun.

un gran hombre	a great man
una gran casa	a great house
but grandes hombres	great men

Position of Adjectives

An adjective normally follows a noun in Spanish, but we have already met with several adjectives such as: primero, cien, alguno, último, which precede the noun. Other adjectives, such as those of nationality or colour, always follow, and there are a number which change their meaning according to their position. Such are, for example:

bueno	un buen hombre	a good fellow
	un hombre bueno	a good man
pobre	mi pobre hijo	my poor son (unfortunate)
	un hombre pobre	a poor man (without money)
grande	un gran hombre	a great man
	un hombre grande	a big man
nuevo	es un nuevo libro	it is a new (another) book
	es un libro nuevo	it is a new (brand new) book
varios	colores varios	various (different) colours
	varios libros	various (several) books

Apart from certain definite cases it is impossible to give a precise rule with regard to the position of adjectives in Spanish. We have said that an adjective normally follows:

una casa hermosa   a beautiful house

One can say, however:

una hermosa casa

The difference is that in the first case the adjective qualifies and defines. It tells us what kind of a house it is, i.e. a beautiful one, not an ugly one.   In the second case (where the adjective precedes) its use is figurative, decorative; it is an addition, an embellishment.   This can be seen more clearly, perhaps, in such a case as:

la blanca nieve   the white snow

An adjective of colour usually follows the noun.   However, as snow is usually considered to be white, it is not *necessary* to describe the colour.   Hence the position of the adjective before the noun.   If, however, we wished to speak of " red snow," we should have to put the adjective after the noun, since in this case the adjective would *define* and not merely act as an embellishment.

We have met with the expression " un vasto territorio." We know that the territory stretching from the United States to Chile *is* vast, therefore it is not necessary to define it as such.   Our adjective is therefore purely decorative and adds to the idea.

To sum up, we can say that:

(1) Adjectives of nationality, colour, qualifying and defining adjectives follow the noun.

un campesino español
una casa blanca
un hombre simpático

(2) Certain adjectives change meaning according to position, such as: grande, nuevo, pobre, etc.

(3) Certain adjectives always precede, such as: cada, cien, mucho, poco, etc.

(4) Qualifying adjectives may precede if used in a figurative or decorative sense.

It will be realised, however, that the position of the adjective is often a question of style.   Observation and reading is the only real guide to the problem.

EXERCISES

(1) Answer the following questions in Spanish:

1. ¿ Cuántas repúblicas hay en la América latina? 2. ¿ En qué parte del continente sudamericano se habla portugués? 3. ¿ En qué año hizo Colón su primer viaje al Nuevo Mundo? 4. ¿ Quién descubrió el océano Pacífico? 5. ¿ Cómo se llamaban los habitantes del Perú? 6. ¿ Qué llevaron los conquistadores españoles a los nuevos territorios? 7. ¿ Qué dificultades confrontaron a los exploradores? 8. ¿ Cuándo perdió España sus últimas colonias? 9. ¿ Han desaparecido por completo las tradiciones de la madre patria? 10. Cuál es la ciudad más grande de la América del Sur? 11. ¿ Cómo se llama el estrecho que separa el continente de la Tierra del Fuego? 12. ¿ Se habla español en la isla de Cuba? 13. ¿ Cuál es el río más largo del mundo? 14. ¿ Puede Vd. decir dónde está el lago de Titicaca? 15. ¿ Qué se cultiva en el Brasil?

(2) Conjugate in full in the preterite tense the following verbs:

aguardar ser escribir volver tener extender estar conocer descubrir hacer

(3) Give the third person singular of (a) present, (b) future, (c) imperfect, (d) preterite indicative tenses of the following verbs:

llevar hacer ver sentarse tener

(4) Put into Spanish:

1. He was a great man. 2. I have a brand new pen. 3. It is a very large house. 4. A new teacher has come to the school. 5. Ramón is a good lad. 6. She has bought several hats.

(5) Write the correct form of the words in brackets and translate the sentences into English.

1. Pizarro fue un (grande) explorador. 2. Es una (grande) señora. 3. Las (grande) ciudades de la América del Sur.

4. Hace muy (malo) tiempo. 5. Vendrá (alguno) día sin duda. 6. Muy (bueno) noches. 7. Una (bueno) comida. 8. Un (bueno) niño. 9. No tengo (ninguno) dinero. 10. Es una iglesia muy (grande).

(6) Complete the following sentences:

1. España es una península; Cuba es una ——.
2. El que hace un viaje es un ——.
3. Hernán Cortés fue un gran ——.
4. El español es una hermosa ——.
5. Cien años es un ——.

(7) Give verbs corresponding to the following nouns:

la extensión   el viaje   el descubrimiento   la conquista
el nacimiento

(8) Give nouns corresponding to the following verbs:

vivir administrar ver buscar gobernar

(9) Put into Spanish:

Except for Brazil, Spanish is spoken throughout the vast territory that stretches from the Mexican border of the United States to Chile. Since the period of colonisation representatives of nearly every nation have gone to Latin America, especially to the Argentine. In 1898 Spain lost the last of her colonies, but many of her traditions, as well as her language, still live on the other side of the Atlantic.

CHAPTER XIII

EL MARINERO

HACE algún tiempo di con un compatriota mío en Nueva Orleáns. Era el propietario de una casa de huéspedes frecuentada por marineros de habla española. Este anciano era alto, fuerte y todavía muy ágil a pesar de sus sesenta años. Quiso saber de qué parte venía yo. Cuando le dije que era natural de la Coruña se conmovió mucho porque él era también de Galicia.

Cuando joven era pescador como su padre pero, al morir éste, se fue (como tantos gallegos) a la América latina a probar fortuna. Trabajó varios años de labriego en el interior de la República Argentina pero, como no le gustaba este trabajo, se decidió a volver a la costa. En Buenos Aires se embarcó en un vapor costanero navegando entre el río de la Plata y los puertos brasileños. Sirvió algunos años con la misma compañía de navegación pero desgraciadamente cayó enfermo en Montevideo, fue trasladado al hospital y tuvo que permanecer varios años en el Uruguay.

Más tarde, no pudiendo resistir a la tentación de volver al mar, dio la vuelta al mundo a bordo de un barco noruego y fue a Europa, al África, al Japón y a Australia.

Sería interminable citar toda la lista de embarcaciones en las cuales sirvió. Tuvo muchas aventuras. Durante una tempestad en el océano Índico se fue a pique el vapor en que navegaba, perdiéndose casi la totalidad de la tripulación. En otra ocasión fue hundido el vapor por un submarino enemigo durante la guerra. Pero el anciano siempre tenía mucha suerte, logrando salvarse de todos los peligros de la vida marítima.

Por fin abandonó esta vida aventurera y vino a los

Estados Unidos, donde con sus ahorros compró la casa de huéspedes.

NOTES

De habla española

Spanish speaking. Of Spanish speech.

To speak Spanish is **hablar español,** and similarly to speak English, French, German is **hablar inglés, francés, alemán,** etc.

The speaker of Castilian Spanish, however, prefers to say **hablar el castellano.** Note the exceptional use of the definite article.

Natural

As a noun the meaning of this word is " native of a country."

La naturaleza—nature. Las bellezas de la naturaleza— the beauties of nature.

Morir

The noun is **la muerte**—death.

We have already met with the opposites: **nacer**—to be born, and **el nacimiento**—birth.

El vapor

A general word for a ship is **un barco** or **una embarcación.**

Un barco de velas—sailing vessel.

Un vapor—steamer.

Un barco mercante—freighter, cargo vessel.

Una barca is a smaller vessel, usually a fishing vessel.

El buque is yet another word usually reserved for larger vessels. **Un buque de guerra**—warship.

La navegación

Related words:

> navegar   —to sail
> navegable   —navigable
> el navegante—navigator

Desgraciadamente

The noun is la desgracia, meaning misfortune.

Another rendering of " unfortunately " is **desafortunada-mente.**

" Unfortunate " is, of course, **desgraciado** or **desafortunado.**

Note the Spanish prefix **des-**, which often corresponds to the English *dis-* or *un-*.   For example :

> desarrollar —to unfold, develop
> desaparecer —to disappear
> desembarcar—to disembark

Noruego

Norwegian.   The country is **Noruega**—Norway.

Citar

Citar un pasaje de Cervantes—to quote a passage from Cervantes.

As a reflexive verb **citarse** has the meaning of " to make an appointment."   Los dos caballeros se citaron para las once—The two gentlemen made an appointment for eleven, decided to meet at eleven.

La cita has thus the two meanings : a quotation or an appointment.

Hundir

Hundir is a transitive verb meaning " to sink."

The intransitive verb is **hundirse.**   El barco se hundió—the ship sank.   Also : el barco se fue a pique, with the same meaning.

Ahorros

The verb is **ahorrar**—to save, economise.

> Una caja de ahorros—savings bank

La tripulación

The crew of a ship.   Note also : **los tripulantes**—members of crew.

GRAMMAR

Preterite Indicative Tense. Radical changing verbs

Radical changing verbs of the first and second conjugations such as, for example, **costar, volver,** are not affected in the preterite tense, since the stress never falls on the root vowel.

				Present Indicative	*Preterite*
costar	.	.	.	cuesta	costó
volver	.	.	.	vuelve	volvió

Radical changing verbs of the *third* conjugation, such as **sentir, dormir,** not only change their root vowel in the present indicative when the stress falls on that vowel, but also modify in the case of the third singular and plural of the preterite, when the modified vowel is NOT stressed. For example:

Present indicative:

sentir   siento, sientes, siente, sentimos, sentís, sienten
dormir   duermo, duermes, duerme, dormimos, dormís,
                  duermen

Preterite:

sentir   sentí, sentiste, SINTIÓ, sentimos, sentisteis, SINTIERON
dormir   dormí, dormiste, DURMIÓ, dormimos, dormisteis,
                  DURMIERON

In other words, when followed by -IO or -IE, the E becomes I, and the O becomes U.

You will remember also a third type of verb of the third conjugation, where in the present indicative the E becomes I when the stress falls on it. Such are **pedir, seguir.** This same modification of vowel takes place in the preterite whenever the E is followed by -IO or -IE (as seen above).

Present indicative:

pedir   pido, pides, pide, pedimos, pedís, piden

Preterite:

pedir   pedí, pediste, PIDIÓ, pedimos, pedisteis, PIDIERON

Similarly:

siguió, siguieron

Present Participles. Irregularities

In the case of radical changing verbs of the third conjugation, such as **sentir, dormir,** the same modification of vowel takes place as with the third person plural of the preterite tense, that is, when the E or the O are followed by -IE.

Thus:

Present Participle

dormir	. .	DURMIENDO
sentir	. .	SINTIENDO
pedir	. .	PIDIENDO

The following three verbs also form their present participle irregularly:

decir	diciendo
venir	viniendo
poder	pudiendo

Past Anterior Tense

The preterite of the auxiliary verb **haber** in conjunction with the past participle forms the past anterior tense.

The preterite of **haber** is irregular:

hube, hubiste, hubo, hubimos, hubisteis, hubieron

The use of the past anterior is limited, however, and is normally used only after certain conjunctions such as: **apenas** (hardly), **cuando** (when).

For example:

> Cuando hubo terminado el trabajo salió.
> When he had finished the work he went out.

The use of this tense may be compared with the French:

> *Quand il eut fini, il sortit.*

Preterite (Irregular verbs)

Other irregular verbs of the preterite tense are:

VER (to see)	vi, viste, vio, vimos, visteis, vieron
IR (to go)	fui, fuiste, fue, fuimos, fuisteis, fueron

Notice that the preterite of ir is exactly the same as that of ser (to be).

QUERER (to love, wish)	quise, quisiste, quiso, quisimos, quisisteis, quisieron
DECIR (to say)	dije, dijiste, dijo, dijimos, dijisteis, dijeron
DAR (to give)	di, diste, dio, dimos, disteis, dieron

Expressions of Time

Note the following:

anteayer	the day before yesterday
ayer	yesterday
anoche	last night
hoy	today
mañana	tomorrow
pasado mañana	the day after tomorrow
mañana por la mañana	tomorrow morning
mañana por la tarde	tomorrow afternoon (evening)
ayer por la mañana	yesterday morning
son las tres en punto	it is three o'clock sharp
a las dos y pico	just after two (i.e. two o'clock and a bit)
a eso de las once	about eleven o'clock
hace dos años	two years ago

Éste, aquél (special use)

Consider the following sentence:

Don Pedro vino a la tertulia con su amiga; ésta era muy hermosa, aquél muy feo.

Don Pedro came to the party with his lady friend; the latter was very beautiful, the former very ugly.

Remember that éste refers to that which is nearest, and aquél to that which is farthest away. Hence, in relation to the order of words in the sentence, aquél is the equivalent of the English " former " and éste the equivalent of " latter."

EXERCISES

(1) Answer the following questions in Spanish:

1. ¿ Qué clase de hotel tenía el viejo marinero? 2. ¿ De qué parte de España venía él? 3. ¿ Qué hace un pescador? 4. ¿ A dónde fue el marinero a probar fortuna? 5. ¿ Qué trabajo hizo en la República Argentina? 6. ¿ Qué es un barco costanero? 7. ¿ Cuál es la ciudad más importante a orillas del río de la Plata? 8. ¿ Conoce Vd. algunos puertos brasileños? 9. ¿ A dónde fue el marinero cuando cayó enfermo? 10. ¿ Sabe Vd. el nombre del gran explorador portugués que dio la vuelta al mundo? 11. ¿ Cuántos países visitó el marinero? 12. ¿ Cómo sabemos que el viejo tuvo mucha suerte? 13. ¿ Por qué abandonó su vida aventurera? 14. ¿ Con qué compró la casa de huéspedes? 15. ¿ Ha hecho Vd. jamás un viaje por mar?

(2) Give the first person singular and third person plural preterite of the following verbs:

contar   ver   ser   ir   dar   querer   haber   morir
decir   seguir

(3) Put into Spanish:

1. There is a boarding-house in the village. 2. There were many people in the square. 3. There will be many guests. 4. When he had finished he went out. 5. Twelve months ago. 6. He will come the day after tomorrow at eight o'clock sharp. 7. He asked him for the book. 8. Did you see her last night? 9. He gave it to me yesterday. 10. It has rained a great deal today.

(4) Write short sentences in Spanish to show the use of the following words:

la vez, la hora, el tiempo; saber, conocer; preguntar, pedir

(5) Give synonyms of the following Spanish words:

anciano   dar con   volver   labriego   permanecer

(6) Give the opposites of the following words:

morir   buscar   viejo   fuerte   ahorrar

(7) Give the English equivalent of the following sentences:

1. Le di la lista. 2. Di con don Jaime en la calle de Atocha. 3. La ventana da al corral. 4. El marinero volvió a Montevideo. 5. La chica volvió a escribir la carta.

(8) Put into Spanish:

The Galicians are a maritime people, living on the coast of the Atlantic. Many of them are sailors; others are farmers. In the nineteenth century thousands of them went overseas to seek work in the new lands of South and Central America. Some stayed there, some returned to Spain, whilst others spent their whole lives sailing on ships of all nations. Today in the seaport towns throughout the world—Cardiff, Buenos Aires, New York—are to be found these old sailors who left their native land so many years ago, but who still remember sadly the days of their youth.

CHAPTER XIV

LA LLEGADA DEL TRANSATLÁNTICO

EL empleado de la agencia me había dicho que el vapor
" Estrella de Méjico " llegaría poco antes de las siete.

Como esperaba a un amigo mío que regresaba en dicho
vapor de la Habana, me apresuré a terminar la cena y
tomé el primer tranvía con rumbo al puerto.

El sol ya se había puesto, pero todavía se podía ver la
magnífica bahía de Vigo (sin duda una de las más hermo-
sas del mundo entero), rodeada de bosques y de colinas.

El agua estaba quieta. Algunas barcas de pesca
regresaban al puerto, cargadas de sardinas ; un barco
mercante, negro y sucio, se hacía a la mar, echando por su
chimenea nubes de humo ; a lo lejos se podía distinguir
la luz de un faro. Detrás del muelle empezaban ya a
centellear las luces de la ciudad y, al otro lado de la ría, el
pueblecito de Marín iba perdiéndose en la oscuridad.

Unos marineros, vociferando ruidosamente a la puerta de una taberna, sólo molestaban la tranquilidad y quietud de la tarde.

A las siete y media pude ver por fin las luces del transatlántico que entraba lenta y majestuosamente en la bahía.

NOTES

Estrella
Star.
Note also:

> la luna　—moon
> el sol　—sun
> hay luna—it is moonlight

Apresurarse
To hurry.
We have already met with the word **prisa** in such expressions as:

> darse prisa—to hurry
> tener prisa—to be in a hurry

Ponerse

> El sol se pone—the sun sets
> The sunset is **la puesta del sol**
>
> El sol sale—the sun rises
> La salida del sol—sunrise

Vigo
The bay of Vigo is counted amongst the world's most beautiful harbours. Perhaps that of Río de Janeiro is the most renowned.

Todo el mundo
This means " everybody." Todo el mundo lo dice— Everybody says so.
The whole world, all the world is: El mundo entero.

Sucio
The noun is **la suciedad**—dirt.
The opposite is limpio—clean, and **la limpieza**—cleanliness.

Hacerse a *la mar*

Generally this word is masculine : El mar Mediterráneo ; el barco se hundió en el mar.

In certain set expressions, however, the word is sometimes feminine, as :

> hacerse a la mar—to set sail
> en alta mar—on the high sea

La chimenea

Chimney.

Used in connection with houses, factories, ships, locomotives. The word has also the meaning of fireplace.

La ría

La ría—estuary.   El río—river.

Ruidosamente

The adjective is, of course, **ruidoso**, and the noun **el ruido**.

Sólo

Distinguish between **sólo** and **solo.**

> El niño fue solo.   The child went alone.
> Café solo.   Black coffee (coffee alone).

> Sólo tiene diez pesetas.   He has only ten pesetas.

In the third sentence **solamente** is synonymous.

Nube

La nube—cloud.
Connected words are :

> la niebla —fog, mist
> la neblina—slight mist, haze

La ciudad de la niebla—The city of fog is a novel by Pío Baroja, the famous Spanish writer.   The city in question is London !

GRAMMAR

Adjectives.   The Superlative

The superlative of an adjective is formed by prefixing **el más** (la más, etc.).

Este lápiz es el más largo.   This pencil is the longest.
Esta bahía es la más hermosa.   This bay is the most beautiful.
   Los edificios de Nueva York son los más altos del mundo.
   The buildings of New York are the tallest in the world.
   ¿ Cuáles de estas plumas son las más fuertes ?
   Which of these pens are the strongest ?

Notice that in such a case as : la casa más alta—the tallest house, the definite article is NOT repeated, as for instance in French : *la maison la plus haute.*

Notice also the use of **de** in such a sentence as : El edificio más alto **del** mundo—The highest building *in* the world.

Similarly : " the least " is rendered by **el menos** (la menos, etc.).

> Este niño es el menos inteligente de todos.
> This child is the least intelligent of all.

Adverbs.   Juxtaposition

When two adverbs ending in **-mente** come together in a sentence the latter only takes the ending.

El vapor entraba lenta y majestuosamente en la bahía.
The steamer was coming slowly and majestically into the bay.

Adverbs.   The regular comparison

As in the case of adjectives, the comparative of adverbs is formed by prefixing **más**.

> Ahora anda el burro más de prisa.
> Now the donkey is walking more quickly.

The comparison of inequality :

> Este burro anda más despacio que aquél.
> This donkey walks more slowly than that one.

Aquí el sol se pone menos rápidamente que en el Ecuador.
Here the sun sets less rapidly than in Ecuador.

The comparison of equality:

> Voy al teatro tan amenudo como usted.
> I go to the theatre as often as you.

The superlative is formed in the same way as the comparative, but **lo** immediately precedes the adverb when the latter is followed by a word or expression denoting possibility.

> Lo que más me sorprende.
> What surprises me most.

But:

Lo más pronto posible. As soon as possible.
Esto es lo menos que Vd. puede hacer. This is the least you can do.

Preterite. Irregular Verbs

PONER (to put)	puse, pusiste, puso, pusimos, pusisteis, pusieron
ANDAR (to walk)	anduve, anduviste, anduvo, anduvimos, anduvisteis, anduvieron
CONDUCIR (to lead)	conduje, condujiste, condujo, condujimos, condujisteis, condujeron
TRAER (to bring)	traje, trajiste, trajo, trajimos, trajisteis, trajeron

Pluperfect Indicative Tense

This tense is formed by the conjunction of the imperfect indicative of **haber** with the past participle.

> Habíamos terminado. We had finished.

Its use is similar to that in English. Study the following sentences:

> Mi primo había escrito dos cartas cuando llegué.
> My cousin had written two letters when I arrived.

El agente me dijo que el vapor había llegado.
The agent told me that the ship had arrived.

We have already met with some irregular past participles
(such as **escrito** (from **escribir**) ; **visto** (from **ver**) ; **dicho** (from
decir)). Other irregular participles are :

MORIR (to die)	muerto
PONER (to put, place)	puesto
HACER (to do, make)	hecho
VOLVER (to return)	vuelto

It is useful and helpful to remember that very often nouns
exist which are connected with these irregular past participles.
For instance :

un puesto	—a stall, booth (where things are set out)
un dicho	—a saying
un hecho	—a deed
un billete de ida y **vuelta**	—a *return* ticket
la muerte	—death

EXERCISES

(1) Answer the following questions in Spanish :

1. ¿ Cómo se llamaba el vapor?   2. ¿ De dónde regresaba
el amigo?   3. ¿ Dónde está la Habana?   4. ¿ A qué hora
se pone el sol hoy?   5. ¿ Cómo estaba el agua en la bahía de
Vigo?   6. ¿ Cómo se llama un barco que lleva mercancías?
7. ¿ Qué echaba el barco mercante por la chimenea?
8. ¿ Qué se podía distinguir a lo lejos?   9. ¿ Dónde está el
pueblo de Marín?   10. ¿ Quiénes molestaban la tranquilidad
de la tarde?   11. ¿ A qué hora llegó el transatlántico?
12. ¿ Cuántos días dura la travesía del Atlántico?   13. ¿ Cuál
es el puerto más importante de Inglaterra?   14. ¿ Qué se ve
de noche en el cielo?   15. ¿ Cuántos pasajeros puede llevar
un transatlántico moderno?

(2) Put the verbs in brackets into the appropriate person and number of the preterite tense.

1. Yo (ponerse) el sombrero. 2. Los guardias (ir) hasta el muelle. 3. El mozo (traer) dos vasos de cerveza. 4. Esta calle (conducir) a la playa. 5. La vieja (querer) saber de dónde venía yo. 6. Los empleados (decir) que el barco había llegado. 7. Ramón (morir) a la edad de setenta años. 8. Nosotros no (hacer) nada. 9. ¿A dónde (irse) tú? 10. ¿Le (dar) Vd. el dinero?

(3) Replace the infinitives in heavy type by past participles.

1. He **acabar** el trabajo. 2. Me dijo que había **ver** la ciudad. 3. El pobre había **morir**. 4. ¿Quién ha **hacer** esto? 5. La luna se había **poner** cuando salí. 6. Hemos **escribir** la carta. 7. El maestro había **interrumpir** al niño. 8. Cuando hubo **comer** fue a dar un paseo. 9. Las barcas han **salir** del puerto. 10. No he **poder** distinguir la luz.

(4) Put into Spanish:

1. Río de Janeiro is one of the world's most beautiful cities. 2. The donkey was walking more slowly than his master. 3. The priest came in silently and sadly. 4. You have finished the work very quickly. 5. He often comes to see me.

(5) Form sentences in Spanish, using the following words or expressions:

rodeado de   a lo lejos   apresurarse a   antes de   después de

(6) Give the Spanish equivalents of the following:

steamer   liner   freighter   fishing vessel

(7) Put into Spanish:

When he reached the quay, the sun was setting over the bay. Already one or two stars were to be seen in the sky, and in the distance twinkled the lights of the little village of Marín. Several fishing boats were returning to the harbour laden with sardines, and a dirty old cargo vessel was putting out to sea. In half an hour the liner would arrive, bringing his friend from South America.

CHAPTER XV

COMUNICACIONES

Por ser España un país muy montañoso las comunicaciones nunca han sido fáciles. Hay pocos ríos navegables y menos canales. Una excepción es el río Guadalquivir. Vapores de ultramar pueden subir hasta el puerto fluvial

de Sevilla, a unos ochenta kilómetros de la desembocadura del río.

Los puertos de mar son numerosos. Basta mencionar los más importantes: Barcelona, Valencia, Alicante, Cartagena y Málaga a orillas del Mediterráneo; Cádiz y Huelva entre Gibraltar y la frontera portuguesa; Vigo, el Ferrol, la Coruña, Santander y Bilbao en la costa del Atlántico y del golfo de Vizcaya.

En cuanto a comunicaciones terrestres grandes líneas ferroviarias unen todas las ciudades, pero en algunas regiones hay varias líneas en construcción que no están terminadas todavía.

Las carreteras principales de España son excelentes por regla general, y en los últimos años se ha desarrollado mucho el servicio de autobuses por todas partes. Sin embargo el carro tradicional, arrastrado por los bueyes lentos y solemnes, no ha desaparecido por completo y, a pesar de las invenciones modernas, se usan todavía burros, caballos y mulas.

¿Cómo serán las comunicaciones del porvenir? Hay personas que creen que es tan inútil como costoso emprender la construcción de nuevas vías férreas. ¿Para qué servirán? El aeroplano será dentro de pocos años el medio de transporte más importante. Ya se ve que en el Nuevo Mundo, como consecuencia de las distancias tan enormes, la aviación desempeña hoy día un papel más importante que en los países europeos de menor extensión. No está lejos el día en que cada ciudad tendrá su aerodromo.

NOTES

Montañoso

> La montaña —mountain
> El montañés—mountaineer

La desembocadura
Derived from **la boca**—mouth.
The verb is **desembocar.**

> The Ebro flows into the Mediterranean.
> El Ebro desemboca en el Mediterráneo.

Puertos de mar
Cartagena and El Ferrol are Spanish naval bases.

Unen
The verb is **unir**—to unite, join.
We have already met the past participle: Los Estados **Unidos.**

Desarrollarse

To unfold, develop.

The noun " development " is **el desarrollo.**

Carro tradicional

On mountainous and precipitous roads in rural districts it is sometimes difficult for vehicles to pass except at certain places. The axles of the bullock carts are often constructed in such a way that when the cart moves along it is accompanied by a shrill squeaking noise. This gives warning to all in the vicinity so that those nearest the crossing places may halt until the other has passed by.

El porvenir

The future. Or: **lo porvenir.** That is: **Lo** que es **por venir**—that which is to come. E.g. En lo porvenir—in the future.

Similarly:

lo presente—the present   **lo pasado**—the past

These words are also used with the masculine articles:

un pasado glorioso—a glorious past

El futuro is a grammatical term.

el futuro perfecto—the future perfect

¿ Para qué servirá ?

Servir para... to be of use for...

Esta pluma no sirve para nada—This pen is no good.
¿ Para qué sirve? What's the use? What is it used for?

Desaparecer

To disappear.

The opposite is **aparecer**—to make an appearance.

Parecer is to " appear " in the sense of " seem."

¿ Qué le parece a Vd. ? What do you think of it? How does it seem to you?

Parecerse—to resemble.

Se parece mucho a su hermano—He is very like his brother.

Línea ferroviaria

La línea ferroviaria, la vía férrea, and el ferrocarril all mean railway.

El aeroplano

A word also used is **el avión**.

el hidroavión	—seaplane
el aviador	—aviator
volar	—to fly
el vuelo	—flight

GRAMMAR

Adjectives.   Irregular comparison

There are a few adjectives in Spanish which have irregular comparatives and superlatives.

pequeño	(small)	menor (smaller)	el menor (the smallest)
grande	(big)	mayor (bigger)	el mayor (the biggest)
bueno	(good)	mejor (better)	el mejor (the best)
malo	(bad)	peor (worse)	el peor (the worst)

These comparatives have the same form for both the masculine and the feminine:

Es el mejor alumno de la clase.	He is the best pupil in the class.
Esta ciudad es la peor del mundo.	This city is the worst in the world.
Sus mayores enemigos.	Their worst enemies.
Las menores dificultades.	The slightest difficulties.

The two comparatives **menor** and **mayor**, when relating to persons, usually mean " younger " and " older " (compare " minor " and " major "). The adjectives **pequeño** and

grande are also compared regularly and relate to size. For example:

Carlos es más grande que María.	Carlos is bigger than María.

But:

Soy mayor que él.	I am older than he is.
Es la iglesia más pequeña.	It is the smallest church.

But:

Es la menor de las hermanas.	She is the youngest of the sisters.

Adverbs. Irregular comparison

Corresponding to the adjectives mentioned in the preceding paragraph are the adverbs:

poco	(little)	menos	(less)
mucho	(much)	más	(more)
bien	(well)	mejor	(better)
mal	(badly)	peor	(worse)

Este niño trabaja bien pero aquél trabaja mejor.
This child works well but that one works better.

Yo trabajo poco, él trabaja menos.
I work little, he works less.

Mi hermano lee mucho más que yo.
My brother reads much more than I.

As stated previously, the superlative has the same form as the comparative, but notice such cases as:

Trabaja lo más despacio posible.
He works as slowly as he can.

Be careful to distinguish: poco   un poco   un poco de.

Carlos come poco.	Carlos eats little (not very much).
Coma Vd. un poco.	Eat a little.
¿ Quiere Vd. un poco de carne ?	Do you want a little meat ?

Tanto... como...

We have already studied the use of **tan... como...** in such a sentence as : No es tan fuerte como yo—He is not so strong as I am. Remember that **tan** qualifies an adjective or an adverb.

Tanto, on the other hand, qualifies a noun, as for instance :

> No tengo tanto dinero como él.
> I have not as much money as he.
> Ramón tiene tantas hijas como Pedro.
> Ramón has as many daughters as Pedro.

The Passive Voice

The passive voice is not used as frequently in Spanish as in English. It is formed by the verb **ser** followed by the past participle.

Study the following examples :

Esta casa fue construída por un arquitecto muy célebre.
This house was built by a very famous architect.

El conde ha sido desterrado.   The count has been banished.

La criada entró sin ser vista.   The servant entered without being seen.

La reina fue seguida del rey.   The queen was followed by the king.

Notice that in all these cases the past participle agrees with the subject. The agent is introduced in Spanish by **por** or **de**. **Por** is generally used when the agent is a living being, and **de** in other cases, after verbs expressing emotion, and in several conventional phrases such as : seguido de, conocido de (known by).

> Fue amada de todos.   She was beloved by all.

The past participle is also used in conjunction with the verb **estar**, the distinction being that *state* rather than *action* is implied.

Compare the following:

La puerta fue abierta.	The door was open*ed*.
and	
La puerta estaba abierta.	The door was open.

El ferrocarril fue construído en tres años.
The railway was built in three years.

and   El ferrocarril no está terminado todavía.
The railway is not finished yet.

Frequently these verbs are replaced by such forms as hallarse, verse, as for example:

La puerta se hallaba abierta.
The door was open (literally " found itself ").

Jaime se vio obligado a marcharse.
Jaime was obliged to leave (literally " saw himself ").

Very often the passive is replaced by the reflexive form. Compare the following for instance:

A lo lejos se vieron muchas casas.	Many houses were seen in the distance.
Aquí se habla español.	Spanish spoken here.
Se bebe mucho té en Inglaterra.	A lot of tea is drunk in England.

Infinitive.   Construction with *por*

Notice the following rather idiomatic construction:

Por estar tan cansado, no quise continuar el viaje.
As I was so tired (through being so tired), I did not wish to continue the journey.

And similarly:

Por estar cansada mi hermana, decidimos no continuar el viaje.
As my sister was tired, we decided not to continue the journey.

The sentence could, of course, be expressed as:

Como mi hermana estaba cansada...

Idiomatic Use of Verbs

Notice particularly the two verbs: **faltar**—to lack, and **bastar**—to suffice.

Me falta dinero.   I am short of money (i.e. money is lacking to me).

Basta mencionarlo.   It is enough to mention it.

Notice also the exclamatory use: ¡ Basta! That's enough! No more!

EXERCISES

(1) Answer the following questions in Spanish:

1. ¿ Hay muchos ríos navegables en España? 2. ¿ Qué es un puerto fluvial? 3. ¿ Cómo se llama la ciudad que se encuentra cerca de la desembocadura del Tajo? 4. ¿ Cuál es el puerto más importante de España? 5. ¿ Qué separa España del África? 6. ¿ Por dónde pasa el ferrocarril París–Lisboa? 7. ¿ Cuántos ferrocarriles atraviesan los Pirineos? 8. ¿ Hay buenos servicios de autobuses en España? 9. ¿ Prefiere Vd. el tren o el autobús? 10. ¿ Le parece a Vd. inútil emprender la construcción de nuevos ferrocarriles? 11. ¿ Ha hecho Vd. algún viaje aéreo? 12. ¿ Por qué, hasta hoy día, ha desempeñado la aviación un papel más importante en la América del Sur que en España? 13. ¿ Cuál es la velocidad de un aeroplano moderno? 14. ¿ Tiene aerodromo la ciudad donde Vd. vive? 15. ¿ Se usan bueyes en Inglaterra?

(2) Translate the English words in brackets.

1. El aeroplano va (more) de prisa (than) un tren. 2. Es la capital (most) bella de Europa. 3. El río Guadalquivir no es (as) largo (as) el Ebro. 4. Carlos es (older than) Juan, pero no es (as tall). 5. España no tiene (as many) barcos mercantes (as) Noruega. 6. El viejo no estaba (as) cansado (as) el joven. 7. El burro anda (slowly) pero el buey anda (more slowly). 8. Trabaja (as little as) posible. 9. Este libro es (the worst) de todos. 10. Ella sabe cantar (better than) su hermana.

(3) Replace the English words in brackets by appropriate forms of ser or estar.

1. El ferrocarril no (is) construído todavía.   2. El ferrocarril (was) construído por un ingeniero muy famoso.   3. El cuarto (was) iluminado por gas.   4. La carta (is) escrita.
5. La carta (was) escrita por un abogado.

(4) Using the reflexive construction, express the following sentences in Spanish :

1. Spanish spoken here.   2. They say he has gone to Cuba.
3. Dancing until midnight.   4. Trade has developed greatly in this country.   5. The door opened.

(5) Replace the infinitive, where necessary, by the correct form of the verb.

1. Cuando hubo terminar su trabajo, salió.   2. Después de escribir la carta, me la dio.   3. Cuando entré, mi hermano escribir una carta.   4. Creo que don José venir mañana.
5. Isabel estaba cantar una canción.

(6) Compose short sentences in Spanish, making use of the following words or expressions :

basta   en cuanto a   desarrollarse   sin embargo   servir para

(7) Complete the following sentences :

1. España es un país muy ——.   2. Muchos autobuses recorren las —— de España.   3. El buey —— el carro.
4. Este actor desempeña un —— muy importante.   5. Sevilla está a unos ochenta kilómetros de la —— del río.

(8) Put into Spanish:

Many of the rivers of Great Britain are navigable, and there are innumerable canals linking the different towns.   It is possible to travel almost anywhere by rail.   There are certain parts of the country, however, where railways do not exist, but excellent bus services have been developed.   Many cities have their aerodromes, and perhaps the day is not far distant when air travel will be universal.

RECAPITULATION III

EXERCISES

(1) Put into Spanish:

1. The magnificent cathedral of Seville is one of the largest in Spain. 2. Coming into the room the servant dropped all the plates. 3. He asked me whether I would go with him. 4. It was very bad weather. 5. He said yesterday that he would like to come too. 6. She is very beautiful but not so intelligent as her sister. 7. Had you read this letter when you came to see me the day before yesterday? 8. As his mother was ill he did not wish to go out. 9. Have you seen as many bull-fights as I have? 10. He thinks that I am older than my brother. 11. A university was founded in Mexico City at the beginning of the fifteenth century. 12. He always spoke slowly and carefully. 13. He set sail five years ago and is still abroad. 14. When we reached the quay the liner had already entered the bay. 15. She used to go shopping every morning. 16. The new road isn't built yet. 17. Who has done it? I don't know. 18. The sailor has been taken to hospital. 19. Grandfather didn't like tinned sardines. 20. The sun was setting as we crossed the lake.

(2) Give the first person (singular and plural) of the preterite of the following verbs:

dar   querer   empezar   sentir   morir   pedir   embarcarse
ser   ir   conducir

(3) Give the third person (singular and plural) of the preterite of the following verbs:

decir   ser   estar   poner   sentir   contar   ver   dar
andar   hacer

(4) Write in Spanish a few lines on each of the following topics:

1. Los gallegos. 2. El descubrimiento de América. 3. La tienda de comestibles. 4. Comunicaciones antiguas y modernas. 5. La bahía de Vigo.

CHAPTER XVI

VIAJE EN TERCERA CLASE

Habíamos sacado los billetes y esperábamos la llegada del tren.

—El tren trae media hora de retraso—había gritado el jefe de estación, pero nadie hizo caso de él.

Cuatro jóvenes, sentados sobre un baúl en el andén,

jugaban a los naipes ; dos niños con su madre comían melones ; un caballero gordo, de pie delante de la sala de espera, fumaba un pitillo y trataba de leer su diario. Sólo se quejaba un pobre viajante de comercio pero se consoló éste por fin con un " No hay remedio " lúgubre... y filosófico.

Tres cuartos de hora más tarde vino el tren y pude encontrar fácilmente un departamento de tercera clase. Subí y el caballero gordo me siguió. Colocó su maleta en la red y se sentó al lado de una señora que charlaba ruidosamente con su amiga.

La locomotora salió de la estación, silbando ansiosa y melancólicamente.

Empezó el caballero a fumar otro pitillo ; siguió charlando la señora ; yo me dormí.

Me despertó un ruido confuso de voces. Estábamos en una estación muy grande. El caballero gordo se levantó, encendió otro pitillo y, diciéndonos que iba a tomar una taza de café, bajó del coche. Cinco minutos después el tren se puso en marcha otra vez.

Súbitamente lanzó la señora un grito terrible : — ¡ Ay ! ¡ El pobre señor ha olvidado su maleta !

Como el tren no había salido todavía de la estación, yo, con la ayuda de la señora, cogí la maleta, arrojándola por la ventanilla. Afortunadamente cayó en el andén.

Y la dama siguió hablando con su amiga : — Como decía, compré el traje y sólo pagué...

Pero no acabó la frase. ¡ El caballero gordo acababa de entrar en el departamento !

— Había tanta gente en la fonda que no pudieron servirme — dijo, — pero, gracias a Dios, pude subir en el último coche.

¡ Nadie sabrá cuántas pesetas pagó la dama y no quiero yo repetir lo que dijo el caballero cuando buscó su maleta !

NOTES

A similar story to the above is developed in the play *No Fumadores* (Non-smoker), by Jacinto Benavente, the famous Spanish dramatist.

Sacar un billete

Sacar   —to take out
Sacar un billete—to take a ticket

un billete de tercera clase—a third-class ticket
un billete de ida y vuelta—a return ticket

Tren

Types of trains are:

un tren correo	—mail train
un tren expreso	—express train
un tren de mercancías	—a goods train
un tren mixto	—a " mixed " train carrying goods and passengers
un tren de recreo	—an excursion train

The train is made up of:

la locomotora	—locomotive
el ténder	—tender
los coches	—coaches, carriages
el coche-comedor	—dining-car
el coche-cama	—sleeper
el furgón	—luggage van

El baúl

A trunk.

La maleta	—suit-case
El equipaje	—luggage

Los naipes

Spanish cards are different from English ones. There are 48 cards in the pack. There is the ace (el as), the cards numbering from 2 to 9, the Jack (la sota), the horse (el caballo), and the king (el rey). The four suits are: espadas (swords); bastos (clubs); oros (sovereigns); copas (wine glasses).

It is curious that **bastos** represent clubs, not as the English, but as actual cudgels!

El pitillo

A cigarette, in Spanish, is **un pitillo, un cigarrillo.** Sometimes the word **el cigarro** is used in the sense of cigarette.

A cigar is **un puro** or **un habano,** i.e. un cigarro puro or un cigarro habano—a cigar of pure leaf, a Havana cigar.

A pipe is **una pipa.** Notice that to smoke a pipe is fumar **en** pipa. After all, it is the tobacco that is smoked in the pipe.

El traje

As has been pointed out before, **el traje** means " man's suit " or " woman's dress."

> Hat—**el sombrero.**
> A woman's dress—**el traje** or **el vestido.**
> Skirt—**la falda.**
> Stockings—**las medias.**
> Blouse—**la blusa.**
> A man's jacket—**una chaqueta** or **una americana.**
> Shirt—**la camisa.**
> Trousers—**el pantalón.**

A sombrero is, in Spanish, **un sombrero mejicano** (i.e. a Mexican hat).

De pie

Compare : **de pie** and **a pie.**

> **Estar de pie**—to be standing
> **Ir a pie** —to go on foot

Consider the following philosophy of oriental origin :

Mejor sentado que de pie.
Mejor echado que sentado.
Mejor muerto que echado.

It is better to be seated than standing, better to be lying down than seated, better to be dead than lying down.

echar means " to throw," but notice **estar echado**—to be lying down.

Similarly :

> **estar sentado**—to be seated

GRAMMAR

Preterite Tense. Changes of spelling

In the case of the following verbs, notice the changes of spelling which occur in the preterite tense.

PAGAR—to pay

Whenever E follows G, as in the first person singular, it is necessary to insert U between the G and E so as to preserve the hard sound of G in the infinitive.

yo pagué   I paid   but él pagó   he paid

Similarly, of course, in the case of any verb ending in -GAR. E.g.:

apagar—to extinguish
obligar—to compel

EMPEZAR—to begin

Whenever E follows Z, as in the first person singular, it is necessary to change the Z into C. Compare, for instance, LUZ (light) which takes the plural LUCES.

yo empecé   I began   but él empezó   he began

Similarly, any verb ending in -ZAR. E.g.:

comenzar—to commence   lanzar—to throw

BUSCAR—to look for

Whenever E follows C, as in the first person singular, it is necessary to replace C by QU in order to preserve the hard sound of C in the infinitive.

yo busqué—I sought   but él buscó—he sought

Similarly, any verb ending in -CAR. E.g.:

sacar—to take out   secar—to dry

Some orthographical changes also affect the third person of the preterite. If the third person singular or plural endings (-IÓ, -IERON) were added to the stem of a verb ending in a vowel, the unaccented vowel " i " would fall between the two vowels. In such cases the unaccented " i " is replaced by " y." For instance:

CAER—to fall

yo caí   I fell | él cayó   he fell
                      | ellos cayeron   they fell

LEER—to read

yo leí   I read

$\begin{cases} \text{él leyó} & \text{he read} \\ \text{ellos leyeron} & \text{they read} \end{cases}$

CONSTRUIR—to build

yo construí   I built

$\begin{cases} \text{él construyó} & \text{he built} \\ \text{ellos construyeron} & \text{they built} \end{cases}$

OIR—to hear

yo oí   I heard

$\begin{cases} \text{él oyó} & \text{he heard} \\ \text{ellos oyeron} & \text{they heard} \end{cases}$

Notice that such changes also affect the present participle:

caer—cayendo   leer—leyendo   construir—construyendo
ir—yendo

In the case of verbs of the second or third conjugation, the stem of which ends in -LL or -Ñ, the " i " of the preterite endings -IÓ, -IERON, disappears completely.

ZAMBULLIR—to dive, plunge

yo zambullí $\begin{cases} \text{él zambulló (and not " zambull-ió ")} \\ \text{ellos zambulleron} \end{cases}$

TEÑIR—to dye

yo teñí $\begin{cases} \text{él tiñó (and not " tiñ-ió)} \\ \text{ellos tiñeron} \end{cases}$

and also the present participles: zambullendo, tiñendo.

Preterite. Irregular verbs

VENIR (to come)   vine, viniste, vino, vinimos, vinisteis, vinieron

PODER (to be able)   pude, pudiste, pudo, pudimos, pudisteis, pudieron

SABER (to know)   supe, supiste, supo, supimos, supisteis, supieron

Notice that **poder** means *to be able* in the sense of physical ability. For instance:

Es cojo.   No puede nadar.   He is lame.   He cannot swim.

On the other hand, **saber** means *to know* or *to know how to.* Thus:

He cannot swim.   No sabe nadar.

In the latter case the meaning is that he does not know how to swim, but he is not incapable of learning.

Poder also corresponds to the English " can " or " may."

¿ Puede Vd. venir mañana ?   Can you come tomorrow ?
Esto no puede ser.   This cannot be.

Reflexive Verbs.   Change of meaning

Some verbs change their meaning when used reflexively. Such are, for instance:

dormir   (to sleep)   dormirse   (to go to sleep)
ir   (to go)   irse   (to go away)
morir   (to die)   morirse   (to be dying)
marchar (to march, walk)   marcharse (to go away)

El niño duerme.   The child is asleep.
Yo me dormí.   I fell asleep.

Va al teatro.   He is going to the theatre.
Se fue en seguida.   He went away at once.

Verbs.   Idiomatic uses
SEGUIR—to follow

This verb, usually meaning " to follow," can also be used with the present participle in the sense of " to go on doing something."

El caballero me siguió.   The gentleman followed me.
La dama siguió hablando.   The lady went on talking.

ACABAR—to finish

When used with the present and imperfect indicative tenses and followed by the preposition DE, the meaning corresponds to the English " to have just."

El zapatero acabó su trabajo.	The shoemaker finished his work.
But Acaba de salir.	He *has* just gone out.
Acababa de salir.	He *had* just gone out.

In this respect the French construction can be compared: *Il vient de sortir.   Il venait de sortir.*

EXERCISES

(1) Answer the following questions in Spanish:

1. ¿ Qué esperábamos? 2. ¿ Cuánto tiempo tardó el tren en llegar? 3. ¿ Quiénes estaban sentados en el baúl? 4. ¿ Le gusta a Vd. jugar a los naipes? 5. ¿ Qué hacía el caballero gordo? 6. ¿ Qué dijo el pobre viajante de comercio? 7. ¿ En dónde colocó el caballero su maleta? 8. ¿ Qué hacía la señora? 9. ¿ A dónde fue el caballero? 10. ¿ Por qué lanzó un grito la señora? 11. ¿ Qué hicimos con la maleta? 12. ¿ Cuándo volvió el caballero? 13. ¿ De qué hablaba la señora cuando entró el caballero en el departamento? 14. ¿ Qué dijo el caballero cuando buscó su maleta? 15. ¿ Prefiere Vd. viajar en primera o en tercera clase?

(2) Replace the infinitives in heavy type by the appropriate form of the preterite.

1. El caballero **fumar** un pitillo. 2. Mi amigo **venir** a las siete de la tarde. 3. No **poder** encontrar mi maleta. 4. El chico no **saber** hacerlo. 5. La maleta **caer** en el andén. 6. Nosotros **buscar** el dinero. 7. Yo **buscar** el dinero. 8. Yo **empezar** el trabajo. 9. Colón **hacer** varios viajes al Nuevo Mundo. 10. Los convidados **sentarse**.

(3) Put into Spanish:

1. I have just read the letter. 2. In spite of the cold he went swimming. 3. He went away sadly. The woman was dying. 4. The travellers got into the train. 5. He threw the newspaper through the window. 6. I took two pesetas out of the box. 7. They were awakened at seven o'clock. 8. We went in again. 9. Why did he light his cigarette? 10. Her father paid no attention to her.

(4) Give the opposites of the following words and expressions:

la llegada   estar de pie   subir   sentarse   afortunadamente

(5) Give the first person singular and third person plural preterite of the following verbs:

jugar decir lanzar saber coger andar conducir querer
seguir ser

(6) Put into Spanish:

The train was ten minutes late and all the passengers were waiting on the platform or in the waiting-room. At last the train arrived and I got into a third-class compartment. A stout gentleman followed me and sat down near the window at the side of two ladies who were talking. There were also two children with their mother, eating melons. When the train reached the next station the stout gentleman got out, saying that he was going to have a cup of coffee.

CHAPTER XVII

ESPAÑA VISTA POR LOS EXTRANJEROS

Vamos a visitar un pueblo español. Este pueblo no tiene nombre porque existe solamente en la imaginación de los extranjeros.

Los hombres que se pasean por las calles de este pueblo son pequeños, morenos, celosos, perezosos y violentos. No trabajan nunca. Fuman interminables pitillos.

Las mujeres son gordas y alegres, tienen los cabellos negros, se visten siempre de negro.

Todos se levantan a una hora avanzada, duermen la siesta por la tarde, cantan y bailan por la noche. Todos huelen a ajo.

El domingo todos los habitantes del pueblo van a la iglesia a oir misa. Después compran entradas para la corrida de toros. La plaza de toros siempre está atestada de gente.

Al anochecer se oye música por todas las calles. Un joven muy guapo está tocando la guitarra a la reja de su novia. La chica le echa una rosa. (Esta diversión se llama en castellano : Pelar la pava.)

Si nos atrevemos a penetrar hasta lo más oscuro de la calle (¡ las calles son siempre muy estrechas y oscuras !) podemos ver hombres misteriosos envueltos en sus capas, bajo las cuales se divisa la forma de una espada o de un puñal. Estos caballeros esperan una víctima.

A la luz pálida de un farol se ve un mendigo que anda tristemente por la callejuela. Pide limosna. Un transeunte le entrega una moneda.

Y cuando volvemos a casa oímos la voz del vigilante :
— ¡ Son las once y... ser-e-no !

Naturalmente muchos escritores españoles han protestado vigorosamente contra esta representación tan exagerada de la vida española.

Por supuesto es verdad que hay en España corridas de toros, bandidos y asesinatos, y hay que admitir también que cuando el extranjero piensa en la patria de don Quijote le saltan inmediatamente a la mente los nombres de tales personajes como don Juan, Carmen y el Barbero de Sevilla. Pero esto es la España tradicional, la España del teatro y de la leyenda.

NOTES

Celoso

Jealous.

The noun **el celo** (in the singular) means " zeal." The plural form **los celos** has the meaning of " jealousy."

Los cabellos

Do not confuse with **caballos** (horses). In this respect compare the French : *cheveux—chevaux*.

Another word used with the meaning of " hair " (either of man or animals) is **el pelo**.

Ella tiene el pelo rubio—She has fair hair.

Oir misa

To hear Mass. Other words connected with the Church are :

la catedral	cathedral
la iglesia	church
el sacerdote	priest
el cura	village priest
el obispo	bishop
el papa	Pope

Note the two words which are masculine although ending in -a.

Gente (la)

People. A word rarely used in the plural.

Había mucha gente allí—Many people were there.

Al anochecer

At nightfall. Notice that the infinitive is here used as a noun.

Similarly:

al amanecer—at dawn

Tocar la guitarra

To play the guitar.

To play a musical instrument is **tocar**, literally " to touch " the strings or keys.

tocar el piano, el violín—to play the piano, the violin

To play a game is **jugar**.

jugar a la pelota, a los naipes—to play at ball, cards

Pelar la pava

An idiomatic expression meaning literally " to pluck the turkey." The sense is " court a lady," particularly at the " reja " in traditional Spanish style.

Gordo

Fat, stout.

Una perra gorda (a fat dog) is a popular word for a 10 centime piece. The lion which figured on the coin resembled a dog, hence the name.

Similarly: **una perra chica** is a 5 centime piece.

The 50 centime coin is often called " dos reales." (**El real** was a former 25 centime coin.) The unit is, of course, **la peseta** (100 céntimos). The 5 peseta coin equivalent to the dollar at par is **el duro**.

Atreverse

To dare.

No me atrevo a entrar—I dare not go in.

The past participle has an active meaning:

un hombre atrevido—a daring man

La capa

This is the long sleeveless Spanish cloak designed to keep out both the cold wind and the hot sun.   Such capes were also useful for concealing weapons!   Highly romantic historical plays are known in Spanish as : comedias de capa y espada.

Extranjero

Foreigner.
This word also means " abroad, in a foreign land."

> estar en el extranjero—to be abroad
> ir al extranjero   —to go abroad

La víctima

Notice the gender of this word.

El farol

A street lamp.
The ordinary lamp is **la lámpara.**

> una lámpara de petróleo—an oil (paraffin) lamp
> una lámpara eléctrica   —an electric lamp

La moneda

Coin.

> La casa de Moneda—the Mint

Money is, of course, **el dinero.**

El sereno

Night-watchman.

El vigilante

It was the custom in old Spain for the night-watchman to go his rounds crying through the streets the hour of the night and the state of the weather.   For instance, he would cry : ¡ Son las dos y sereno !—It is two o'clock and a fine night !   Hence the term **sereno** for " night-watchman."

El caballero

Originally a knight, horseman. Then by extension a man of sufficient means to possess a horse. Now it has much the same meaning as the English " gentleman." It is also used in the sense of " señor ":

> Pase Vd., caballero—Come in, sir.

GRAMMAR

Neuter Article. Lo

We have already met with this form in connection with the superlative of the adverb:

> Lo mejor es no decir nada.
> The best thing is to say nothing.

and also as a relative:

> Lo que me gusta. What I like.
> No sé lo que quiere decir esto. I don't know what this means.

Before an adjective (for example: **importante**), **lo** has the meaning of " that which is important ":

> Lo importante es no ir demasiado lejos.
> What is important is not to go too far.

It may also have the force of a substantive:

> Desde lo alto de la torre.
> From the top of the tower.

Lo may also precede an adverb in an exclamatory sense:

> ¡ Lo bien que lee este niño !
> How well this child reads !

Adjectives and Adverbs. Absolute Superlative

If we say, for example, that a girl is " most beautiful," we do not compare her with any other girl. The meaning could be expressed by " very beautiful," " extremely beautiful."

Similarly in Spanish:

A most beautiful girl $\left\{\begin{array}{l}\text{Una chica muy hermosa.}\\\text{Una chica sumamente hermosa.}\end{array}\right.$

There is also another method which consists of adding -ísimo (-ísima, -ísimos, -ísimas) to the stem of the positive adjective.

Una chica hermosísima.

This form is extensively used in Spanish. Sometimes a change of spelling is involved when -ísimo is added to the stem:

rico	(rich)	riquísimo	(very rich)
feliz	(happy)	felicísimo	(very happy)
largo	(long)	larguísimo	(very long)

These endings may also be added to an adverb:

temprano (early) tempranísimo (very early)

Idiomatic Use of Verbs

OLER—to smell

This verb is radical changing, but has a further peculiarity. The present indicative is:

huelo, hueles, huele, olemos, oléis, huelen

The H precedes the modified vowel, since an unaccented U cannot stand alone at the beginning of a word.

Notice particularly:

oler a—to smell of

Estos guantes huelen a pescado.   These gloves smell of fish.

Infinitive.   Prepositions

An infinitive dependent on another verb may be preceded by a preposition (e.g. El niño aprende a escribir), or may follow directly without a preposition (e.g. ¿ Quiere Vd. ir conmigo ?).

The direct infinitive is used after the following verbs:

deber	Vd. no debe decir eso.	You must not say that.
poder	No puedo venir mañana.	I cannot come to-morrow.
desear	¿ Desea Vd. comprarlo ?	Do you wish to buy it ?
soler	Suele salir a las ocho.	He usually goes out at eight.
aconsejar	¿ Qué me aconseja Vd. hacer ?	What do you advise me to do ?
pensar	¿ Qué piensa Vd. hacer ?	What do you intend to do ?

The direct infinitive is also used after certain impersonal verbs and expressions, as:

Basta decirlo una vez.	It is enough to say it once.
Es imposible hacer eso.	It is impossible to do that.
Se prohíbe fumar.	Smoking prohibited.
No me fue posible contestarle.	It was impossible for me to reply to him.
Es lástima no comerlo.	It is a pity not to eat it.
Es necesario (preciso) hacerlo.	It is necessary to do it.

Followed by " a ":

apresurarse	Se apresuró a vestirse.	He hastened to dress.
ir	Voy a escribirle.	I am going to write to him.
empezar	Empezó a cantar.	He began to sing.
comenzar	Comenzó a escribir.	He began to write.
aprender	Aprende a dibujar.	He is learning to draw.
enseñar	Me enseña a dibujar.	He is teaching me to draw.
atreverse	No me atrevo a hacer eso.	I dare not do that.
volver	Volvió a embarcarse.	He went to sea again.

Followed by " de ":

tratar	Trataré de hacerlo.	I shall try to do it.

| cesar | Cesó de trabajar. | He stopped working. |
| cansarse | Se cansó de escribir. | He got tired of writing. |

Followed by " en ":

insistir	Insistió en mostrármelo.	He insisted on showing it to me.
consentir	Consintió en ir con ellos.	He consented to go with them.
tardar	El tren tardó en llegar.	The train was late in arriving.
vacilar	No vacile Vd. en decir la verdad.	Don't hesitate to tell the truth.

Followed by " por ":

acabar	Acabó por echarlo al fuego.	He finished by throwing it into the fire.
empezar	Empezó por escribir la fecha.	He began by writing the date.
esforzarse	Se esfuerza por acabar la tarea.	He strives to finish the task.

" para " is, of course, used before the infinitive in the sense of " in order to."

Tomó papel y tinta para escribir la carta.   He took paper and ink to write the letter.

Comemos para vivir.   We eat to live.

Make a point of learning the correct use of these prepositions by memorising a whole phrase or sentence and by making special note of unusual cases.

deber, tener que, haber de
Compare the following :

Tengo que marcharme mañana.—I have to go away tomorrow.
Debo marcharme mañana.   —I must go away tomorrow.
                            (This form is a little less emphatic.)

He de marcharme mañana.   —I am to go away tomorrow. (This form is still less emphatic and rather implies immediate future action.)

Notice also:

deber de

¿ No ha venido doña Antonia?   Debe de estar enferma. Hasn't doña Antonia come?   She must be ill.

In this case the verb does not, of course, express obligation but assumption. That is, we must assume that she is ill.

debería

Vd. no debería hacer eso.   You should not (ought not to) do that.

The form **debiera** (conditional subjunctive) is also very common in the same sense:

Yo debiera ir en seguida.   I ought to go at once.

deber—to owe

Do not forget this other meaning of " deber ":

¿ Cuánto le debe Vd.?   How much do you owe him?

EXERCISES

(1) Answer the following questions in Spanish:

1. ¿ Cómo se llama este pueblo español?   2. ¿ Cómo son los españoles según la idea tradicional?   3. ¿ Cómo se visten las mujeres?   4. ¿ A dónde van los habitantes de este pueblo el domingo?   5. ¿ Qué se oye de noche por las calles? 6. ¿ Quiénes andan por las calles?   7. ¿ Qué se divisa bajo sus capas?   8. ¿ Quién anda tristemente por la callejuela? 9. ¿ Hay muchos mendigos en Inglaterra?   10. ¿ Quién escribió " don Quijote "?   11. ¿ Cómo se alumbran las calles de una ciudad moderna?   12. ¿ Por qué han protestado muchos escritores españoles?   13. ¿ Cómo se llama el legen-

dario bandido inglés? 14. ¿ Hay todavía serenos en Inglaterra? 15. ¿ Para qué va la gente a la iglesia?

(2) Give the English equivalents of the following:

1. Hay que hacerlo en seguida. 2. Vd. tiene que trabajar. 3. El viejo debe de estar muy cansado. 4. ¿ Cuánto me debe Vd.? 5. No debemos venderlo. 6. Vd. no debería hablar tan de prisa. 7. He de visitarle mañana. 8. Lo importante es no llegar tarde. 9. Este pañuelo huele a pescado. 10. Esta iglesia es hermosísima.

(3) Replace the blanks by the correct preposition, if one is needed.

1. No puedo —— hacerlo. 2. Había empezado —— escribir la carta. 3. Pienso —— ir a Barcelona. 4. El caballero trataba —— encender el pitillo. 5. ¿ Quiere Vd. —— venir conmigo? 6. Es imposible —— llegar antes del anochecer. 7. El marinero se decidió —— volver a Nueva York. 8. ¿ Se atreve Vd. —— entrar en aquella casa? 9. Volvió —— subir al árbol. 10. Acabó —— leer este libro.

(4) Give synonyms of the following:

solamente pasearse guapo echar aguardar

(5) Put the verbs in heavy type into the preterite tense.

1. **Voy** a la ciudad. 2. Tú no **tienes** mucha suerte. 3. El camarero no **trae** el vino. 4. **Pago** cincuenta pesetas. 5. **Decimos** la verdad. 6. No me **es** posible. 7. El viejo **muere.** 8. No **hacemos** caso de él. 9. La chica **se pone** muy pálida. 10. El soldado **se levanta** temprano.

(6) Put into Spanish:

Young men playing the guitar at their lover's window, mysterious men wrapped in their black cloaks waiting at the street corner, beggars asking alms in the pale light of a street lamp, the voice of the night-watchman—such is the traditional representation of Spanish life. Does the Spain of Carmen really exist, or does it exist only in the imagination of foreigners? Do we find the answer to this question if we go to Barcelona or Madrid, or must we visit some small country town?

CHAPTER XVIII

CONTRASTE

EL hotel de las Cuatro Naciones (nadie sabe por qué lleva este nombre) está situado en la falda de la sierra. Desde la terraza el turista puede contemplar el magnífico paisaje, la estupenda perspectiva de los elevados picachos de la Cordillera. Este hotel es un magnífico ejemplo de la

arquitectura moderna. Fue construído por un arquitecto europeo de fama universal. Ofrece al turista toda clase de comodidades. Hay más de cien habitaciones lujosas, calefacción central, teléfonos y ascensores. Además ofrece facilidades para los deportistas, y en invierno los aficionados al alpinismo pueden dedicarse a los deportes de nieve.

Pero el viajero a quien sorprende la noche en lo alto de la sierra tiene que trasnochar en la venta del Gato, mesón bajo y negro, de aspecto pobre y _mugriento_. Aquí se reúnen por la tarde, después del trabajo del día, _pastores_ y _cabreros_ de la vecindad y, de vez en cuando, _llegan arrieros_ con sus animales. En esta venta pasan la noche antes de continuar el viaje al día siguiente.

Por la puerta del mesón pueden verse los viajeros sentados alrededor de la mesa. La pieza está iluminada de noche por una lámpara de petróleo. Un brasero debajo de la mesa calienta el cuarto. Las alcobas, frías en invierno, calientes en verano, ofrecen sus duras camas al viajero.

NOTES

La falda
This word has two meanings: (1) lower slope of a hill, mountain; (2) skirt (article of clothing).

El picacho
From **pico**. Literally " a big peak." -**acho** is one of the augmentative suffixes used in Spanish.

El pico (suggesting " sharp-pointed ") is also the word used for a bird's beak. **Picar** is " to prick " or " to pinch."

Un pico (a bit) is familiarly used in such expressions as:
Son las tres y pico—It is just after three o'clock (i.e. three and a bit).

La comodidad
The adjective is **cómodo**—comfortable.
La cómoda—chest of drawers.

Lujoso
El lujo—luxury. Un hotel de lujo—luxury hotel.

Calefacción
We have already met with **calentar**—to heat. Related words are:

el calor—heat	Tengo calor—Hace calor.
caliente—hot	El agua está caliente.

cálido, caluroso—hot   Por un día muy caluroso. Un
                                       país cálido
la calefacción—heating   La calefacción central
el calorífero—furnace   (for central heating). There are
   several types :

                          ⎧ de agua caliente
             calorífero ⎨ de vapor
                          ⎩ de combustión lenta

El deportista — *sports man*

   El deporte—sport. Los deportes de nieve—winter sports.
   A pastime is **un pasatiempo.**

Aficionado
   Connected with **la afición** (liking, fondness).

Tiene mucha afición a la música—He is very fond of music.
Es muy aficionado a los deportes—He is very fond of sports.

   Hence :
       un aficionado—an amateur, a lover of something.

La venta
   La venta, el mesón—usually country inns.
   La posada—usually an inn in town or village.
   La fonda—eating house, restaurant, station buffet.
   Of course the words **el hotel** and **el restaurant** (sometimes
written **restaurante**) are not of Spanish origin, and usually
refer to modern establishments.
   El ventero, el posadero—landlord of an inn.

Mugriento
   La mugre—dirt, filth. Synonymous : la suciedad.

El Arriero
   Muleteer, carter.
   Note : ¡ Arre ! Word used to encourage donkeys, horses,
etc. Equivalent to " gee-up ! "

De noche

Note the two expressions:

> de noche—by night
> de día   —by day

El brasero

The brasier is still used in rural Spain for heating rooms. Frequent deaths are caused through inadequate ventilation since, in cold weather, charcoal brasiers are often placed in the sleeping quarters during the night. It was often the custom to put hot embers under the table to warm the feet and legs of those taking meals.

GRAMMAR

Tan, tal

Compare the uses of these two words:

Una muchacha tan hermosa.	Such a beautiful girl.
Vd. no debiera decir tal cosa.	You ought not to say such a thing.
Hoy día no se leen tales libros.	Such books are not read nowadays.

Notice that **tan** qualifies an adjective, and **tal** (plural—*tales*) qualifies a noun.

Notice also the exclamatory use:

¡ Qué muchacha tan hermosa !   What a beautiful girl!

Semejante (such, similar) may replace **tal** with the same meaning:

Semejante mentira es increíble.	Such a lie is unbelievable.

Por and para

Generally speaking, **para** is used to denote destination or purpose, and **por** to denote agency, motive, means, equivalence, exchange, and is used in connection with certain expressions of time and place. These prepositions have also many idiomatic uses, and it is advisable to note all examples met with in reading.

Study the following examples:

Para

Comemos para vivir.	We eat to (in order to) live.
Este libro es para mí.	This book is for me.
Para mí es muy importante.	For me it is very important.
¿ Para qué sirve esto ?	What's this used for ?
¿ Tiene Vd. bastante dinero para comprarlo ?	Have you enough money to buy it ?
Soy demasiado pobre para comprar tales cosas.	I am too poor to buy such things.
Mañana sale mi hermano para Madrid.	Tomorrow my brother is setting out for Madrid.
Carlos estaba leyendo para sí.	Carlos was reading to himself.
El tren está para salir.	The train is about to start.

Por

Esta casa fue edificada por un arquitecto catalán.	This house was built by a Catalan architect.
¿ Por qué lo hace Vd. así ?	Why are you doing it like that ?
Le llamé por teléfono.	I rang him up.
Mañana por la tarde.	Tomorrow afternoon.
Pasamos por la ciudad.	We went through the town.
Dió un paseo por las calles.	He went for a walk through the streets.
Tres veces por semana.	Three times a week.
Lo compré por dos pesetas.	I bought it for two pesetas.
Por ejemplo.	For example.
Por consiguiente.	Therefore, as a result.

Past Participle.   Use with *tener*

We have seen already how the perfect (and related tenses) are formed by the verb **haber** and the past participle.

La casa que he visto.	The house I have seen.

And also in reflexive verbs, where the auxiliary **haber** is always used:

La señora se había levantado.   The lady had got up.

Tener is also found with the past participle, with a slight difference in meaning.   Compare:

Ha escrito dos cartas.   He has written two letters.

Tiene escritas dos cartas.   He has two letters already written.   (The sense is that he has two letters which are completed.)

Notice that in such cases the past participle agrees with the direct object.

Tener cannot be used, however, with reflexive verbs.

Past Participles.   Irregular forms

> CUBRIR (to cover)   cubierto—covered
> ABRIR (to open)   abierto —open(ed)
> ROMPER (to break)   roto   —broken

Past participles may be used as pure verbs or with adjectival force.   For instance:

¿ Quién ha abierto la puerta ?   Who has opened the door?
La puerta está abierta.   The door is open.

Se ha roto el brazo.   He has broken his arm.
Su reloj está roto.   His watch is broken.

EXERCISES

(1) Answer the following questions in Spanish:

1. ¿ Qué nombre lleva el hotel ?   2. ¿ Dónde está situado ?
3. ¿ Qué se puede ver desde la terraza de este hotel ?   4. ¿ Qué es una cordillera ?   5. ¿ Por quién fué construído este hotel ?
6. ¿ Cuántas habitaciones hay ?   7. ¿ Qué facilidades ofrece el hotel ?   8. ¿ Cómo se llama la venta en lo alto de la sierra ?   9. ¿ Puede Vd. describir el mesón ?   10. ¿ Quiénes

se reúnen en la venta? 11. ¿Cómo está iluminada la cocina? 12. ¿Le gustaría a Vd. pasar la noche en esta venta? 13. ¿Qué animales guardan los pastores? ¿los cabreros? 14. ¿Hay calefacción central en este mesón? 15. ¿Cómo son las alcobas?

(2) Complete the following sentences:

1. Desde aquí se pueden ver los elevados —— de los Pirineos. 2. El hotel fue construído por un —— moderno. 3. Edificios muy altos tienen generalmente ——. 4. Los arrieros —— en la venta. 5. En las aldeas se usan —— para calentar los cuartos.

(3) Give synonyms of the following:

la sierra   la alcoba   célebre   la venta   me gusta más

(4) Replace the blanks by **por** or **para**.

1. Este vino es —— tí. 2. El barco sale —— Buenos Aires. 3. El mendigo andaba —— las calles. 4. Hay que estudiar mucho —— hacerse médico. 5. Le llamé —— teléfono. 6. Viene generalmente —— la tarde. 7. Es demasiado estúpido —— comprender. 8. Fué matado —— el toro. 9. El dependiente gana 80 pesetas —— semana. 10. Hay que comer —— vivir, no vivir —— comer.

(5) Translate the English words in brackets.

1. Sé que vendrá (some) día. 2. Nunca he visto (such) montañas. 3. El cabrero no tiene (no) dinero. 4. El inglés quería (another) vaso de cerveza. 5. (Such a) situación es imposible.

(6) Replace the infinitives in heavy type by past participles.

1. He **romper** la taza. 2. ¿Ha **volver** su hermano ya? 3. La sierra estaba **cubrir** de nieve. 4. ¿Quién ha **hacer** esto? 5. El camarero ha **traer** dos vasos. 6. ¿Ha **ver** Vd. esta ciudad? 7. Don Carlos ha **escribir** dos cartas. 8. Los arrieros han **llegar** a la venta. 9. ¿Quién ha **descubrir** el Pacífico? 10. La pobre mujer ha **caer** enferma.

(7) Put into Spanish:

Spain, as we have seen, is a land of contrasts. Modern hotels can be found in most places frequented by tourists, but the traveller can still discover old inns where shepherds and goatherds come to spend their evenings, and where carters, travelling from town to town, pass the night before continuing their journey on the following day. In such inns the traveller is given a simple meal of soup, bread, vegetables, and wine. The beds are often hard, but the real traveller does not mind that!

CHAPTER XIX

VISITA A UNA FÁBRICA

LLAMÉ a la puerta.

— ¡ Adelante ! dijo una voz.

Entré en la oficina de la gran fábrica de tejidos. Pregunté por mi amigo don Carlos.

— Haga Vd. el favor de tomar asiento, caballero—me dijo uno de los dependientes,— El señor González estará libre dentro de algunos minutos.

Al poco tiempo entró don Carlos. — ¡ Qué tal ! ¿ Has tenido buen viaje ?   ¿ Cómo está la familia ?

Después de charlar un rato fuimos a visitar la fábrica, y don Carlos me describió los varios procedimientos relacionados con la manufactura de los tejidos de lana.

— Como sabes, la lana, materia prima de la industria, procede del carnero.   La mejor raza, la del merino, es de origen español.

— Es un animal bastante pequeño ¿ verdad ?

— Sí. Generalmente la lana procedente de animales de cuerpo pequeño es la más fina, pero en algunos países se da más importancia a la producción de carne. En este caso el animal es más grande pero la lana no es tan fina.

— ¿ Cómo se vende la lana ?

— Se vende generalmente en pública subasta. Primero el comprador tiene que estimar con exactitud el rendimiento de la lana que va a comprar.

— ¿ Rendimiento ?

— Sí. La lana natural está llena de grasa y a veces está muy sucia. El rendimiento es la proporción de lana pura, sin impurezas. Por ejemplo una lana muy limpia puede tener un rendimiento de un 75 por ciento, es decir, al lavarse se pierde sólo la cuarta parte de su peso.

Después del lavado el primer procedimiento de importancia es el de cardar o peinar.

— ¿ Cardar ? ¿ Qué significa eso ?

— Significa casi lo mismo que peinar. Se introduce la lana en una máquina que separa las fibras. Después es preciso hilar la lana y por último se teje. El telar mecánico es una máquina verdaderamente maravillosa.

— ¿ Cuántos obreros se necesitan para operar un telar ?

— Como verás, un solo operario puede a veces manejar varios telares.

— ¿ Cuándo se tiñe la lana ?

— Algunas veces se tiñe antes de hilar, otras veces después.

Sabes sin duda que en algunas partes aisladas se hacen todavía todas estas operaciones a mano y con máquinas muy primitivas, tales como el torno de hilar, el telar de madera. Se usan tintes naturales—vegetales o minerales. Pero ahora se ha concentrado la industria en la provincia de Barcelona, donde se fabrican tejidos de todas clases, de lana, de algodón, de seda, etc.

NOTES

Adelante

Come in !   Forward !   Also : ¡ **Pase Vd. !**
Adelantar—to bring forward, advance.

Mi reloj adelanta mucho.   My watch is very fast.
Un niño muy adelantado.   A very precocious child.

The opposite is **atrasar** :

Mi reloj atrasa.
Un niño atrasado (backward).

Haga el favor de

Other variants are :

Hágame Vd. el favor de darme ese libro.
Sírvase Vd. darme ese libro.
Tenga Vd. la bondad de darme ese libro.

All these forms are equivalent to the English " please."

One also says : ¿ Quiere Vd. darme el libro ? which often has
the force of " please give me the book."

Tomar asiento ’

To take a seat.   Note the omission of the article.
Also, of course, **sentarse.**

Tejidos

Los tejidos—textiles.
Textil is the adjective.   Las industrias textiles.

El merino

A wool of Spanish origin, the characteristics of which are
fineness of fibre and elasticity.   The finest Merino wools now
come from Australia.   Other countries, such as New Zealand,
South America, are generally more concerned with meat
production than with wool of the finest quality, and the sheep
from these parts are larger bodied.   The ideal would be, of
course, a large bodied sheep with first quality wool, and
experiments are continually being carried out to improve the
size of the animal and the quality of the wool.

El comprador

Buyer.

The opposite is **el vendedor**—vendor, salesman.

El peso

Weight.

From the verb **pesar**—to weigh.

El peso is also the name given to the dollar of Latin America.
The North American dollar is called **el dólar**.

In Spain, the five peseta coin, equivalent to the dollar, is **el
duro,** similar in size to the former English five shilling piece.

La máquina

Machine.

> la sala de máquinas—engine room
> el maquinista—engine driver, mechanic.

Do not confuse **el maquinista** with **el ingeniero** who is the
trained engineer with technical or university qualifications.

La seda

Silk.

The silkworm is **el gusano de seda.**

Hilar

> la hilandería—spinning mill
> el hilandero—spinner.

" Las Hilanderas " is the famous painting by Velázquez.

¿ Verdad ?

Note this use of " verdad," equivalent to the French
n'est-ce pas?

Lo ha visto Vd. ¿ verdad?	You have seen it, haven't you ?
Hace frío ¿ verdad?	It's cold, isn't it ?
Iremos mañana, ¿ verdad?	We shall go tomorrow, shan't we ?

The longer form : **¿ no es verdad ?** (isn't it so?) is also used.

GRAMMAR

The Present Subjunctive

The complete conjugation of this tense, which has been mentioned in connection with the polite imperative, is as follows:

HABLAR	COMER	VIVIR
hable	coma	viva
hables	comas	vivas
hable	coma	viva
hablemos	comamos	vivamos
habléis	comáis	viváis
hablen	coman	vivan

Notice that the second and third conjugations have identical endings.

Radical Changing Verbs. If a verb is radical changing in the present indicative, the same change of root vowel takes place in the subjunctive.

	Present Indicative	*Present Subjunctive*
contar . .	cuento, cuentas, etc.	cuente, cuentes, etc.
perder . .	pierdo, pierdes, etc.	pierda, pierdas, etc.

With radical changing verbs of the class **pedir,** there is an additional modification:

pedir Present indicative: pido, pides, pide, pedimos, pedís, piden

Present subjunctive: pida, pidas, pida, **pidamos, pidáis,** pidan

That is, the E becomes I even when the stress does not fall on the vowel. Compare the preterite of **pedir**: pidió, pidieron (third person singular and plural).

Similarly in the case of third conjugation verbs of the **morir, sentir** class, the O becomes U, and the E becomes I, before -amos, -áis.

morir   Present indicative: muero, mueres, muere, morimos, morís, mueren

   Present subjunctive: muera, mueras, muera, muramos, muráis, mueran

sentir   Present indicative: siento, sientes, siente, sentimos, sentís, sienten

     Present subjunctive: sienta, sientas, sienta, sintamos, sintáis, sientan.

Compare the preterite: murió, murieron; sintió, sintieron (third persons singular and plural).

Irregular Verbs. In practically all cases the present subjunctive follows the same form as the first person singular of the present indicative. Thus:

tener   Present indicative: tengo   Present subjunctive: tenga, tengas, tenga, tengamos, tengáis, tengan

decir   Present indicative: digo   Present subjunctive: diga, etc.

poner   Present indicative: pongo   Present subjunctive: ponga, etc.

Some verbs do not follow this rule:

ser   Present subjunctive: sea, seas, sea, seamos, seáis, sean
saber   Present subjunctive: sepa, sepas, sepa, etc.
ir   Present subjunctive: vaya, vayas, vaya, etc.
haber   Present subjunctive: haya, hayas, haya, etc.

Apart from the accents, the present subjunctive of **dar** and **estar** has regularly the same form as a first conjugation verb.

         dar   dé, des, dé, demos, deis, den
         estar   esté, estés, esté, estemos, estéis, estén

Changes of Spelling.   The same rules apply as in the case of the present indicative and the preterite:

	Present Indicative	*Preterite*	*Present Subjunctive*
buscar .	busco	busqué	busque
alcanzar .	alcanzo	alcancé	alcance
pagar .	pago	pagué	pague
vencer .	venzo	vencí	venza
distinguir .	distingo	distinguí	distinga
dirigir .	dirijo	dirigí	dirija
conocer .	conozco	conocí	conozca

As we have discussed before, the polite imperative is formed from the present subjunctive:

Hágalo Vd. en seguida.	Do it at once.
No se marchen Vds.	Don't go away.

The imperative of the first person plural is also formed from the subjunctive:

Sigamos este camino.	Let us follow this road.
Escribámosle.	Let us write to him.

Notice the accent.
In the case of reflexive verbs there is contraction:

Levantémonos.	Let us get up.
(instead of Levantémosnos)	

A command in the other persons is usually accompanied by "que."

¡ Que muera !	Let him die !
¡ Que venga ella !	Let her come !

Note the use of the subjunctive in such a sentence as:

Tradúzcanse **las** siguientes frases.	Translate the following sentences (i.e. let the sentences be translated).

Government of Verbs

A verb may govern a direct object both in Spanish and English, as for instance:

> Busca su reloj.   He seeks his watch.

Or it may be followed by a preposition the usage of which is similar in both languages:

Pagó diez pesetas **por** el reloj.   He paid ten pesetas *for* the watch.

Sometimes usage differs:

Piensa **en** lo que ha hecho.   He thinks *of* what he has done.

Such usages are best learnt by observation.   It is important to learn a whole phrase or sentence rather than to try to remember which preposition governs the object after certain verbs.   Here is a list of verbs which have occurred:

No preposition:

buscar	Está buscando trabajo.	He is looking for work.
pedir	No pida Vd. pan.	Don't ask for any bread.
esperar	Esperamos el tren.	We are waiting for the train.
escuchar	Los niños escuchan la música.	The children are listening to the music.

Followed by preposition:

A

oler	Huele a ajo.	It smells of garlic.
acercarse	Se acercó a la puerta.	He approached the door.
parecerse	Se parece a su padre.	He resembles his father.
jugar	Le gusta jugar a los naipes.	He likes playing cards.

| comprar | Compra un reloj al relojero. | He buys a watch from the watch-maker. |

De

acordarse	¿ Se acuerda Vd. de ella ?	Do you remember her ?
maravillarse	Me maravillé de lo que dijo.	I wondered at what he said.
pensar	¿ Qué piensa Vd. de esto ?	What do you think of this ?

En

consentir	Consintió en el matri-monio.	He consented to the marriage.
entrar	Entró en la casa.	He entered the house.
pensar	¿ En qué piensa Vd. ?	What are you think-ing of ?

Con

soñar	Sueña con los días pasados.	He dreams of past days.
casarse	Se casó con la mu-chacha.	He married the girl.
contar	Cuento con Vd.	I count on you.

Para

| servir | No sirve para nada. | It's no use at all. |

Por

| pagar | Pagó dos pesetas por la pluma. | He paid two pesetas for the pen. |

But:

| | Pagó la pluma. | He paid for the pen. |

(i.e. with the direct object when no sum of money is mentioned)

| preguntar | Preguntaba por Vd. | He was asking for (about) you. |

Notice that some verbs are followed by different prepositions, according to meaning:

> pensar de   to think about, be of the opinion
> pensar en   to think of, to dwell upon

And do not forget the normal use of the " personal **a** ":

> Vio **a** su padre—he saw his father.

Prepositions followed by Verbs

All prepositions are followed by the *infinitive*. Note particularly:

Lo hizo sin querer.	He did it unwillingly.
Después de escribir la carta, salió.	After writing the letter he went out.
¿ Qué hará Vd. antes de salir ?	What will you do before going out ?

Alguien, nadie

Compare these pronouns with those we have already studied:

> algo (something)   alguien (somebody)
> nada (nothing)   nadie   (nobody)

Alguien ha venido.	Someone has come.
No ha venido nadie.	Nobody has come.
(or) Nadie ha venido.	

" No " must precede the verb when the pronoun follows.

Notice particularly:

Nunca da nada a nadie.   He never gives anything to anybody.

EXERCISES

(1) Answer the following questions in Spanish:

1. ¿ Qué clase de fábrica es? 2. ¿ Cuándo estará libre el señor González? 3. ¿ Qué dijo don Carlos? 4. ¿ Cuál es la

materia prima de la industria? 5. ¿ Cuál es la mejor raza de carnero? 6. ¿ Cómo se vende la lana? 7. ¿ Se produce mucha lana en la República Argentina? 8. ¿ Qué se hace después de hilar la lana? 9. ¿ Ha visto Vd. funcionar un telar mecánico? 10. ¿ Se hacen todavía estas operaciones a mano? 11. ¿ En qué parte de la Gran Bretaña se hacen todavía tejidos en casa? 12. ¿ Ha visitado Vd. una fábrica moderna? 13. ¿ Se usan tintes vegetales o minerales para teñir? 14. ¿ Cuántas clases de tejidos se fabrican en la provincia de Barcelona? 15. ¿ Cómo se llama una persona que trabaja en una fábrica?

(2) Give Spanish verbs corresponding to the following nouns:

asiento   fábrica   tejido   peine   tinte   operario   viaje

(3) Replace each of the blanks by an appropriate word taken from the following list: jamás, alguien, nunca, nadie, tampoco, algo, nada. Translate the resultant sentences into English.

1. ¿ Estás seguro de que —— te vio? 2. —— entró en la casa. 3. Desgraciadamente no tengo ——. 4. ¿ Quiere Vd. darme —— que hacer? 5. No me gusta a mí ——. 6. No he visto —— a su tío. 7. ¿ Ha visitado Vd. —— esta ciudad? 8. No hay que darlo a ——. 9. ¿ Quiere Vd. darlo a ——? 10. No tiene —— que decir.

(4) Replace the blanks by appropriate prepositions where they are necessary.

1. Pregunté —— don Carlos. 2. El mendigo pedía —— limosna. 3. El viejo piensa muchas veces —— los días pasados. 4. ¿ Quiere Vd. ver —— el negociante? 5. ¿ Qué piensa Vd. —— esta idea? 6. Hay que comer —— vivir. 7. Pagué diez pesetas —— este libro. 8. Compré el reloj —— el joyero. 9. Lo hizo —— mí. 10. El hombre salió después —— comer. 11. El caballero estaba buscando —— la maleta. 12. El padre consintió —— el matrimonio. 13. Acabo —— terminar el trabajo. 14. ¿ Tiene Vd. —— hacerlo en seguida? 15. No vuelva Vd. —— decir tal cosa.

(5) Put the following verbs into the polite imperative (singular and plural).

(Example: **Comprarlo** para la familia. Cómprelo Vd. para la familia. Cómprenlo Vds. para la familia.)

1. **Sentarse.** 2. **Hacerlo** inmediatamente. 3. **Escribir** la carta. 4. **Permanecer** aquí. 5. **Pedirle** permiso. 6. **Buscar** al jefe de estación. 7. **Empezar** el trabajo. 8. **Volver** en seguida. 9. **Decir** siempre la verdad. 10. **Ponerlo** sobre la mesa.

(6) Repeat the above sentences in the negative.

(Example: Cómprelo Vd. para la familia. No lo compre Vd. para la familia.)

(7) Put into Spanish:

1. He went out without speaking. 2. Before writing the letter Juan closed the door carefully. 3. After eating his dinner the manager went to the office. 4. I am going to see her now. 5. Entering the station he met his friend.

(8) Put into Spanish:

In some parts of Great Britain woollen textiles are still manufactured in the home. The processes employed in a modern factory, however, are almost the same. The wool is first washed to remove the dirt and grease, and then combed or carded to separate the fibres. Afterwards it is spun, dyed, and woven.

CHAPTER XX

EL INDIANO

ESTIMADO AMIGO : Fué para mí una gran sorpresa recibir su carta del 18 de mayo, y siento mucho haber tardado tanto en contestarle.

¿ Se da Vd. cuenta de que hace más de quince años que me despedí de mi tierra natal ? Me fui, como Vd. sabe, a la Habana. No tengo recuerdos muy gratos del viaje. La travesía fue terrible, me mareé casi todos los días y el barco iba atestado de gente. Vd. comprenderá que cuatro personas no caben muy bien en un pequeño camarote. ¡ No es exagerar decir que pasé las de Caín ! Llegué a la Habana cansado y lleno de nostalgia.

Me dirigí en seguida a la hacienda de mi tío Augusto cerca de Matanzas, donde durante algunos años me dediqué con entusiasmo al cultivo de la caña de azúcar. Andando el tiempo hice muchos amigos y, a los cinco años de estar allí, me casé con una hermosísima cubana, cuyas virtudes y excelencias no tengo palabras para alabar. Ahora, gracias a Dios, tenemos dos hijos.

Hace dos años mi señor tío (¡que en paz descanse!) murió después de una enfermedad muy grave, y yo heredé la hacienda.

La semana pasada desembarqué con mi familia en la Coruña. Pensamos pasar unos seis meses aquí en Galicia en casa de mis padres antes de regresar a Cuba.

Tendré mucho gusto en ir a verle a Vd. algún día si no tiene inconveniente. Sin duda tendrá Vd. muchas cosas que decirme. ¿ Se encuentra Vd. todavía soltero ?

¿ Trabaja Vd. todavía en la misma Compañía de Teléfonos ?

Aquí en el pueblo todos me llaman " el indiano " y creen que soy millonario. ¡ Mi señora, la " cubana," no entiende muy bien el gallego !

Aprovecho esta ocasión para darle mis más expresivas gracias por su amabilidad y espero con impaciencia sus próximas noticias.

Siempre de Vd. S.S. y amigo,
ENRIQUE CASTROL.

NOTES

La sorpresa

The verb is **sorprender**—to take by surprise, to surprise.
Me sorprendió la noche—Nightfall overtook me.
Lo que dice me sorprende mucho—What he says surprises me.

Sentir

To feel. Jaime se siente malo. Jaime feels ill.

Note also the meaning of " to regret ":
Lo siento mucho—I am very sorry (literally: " I feel it very much ").
Siento mucho haber hecho eso—I am very sorry I did that.

Darse cuenta de

To realise. Compare the French: *se rendre compte*.

¿ Se da Vd. cuenta de lo serio de esto ?   Do you realise how serious this is ?
No se da cuenta de que soy pobre.   He doesn't realise that I am poor.

Be very careful with the verb **realizar**, which means " to realise " in the commercial sense, to carry into effect, to turn into cash.

Despedirse

To say good-bye.
The noun is la despedida—the leave-taking.

Camarote

Note la cámara as, for example, in la cámara de comercio—Chamber of Commerce.

La cámara de aire—inner tube.

Camarote is an augmentative form of cámara but has acquired the individual meaning of " cabin, berth " on a ship.

Pasar las de Cain

To suffer the tortures of Cain—i.e. to have an awful time.

Alabar

The noun is la alabanza—praise.

Que en paz descanse

Expression used when the name of a dead person is mentioned. Compare: R.I.P.

Also : ¡ Que en el paraíso esté !   May he be in heaven !

Soltero

Bachelor.

A spinster is la soltera.

El Indiano

Name given to one who has returned to Spain from the " Indies." Compare the English " rich uncle from Australia," which is the nearest equivalent.

Dar las gracias por

Note the use of the article.

Another word, agradecer, means " to be grateful for."

A Vd. le agradezco mucho su amabilidad—I am very grateful to you for your kindness.

Se lo agradezco mucho— I am very grateful to you for it.

Another variant is :

Le estoy muy agradecido por su amabilidad—I am grateful to him for his kindness.

Amable

Kind, friendly.

A very common expression in Spanish is : Es Vd. muy amable, equivalent to " That is very kind of you."

GRAMMAR

Caber—to be able to be contained.

An irregular verb.

Present indicative: quepo, cabes, cabe, cabemos, cabéis, caben

Present subjunctive: quepa, quepas, quepa, quepamos, quepáis, quepan

Preterite: cupe, cupiste, cupo, cupimos, cupisteis, cupieron

Future indicative: cabré, cabrás, cabrá, cabremos, cabréis, cabrán

Notice the uses of this verb:

No cabemos aquí.   There's no room for us here (literally: " We do not fit here ").

No cabe duda.   There is no room for doubt.

¿ Cuántas cerillas caben en esta caja?
How many matches does this box hold?

Expressions of Time

Hace dos días.   Two days ago.

Hace dos días que me despedí de él.
It is two days since I bade farewell to him.

Notice the logical use of the Spanish in such a sentence as:

Hace dos semanas que estoy en Madrid.
I have been in Madrid for two weeks. (That is: I *am* in Madrid at the time of speaking, therefore the present tense.)

Similarly:

Hacía dos días que trabajaba en aquella fábrica.
He *had* been working in that factory for two days.   (That is: He was working there at the time.)

The following are of common occurrence:

el año que viene (or) el año próximo   next year
de hoy en ocho (días)   a week today
de hoy en quince (días)   a fortnight today

        quince días—a fortnight
        ocho días　—a week

Compare the French: *huit jours; quinze jours.*

Letters
The date is **la fecha.**

What is the date?　¿ Qué fecha es hoy?　¿ A cuántos estamos?

It is March the first.　Es el primero de marzo. Estamos a primero de marzo.

16th of June, 1940.　El diez y seis de junio **de** mil novecientos cuarenta.

Months are not usually written with capital letters in Spanish.

Letter Openings
To relatives: Querido papá — Dear Father
Mi querida Anita — My dear Anita

To friends: Querido Carlos — Dear Carlos
Estimado amigo (more formal) — Dear Friend

Business: Muy señor mío — Dear Sir
Muy señores míos (nuestros) — Gentlemen
Muy señor mío y amigo (less formal) — My dear Sir

Letter Endings
To relatives: Tu hijo Jaime que te quiere — Your loving Jaime
Your affectionate Jaime

LETTERS

To friends:	Con un cordial apretón de manos	(literally: with a friendly hand-shake)

	Siempre de Vd. S.S. y amigo	Your friend, yours
	Soy de Vd. su buen amigo y S.S.	

Business:	Quedo de Vd. atento y S.S. Q.B.S.M.	I (we) remain, yours faithfully
	Quedamos de Vd. atentos y S.S. Q.E.S.M.	

Abbreviations

atento y S.S.—atento y seguro servidor (literally: attentive and faithful servant)

Q.B.S.M.　　—que besa sus manos (literally: who kisses your hands)

Q.E.S.M.　　—que estrecha su mano (literally: who shakes your hand)

The form Q.B.S.M. is not much used in South America. The formula preferred is: Q.E.S.M. or Q.L.E.L.M. (que le estrecha la mano—who shakes your hand).

When writing to a lady it was once the custom for a gentleman to end the letter: Q.B.S.P.—que besa sus pies—who kisses your feet.

These few examples do not by any means exhaust the many letter endings and openings which are used in Spanish, but they are perhaps amongst the more usual.

EXERCISES

(1) Answer the following questions in Spanish:

1. ¿Qué fecha llevaba la carta que Castrol recibió? 2. ¿Cuánto tiempo tardó en contestar? 3. ¿Cuándo se despidió de su tierra natal? 4. ¿Cuántas personas caben en un transatlántico moderno? 5. ¿Cómo llegó el señor

Castrol a Cuba? 6. ¿Cómo se llamaba su tío? 7. ¿Qué
trabajo hizo en Cuba? 8. ¿Con quién se casó? 9. ¿Cómo
fue la travesía? 10. ¿Por qué heredó Castrol la hacienda?
11. ¿En qué puerto desembarcó? 12. ¿Cuántos meses
piensa pasar en Galicia? 13. ¿Por qué le llaman "indiano"
los vecinos? 14. ¿Por qué tiene la señora Castrol mucha
dificultad en entender el gallego? 15. ¿Escribe Vd. muchas
cartas?

(2) Put into the negative:

1. Tráigame Vd. dos vasos. 2. Abra Vd. la caja.
3. Síganme Vds. 4. Venga Vd. a verme mañana. 5. Atra-
viese Vd. la calle.

(3) Put into Spanish:

1. I have been here two years. 2. Ten days ago. 3. I am
sorry I have written that letter. 4. We had an awful time.
5. Do you intend to live in Cuba? 6. There is no room for
you here. 7. We shall be pleased to see you next week.
8. Were you sea-sick? 9. As time went on I got another job.
10. Did you thank him?

(4) Replace the infinitives in heavy type by present
participles.

1. El viejo se está **morir**. 2. ¿Quién está **leer** en alta voz?
3. Están **construir** una casa. 4. La chica estaba **pedir**
dinero. 5. ¿En qué estás **pensar**?

(5) (a) What verbs correspond to the following nouns?

la sorpresa   la contestación   el recuerdo   la dirección

(b) What nouns correspond to the following verbs?

gustar   atravesar   cultivar   telefonear

(c) What adjectives correspond to the following nouns and
verbs?

tardar   la gratitud   la amabilidad   la enfermedad   el mar

(6) Put into Spanish:

10*th April*, 194–.

DEAR ANTONIA,

I received your letter yesterday. I am sorry to have to tell you that I shall be unable to come and see you next Wednesday, since my mother is very ill and I must stay at home and help my sister.

Did you know that Juan has returned home from Cuba? I saw him the day before yesterday in the street. Everybody thinks that he must be a millionaire, but he told me that he had only enough money to pay for his ticket!

Please write to me again as soon as possible.

Your affectionate friend,

ANITA.

RECAPITULATION IV

EXERCISES

(1) Put into Spanish:

1. He read the whole of the newspaper. 2. We were not able to reach the summit. 3. The child fell asleep in the bus. 4. She had just finished writing the letter when the door opened. 5. You must try to speak more fluently. 6. You ought not to say such things. 7. The mountains were covered with snow. 8. We used to walk along the streets every afternoon. 9. Nobody has started to work yet. 10. How many matches does this box hold? 11. Do you realise the seriousness of the situation? 12. It has been snowing for a week. 13. He knew it two days ago. 14. He was born on July 7th, 1899. 15. What have you got for me? 16. That man is too old to work. 17. What a pretty girl! 18. Is that wool strong enough for spinning? 19. He must have a lot of money. He buys everything he sees. 20. What are you thinking about?

(2) Write in the correct preposition, if one is necessary:

1. El niño aprende —— leer.
2. Voy —— comprar esos libros.
3. Pagó diez pesetas —— la pluma.
4. No podré —— acompañarle a Vd. mañana.
5. ¿ Sabe Vd. —— nadar?
6. Insistió ella —— venir conmigo.
7. Lo haré antes —— acostarme.
8. El cazador ha sido matado —— el león.
9. ¿ Tiene Vd. ganas —— vivir en la ciudad?
10. Es imposible —— vivir sin comer.

(3) Write a continuation in Spanish to the story in Chapter XVI, based on the following outline:

El caballero—furioso—llegar a la próxima estación—bajar del tren—telefonear—conversación con el jefe de estación—salir el tren—tener que pasar la noche en el pueblo.

CHAPTER XXI

LAS REGIONES DE ESPAÑA

Si examinamos un mapa de España veremos que es un país muy montañoso. Tiene la forma de una elevada meseta dividida en fajas por las grandes cordilleras que la atraviesan. Se estima que las tres quintas partes del territorio se encuentran a más de 500 metros sobre el nivel

del mar. Madrid, situada en el centro de esta meseta, es la capital más alta de Europa. España tiene sólo siete u ocho ríos importantes pero, como ya hemos visto, éstos son generalmente demasiado caudalosos e impropios para la navegación.

Desembarquemos en la Coruña y hagamos un viaje imaginario por este hermoso país.

Desde el extremo occidental de la península hasta la frontera francesa se extiende la Cordillera Cantábrica, continuación de los Pirineos. Esta región comprende Galicia, Asturias y las Provincias Vascongadas. Es una comarca muy fértil, de clima templado y lluvioso.

El río Ebro, que nace en los Montes Cantábricos y que desemboca en el mar cerca de Tarragona, ofrece el camino más fácil para llegar al Mediterráneo. Numerosos ríos y arroyos, pasando por Navarra, Aragón y Cataluña, bajan de las cumbres de los Pirineos, y por toda esta región encontramos encantadores paisajes y hermosos valles. Y no olvidemos tampoco la pequeña república de Andorra, escondida y aislada en un valle de la Cordillera entre España y Francia.

Antes de despedirnos de la hermosa Cataluña, una de las partes más ricas de España, visitemos la ciudad de Barcelona, puerto de mar y centro industrial, y sigamos la costa del Mediterráneo, pasando por las célebres huertas de Valencia, Alicante y Murcia.

Por fin llegamos a Andalucía, antiguo reino de los moros. Aquí el clima es seco, caluroso y muy parecido al de Marruecos al otro lado del estrecho de Gibraltar. Se ha llamado esta región " el jardín de España " por la riqueza de su suelo y la gran variedad de sus frutos. El punto culminante de Andalucía es el Mulhacén, pico de la Sierra Nevada, el cual alcanza una altitud de unos 3500 metros, siendo el monte más alto de toda la península.

NOTES

La cordillera

Long chain of mountains.

La Cordillera de los Andes.

Templado

Temperate. **Un clima templado**—a temperate climate. From the verb **templar**—to soften, moderate, temper. In the latter sense : **el temple**—temper (of metals).

El temple del acero toledano—The temper of Toledo steel.

Lluvioso
  Rainy.

la lluvia—rain

Nacer
  To be born ; to rise (of rivers).

el nacimiento —birth
el renacimiento—Renaissance

La fuente is a spring or fountain.   Note : **Las fuentes del Ebro**—the source of the Ebro.

We have already met with the word **desembocar**—to flow into the sea.   Another word is **desaguar.**

El Duero desagua en el Atlántico.

Encantador
  Enchanting.

el encanto—enchantment, charm
encantar   —to charm, enchant

Las huertas de Valencia
  Life in the " huertas " of Valencia is described in many of the earlier novels of Blasco Ibáñez.   One of the most outstanding of these is *La Barraca.*

Los frutos
  Distinguish between **los frutos** and **las frutas.**

  Los frutos de la tierra—The fruits of the earth (i.e. products).
  Como postres hay frutas.   For dessert there is fruit.

  Frutos is also used in a figurative sense, as :

Los frutos de su trabajo—The fruits of his work.

Suelo
  This word means either (1) soil, or (2) floor, ground.

El suelo de España es muy rico en minerales.
El niño se sentó en el suelo.

Sierra nevada

Literally " snowy range."

> **la nieve**—snow
> **nevar**   —to snow

Nieva mucho en los Pirineos—It snows a great deal in the Pyrenees.

La sierra has the first meaning of " saw " (cutting instrument). Hence the extension of meaning to "mountain chain," i.e. a serrated line of jagged mountain peaks.

Reino

Be careful not to confuse **el reino**—kingdom, with **el reinado**—reign.

> **el rey**   —king   **la reina**   —queen
> **el príncipe**—prince **la princesa**—princess

GRAMMAR

Gender of Nouns

A number of examples have occurred of nouns which, although ending in -A, are masculine:

el día (the day)   el tranvía (tramcar)   el guardia (policeman)

Similarly, words ending in -A of Greek origin are masculine:

el panorama (panorama)   el drama (drama)   el mapa (map)
el idioma (language)

Words ending in -D are usually feminine, but notice:

el huésped (guest)   el sud (south)

Words ending in -z are usually feminine, but notice:

el lápiz (pencil)   el pez (fish)   el arroz (rice)

Words ending in -IÓN are also usually feminine, but notice:

el camión (the lorry)

Y, O

Before -I or -HI Y (and) becomes E:

> Ignacio y Carlos
> but Carlos e Ignacio
> Naranjas e higos—Oranges and figs.

Similarly O (or) becomes U before O or HO:

> Dos o tres
> but Siete u ocho
> Ayer u hoy

Más, Menos.   Followed by a numeral

The use of these words where a comparison is made will be remembered:

> Tiene más dinero que yo—He has more money than I.

But, when there is no comparison:

> Tiene más de cincuenta ovejas.
> He has more than fifty sheep.
>
> ¿ Tiene Vd. menos de diez pesetas?
> Have you less than ten pesetas?

In the negative, however, **de** is usually replaced by **que**:

> No he escrito más que dos cartas.
> I have not written more than two letters (i.e. only).

Más, Menos.   Followed by a clause

In this case the following forms are used: el que, los que, la que, las que.   E.g.:

> Me mandó más libros de los que pedí.
> He sent me more books than (those) I ordered.
>
> Recibí menos cartas de las que escribí.
> I received fewer letters than (those) I wrote.

Finally, note the use of **lo que** when no definite noun is referred to:

> Es más inteligente de lo que Vd. cree.
> He is more intelligent than you think (he is).

Si

This word (when unaccented) has two meanings: *if* and *whether*.

> Si viene mañana, déle este libro.
> If he comes tomorrow, give him this book.

Notice that **si** (meaning *if*) is followed by the present indicative as in English.

Me preguntó si vendría.   He asked me whether I would come.

> ¿ Por qué le pregunta Vd. si vendrá?
> Why do you ask him whether he will come?

Inversion

The question of inversion in Spanish is largely one of balance and style.   In such a sentence as:

> ¿ Tiene Ramón bastante dinero ?
> Has Ramón enough money?

the normal order is retained, since the object " bastante dinero " is " longer " than the subject " Ramón " and falls naturally at the end of the sentence.   But if the predicate is shorter than the subject, a better order would be:

> ¿ Tienen vino todos los convidados?
> Have all the guests got wine?

The subject of a sentence is often placed after the verb when the sentence begins with an adverb or an adverbial phrase:

> Desgraciadamente no vino don Carlos hasta la diez.
> Unfortunately don Carlos did not come until ten.

After direct speech inversion is usual in English and compulsory in Spanish with such verbs as **decir**.

> — No lo sé—dijo el cura.
> " I don't know," said the priest.

Inversion of subject and verb may occur at the beginning of any sentence in Spanish for reasons of euphony, balance, or style.

> Llegó el caballero a las once.
> The gentleman arrived at eleven.

A form found in many Spanish writings, although it is not strictly grammatical, is:

> Sentóse el viejo en el sillón (i.e. instead of se sentó).
> The old man sat down in the arm-chair.

Note that the accent is retained.

EXERCISES

(1) Answer the following questions in Spanish:

1. ¿ Qué forma tiene España? 2. ¿ Dónde está situada Madrid? 3. ¿ Cuántos ríos importantes tiene España? 4. ¿ Son navegables estos ríos? 5. ¿ Cómo se llama la Cordillera que se extiende desde la Coruña hasta los Pirineos? 6. ¿ Cómo es el clima de los Países Vascongados? 7. ¿ Dónde desemboca el río Ebro? 8. ¿ Dónde está la república de Andorra? 9. ¿ Dónde está situado el centro industrial de Cataluña? 10. ¿ Por dónde pasamos si seguimos la costa del Mediterráneo desde Barcelona hasta Andalucía? 11. ¿ Por qué se llama la región andaluza " el jardín de España "? 12. ¿ Cuál es el punto culminante de la Sierra Nevada? 13. ¿ Cómo es el clima de Andalucía? 14. ¿ Tiene montañas la Gran Bretaña? 15. ¿ Cuántos ríos españoles penetran también en Portugal?

(2) Put into Spanish:

1. Barcelona is bigger than Seville. 2. He has more than a hundred pesetas. 3. I haven't more than two letters to write. 4. He is not so ill as I am. 5. He has more money than you think. 6. This house has more windows than that one. 7. If he comes, give him this. 8. The waters of the North Sea are not as warm as those of the Mediterranean. 9. How many maps have you? 10. Four-fifths of the farm were under water.

(3) Complete the following sentences:

1. Una llanura elevada se llama una ——. 2. El Mulhacén se encuentra a unos 3500 metros sobre el —— del mar. 3. El clima de Inglaterra es por lo general ——. 4. Un río —— en el mar. 5. El alpinista alcanzó la —— de la sierra. 6. Una larga cadena de montañas se llama una ——. 7. Lisboa es la capital de ——. 8. Algunas partes de España son muy áridas pero Andalucía es muy ——. 9. El que ha estudiado la ciencia de la navegación es un ——. 10. Un barco costanero es un barco que sigue la ——.

(4) The following two lines contain words opposite in meaning. Pair them.

(a) montaña   riqueza   nacer   bajar   seco   rápido occidental   alto

(b) bajo   morir   subir   lento   oriental   llanura lluvioso   pobreza

(5) Give synonyms of the following words:

antiguo   caluroso   parecido a   región   hermoso

(6) Put into Spanish:

The coasts of Great Britain are much longer than those of Spain. On the other hand, Spain is a much more mountainous country. The climate of Spain is generally much drier, but in the north-west corner of the peninsula it is almost as rainy as in Ireland. Both countries have many important sea-ports, but whereas the rivers of Great Britain are mostly navigable, those of Spain are too rapid. On account of the fertility of her soil Andalusia has been named the garden of Spain and produces many fruits which cannot be grown in this country.

CHAPTER XXII

LAS REGIONES DE ESPAÑA (*continuación*)

LA región limitada por Portugal al oeste y que se extiende desde Andalucía hasta León era antes la antigua provincia de Extremadura, comarca fría, elevada, de vastas soledades.

Consideremos ahora las provincias del centro, tales como la Mancha, Castilla la Nueva, Castilla la Vieja, cuna de la lengua castellana. Es la tierra de castillos, el campo de batalla de moros y cristianos, país de llanuras áridas e interminables, en muchas partes sin agua ni árboles, de temperaturas extremas.

Grandes cadenas de montañas surcan este territorio. Castilla la Vieja está separada del Golfo de Vizcaya por los Montes Cantábricos ; Castilla la Nueva está limitada al sur por la Sierra Morena ; las Sierras de Gredos y de Guadarrama separan estas dos mesetas.

Desde todos los puntos de vista España es un país de variedad y de contrastes. Aquí encontramos la soledad de las montañas y el bullicio de las grandes ciudades ; la melancolía de las rías bajas de Galicia y la alegría de las poblaciones andaluzas ; las aguas tranquilas del Mediterráneo y las tempestades del Atlántico ; la aridez y pobreza de los despoblados y la fertilidad de las huertas ; el cielo despejado de Málaga y las nieblas de Santiago de Compostela.

También ofrece España variedad de idiomas. Además del castellano se hablan otros idiomas tales como el gallego (hablado en Galicia, y muy parecido al portugués), el vascuence (lengua quizás de los antiguos iberos) y el catalán (hablado en Cataluña, Valencia y las islas Baleares).

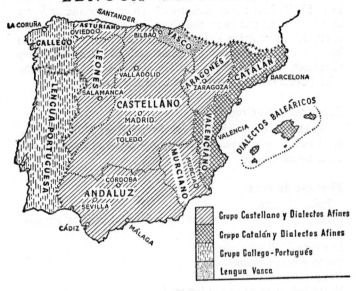

LENGUA ESPAÑOLA

Grupo Castellano y Dialectos Afines

Grupo Catalán y Dialectos Afines

Grupo Gallego-Portugués

Lengua Vasca

NOTES

Soledad

The adjective is solitario.

Los moros

The Arabs invaded Spain in the year 711, defeated Rodrigo, the king of the Visigoths, and within a few years had overrun the whole of the country with the exception of the mountainous districts of Asturias. It was here that the first effective resistance was organised, and in 718 the Spaniards, under the command of Pelayo, inflicted defeat on the Arabs at the battle of Covadonga, near to Oviedo. This was the beginning of the re-conquest of Spain. The end of this long struggle was marked by the conquest of the Moorish kingdom of Granada, when the Catholic sovereigns Ferdinand and Isabella entered the Alhambra in triumph on January 2nd, 1492. The many walled towns and castles of the Central Plateau bear witness to the intermittent struggles between the Moors and the Christians which took place during this long period. In the second half of the eleventh century the most outstanding figure of the re-conquest was the Castilian noble, el Cid, who succeeded in wresting Valencia from the Moors. El Cid has become the national hero of Spain and, as a semi-legendary character, was the subject of the nation's first epic poem, " El Poema del Cid," and of innumerable ballads.

Temperaturas extremas

The climate of Madrid has been described as : " Nueve meses de invierno, tres meses de infierno "—Nine months winter, three months hell.

El punto de vista

Point of view.

Distinguish between el punto—point, dot, and la punta—tip.

El punto—full stop, period.

Punto y coma—semi-colon.

Dos puntos—colon.

Punto interrogante—question mark.

Punto de admiración—exclamation mark.

Estaba a punto de salir—He was on the point of going out.

La punta de la espada—the point of the sword.

Punta de Europa—Europe Point (the tip of land at the end of the Gibraltar peninsula).

Surcar

The noun is el surco—furrow.

El arado surca la tierra—The plough furrows the earth.

El bullicio

Bustle, confusion.

Connected with the verb bullir—to boil.

La aridez

Adjective is árido—dry, arid.

Los despoblados

From the verb **despoblar**—depopulate.

Name given to those regions, semi-desert in character, where vegetation is scant. One of the most desolate regions of Spain is that of Las Hurdes, in the province of Cáceres. Certain parts of this territory, which is rocky and extremely mountainous, are even devoid of soil. For purposes of cultivation, the inhabitants are often forced to carry silt from the river beds to prepared terraces on the hill-sides.

Despejado

In weather reports, for example, **cielo despejado** means a clear, cloudless sky.

El vascuence

The origins of the Basque language, spoken on both sides of the Pyrenees, are unknown. It is in no way related to any other language of the Peninsula. It is thought by some to be the language of the ancient Iberians.

GRAMMAR

Use of Articles

The definite article is used in Spanish and not in English in the following cases:

With nouns used in a general sense.

Le gusta el té.	He likes tea.
Los burros son estúpidos.	Donkeys are stupid.

With titles.

El rey Alfonso.	King Alfonso.
El señor González.	Señor González.

Notice, however, "Buenos días, señor González," where the article is omitted in direct address.

With proper names qualified by an adjective, or by an adjectival phrase.

La hermosa Cataluña.	Beautiful Catalonia.
La España del siglo XII.	Spain of the 12th century.
El viejo Ramón.	Old Ramón.

With the names of certain countries.

El Perú, el Brasil, etc.

With parts of the body.

Lo tenía en la mano.	He held it in his hand.
Lavarse la cara.	To wash one's face.

With certain idiomatic and set expressions.

10 pesetas la botella.	10 pesetas a bottle.
Estar en la escuela.	To be at school.
Ir a la iglesia.	To go to church.
El 60 por ciento.	60 per cent.

The articles are used in English and not in Spanish in the following:

Es médico.	He is a doctor.
Alfonso, rey de España.	Alfonso, *the* king of Spain.
Vendrá otro día.	He will come *an*other day.
Mil soldados.	*A* thousand soldiers.
Cien casas.	*A* hundred houses.
Tal hombre.	Such *a* man.
¡ Qué día !	What *a* day !
Carlos quinto.	Charles *the* Fifth.

Tal... como...

Notice the use of these words:

Tales hombres como éstos.   Such men as these.

and compare it with:

Nunca he visto hombres tan estúpidos como éstos.
I have never seen such stupid men as these.

(i.e. **tal** qualifies a noun and **tan** qualifies an adjective).

Sin... ni...

Notice carefully such sentences as:

Sin pluma ni tinta.	Without pen *or* ink.
Sin árboles ni vegetación.	Without trees *or* vegetation.

Compare the sentence:

No tengo nada—I haven't anything.

Poder.   **Idiomatic uses**

No puedo hacerlo.	I cannot do it.
No podría hacer eso.	I could not do that (i.e. I would not be able).
No pude hacerlo.	I could not do it (i.e. I was not able to do it).
No puedo menos de admirarla.	I cannot help admiring her (i.e. I cannot do less than admire her).

Valer.   **Idiomatic uses**

¿ Cuánto vale?	How much does it cost?
No vale nada.	It is worthless.
No vale la pena de hacerlo.	It is not worth doing.
Más vale tarde que nunca.	It is better late than never.

Valer is irregular in some forms:

Present indicative: **valgo**, vales, vale, valemos, valéis, valen

Future indicative: **valdré**, valdrás, valdrá, valdremos, valdréis, valdrán

Present subjunctive: **valga**, valgas, valga, valgamos, valgáis, valgan

EXERCISES

(1) Answer the following questions in Spanish:

1. ¿ Cómo se llama la parte de España limitada por Portugal al oeste?   2. ¿ Puede Vd. hacer la descripción de esta región? 3. ¿ Cómo es el clima de la meseta central?   4. ¿ Conoce Vd. el nombre de alguna cordillera sudamericana?   5. ¿ En qué parte de España nació la lengua castellana?   6. ¿ Cuántos idiomas se hablan en la península ibérica?   7. ¿ Se habla el castellano en el Brasil?   8. ¿ Qué parte de España le gustaría a Vd. visitar?   9. ¿ Prefiere Vd. la soledad de la sierra al bullicio de la ciudad?   10. ¿ Es verdad decir que las aguas del Mediterráneo están siempre tranquilas?   11. ¿ Cuántos lagos hay en España?   12. ¿ Sabe Vd. de dónde viene el nombre de " Castilla "?   13. ¿ Cómo se llama la sierra que está situada al norte de Madrid?   14. ¿ Puede Vd. enumerar algunas ciudades de Castilla?   15. ¿ Cómo se describe el clima de Madrid?

(2) Put into Spanish:

1. Tea is not grown in Spain.   2. King Alfonso X was called the Wise.   3. Señor González came to dinner.   4. How do you do, Señor González?   5. The children were going to church.   6. Give me your hand.   7. He was washing his face. 8. He is a lawyer.   9. This wine costs 10 pesetas a bottle. 10. This farmer has a hundred sheep and a thousand pigs. 11. I saw her the other day.   12. Can you give me another glass, please?   13. Such a thing is impossible.   14. He is an architect of universal fame.   15. It is such a large house.

(3) Give the English equivalents.

1. No puedo menos de admirarla.   2. ¿No puede Vd. venir mañana?   3. ¿No podría Vd. hacer lo mismo?   4. Eso no vale la pena.   5. ¿Cuánto vale ese libro?   6. Esta pluma no vale nada.   7. Más vale tarde que nunca.   8. ¿Cuánto me debe Vd.?   9. Vd. no debería decir eso.   10. Debe de estar muy enfermo.

(4) Complete the following sentences:

1. ¿Le gusta a Vd. la —— de las montañas?   2. Las poblaciones andaluzas son muy ——.   3. Lo opuesto de riqueza es ——.   4. Una región sin vegetación es un ——. 5. Castilla la Vieja es la —— del idioma castellano.   6. El buque se fue a pique en una ——.   7. La carretera sigue el —— del río Ebro.   8. Un cielo sin nubes es un cielo ——. 9. Roma es una ciudad muy ——.   10. En Barcelona y en Valencia se habla ——.

(5) Put into Spanish:

The plains of the Central Plateau were once the battlefields of Moors and Christians. The Arabs landed in Spain in about 711, conquered most of the country, and established independent kingdoms. They even crossed the Pyrenees and succeeded in getting as far as Poitiers in France. In the year 1492, after more than seven centuries, the Moors lost their last Spanish city—Granada. The re-conquest of the country by the Christians began in the Cantabrian Mountains, and in the reign of the Catholic sovereigns the various kingdoms of Spain were united.

CHAPTER XXIII

DON QUIJOTE

Uno de los libros más célebres de la literatura universal es sin duda la obra maestra de Cervantes: *El ingenioso hidalgo don Quijote de la Mancha.*

Cervantes pinta un cuadro de los españoles de su tiempo,

un panorama de la sociedad y civilización de la nación española, pero es también una pintura del hombre universal y eterno, de todas las épocas y de todos los países. En esta novela encontramos una descripción de todo: montañas y llanuras, palacios y ventas, nobles y ladrones, sacerdotes y cabreros.

Pero "el Quijote" no es solamente una novela descriptiva sino también una obra filosófica. Don Quijote es el idealista, el caballero andante que quiere ayudar a los débiles y proteger a las mujeres, mientras que

Sancho Panza, su escudero, es el realista que ayuda a su amo a llevar a cabo sus aventuras fantásticas. En Dulcinea del Toboso ve don Quijote la perfección de las virtudes femeninas, pero Sancho no se engaña. En el famoso combate de los molinos de viento el caballero de la Triste Figura ve gigantes pero Sancho le dice : — Mire Vuestra Merced que aquéllos que allí se parecen no son gigantes, sino molinos de viento, y lo que en ellos parecen brazos son las aspas.

Don Quijote, montado en su caballo Rocinante, caminando por las tristes llanuras de la Mancha, sueña con ideales utópicos, y Sancho Panza, grosero e ignorante pero lleno de sentido común, sigue con su burro.

Estos dos personajes representan los dos tipos principales del alma española : el soñador y el práctico.

NOTES

La obra

Be careful not to confuse this word with **el trabajo.**

el trabajo—work, labour, task
la obra—a finished work, for example of painting, writing, architecture

Las obras de Cervantes.	The works of Cervantes.
La obra maestra.	The masterpiece.

Hidalgo

This is a contracted form of " hijo de algo "—" son of something," i.e. one possessing wealth and position, a noble or a gentleman.

In this respect the word **caballero** (one who possesses a horse, hence a person of means) can be compared.

El cuadro

Picture.

la pintura—painting
el dibujo —sketch

Do not confuse:

el cuadro	picture
el cuarto	room
cuatro	four
cuarto	fourth

La llanura
Plain, flat country.
The adjective is llano—flat.

El escudero
Squire.
From the word el escudo (shield), which the squire bore for his master.

Dulcinea del Toboso
The lady whom don Quixote endowed with all the virtues and perfections of womanhood, and to whom he dedicated his deeds of prowess.

Molinos de viento
Wandering over the bare plains, don Quixote and his squire Sancho Panza came across a number of windmills. The Knight was convinced that they were wicked giants, waving their arms in the air. Sancho endeavoured to dissuade his master, but don Quixote charged with his lance at the sails, was carried into the air, and dropped to the earth bruised and bleeding.

Engañarse
To be deceived.
el engaño—deceit

Rocinante
Don Quixote's famous nag.

Soñar
To dream.
The noun el sueño means either " dream " or " sleep."
Tengo sueño—I am sleepy.
" El sueño de una noche de verano "—" A Midsummer Night's Dream."

El sentido

Sense.

> los cinco sentidos—the five senses
> el sentido común—common sense

Notice: **sensible**—sensitive (one capable of feeling. From **sentir**—to feel).

GRAMMAR

Pero... sino...

Pero links together two separate sentences. For example:

> Juan tiene hambre/pero/Jaime tiene sed.

After a negative sentence, however, " but " is translated by **sino** when it introduces opposition to the negative statement.

No tengo hambre sino sed.	I am not hungry but thirsty.
No voy hoy sino mañana.	I am not going today but tomorrow.

Familiar Imperative

We have already dealt with the polite imperative, but it is important to be able to recognise and understand the familiar imperative. The familiar imperative (corresponding to **tú** and **vosotros**) is formed as follows:

Statement	Command
tú hablas	habla (speak)
vosotros habláis	hablad (speak)
tú comes	come (eat)
vosotros coméis	comed (eat)
tú escribes	escribe (write)
vosotros escribís	escribid (write)
tú te sientas	siéntate (sit down)
vosotros os sentáis	sentaos (sit down)

In the imperative, note particularly that (1) pronouns are placed at the end of the verb; (2) an accent is sometimes necessary in order to maintain the original stress; (3) the D is elided in the case of the plural form when os is added. The only exception to this latter rule is **idos**—go away (from **irse**).

The familiar imperative exists, however, only in the **positive** form. When the negative sense is intended, the subjunctive must be used.

Compare:

habla (speak)	no hables (don't speak)
hablad	no habléis
come	no comas
comed	no comáis
escribe	no escribas
escribid	no escribáis
siéntate	no te sientes
sentaos	no os sentéis

Remember that when the verb is made negative, the pronouns precede.

There are a number of irregular imperatives. It is important to be able to recognise these.

di (decir)	¡ Dime la verdad !	Tell me the truth ¡
haz (hacer)	¡ Hazlo en seguida !	Do it at once !
ve (ir)	¡ Vete !	Off with you !
oye (oír)	¡ Oye !	Listen !
pon (poner)	¡ Ponlo en la mesa !	Put it on the table !
ten (tener)	¡ Ten ciudado ¡	Be careful !
ven (venir)	¡ Ven acá !	Come here !
sal (salir)	¡ Sal conmigo !	Come out with me !

The plural form of these is regular: decid, haced, id, oíd, poned, tened, venid, salid.

Prepositions

A, en

The preposition " a " normally expresses motion towards, whereas " en " expresses rest at a place.

Voy a Madrid.	I am going to Madrid.
Está en Madrid.	He is in Madrid.

Notice, however:

Está a la puerta.	He is at the door.
Está en la puerta.	He is in the doorway.

Sobre, en

In the sense of " on " these words are often interchangeable.

El libro está en (sobre) la mesa.
The book is on the table.

But Se sentó en un sillón.	He sat down in an arm-chair.
El día en que llegó.	The day on which (when) he arrived.

Escribió un libro sobre sus aventuras.
He wrote a book on (about) his adventures.

Por in conjunction with a preposition. Compare the following sentences:

El aeroplano estaba encima de la ciudad.	The plane was over the city.
El aeroplano voló por encima de la ciudad.	The plane flew over the city.
El barco estaba debajo del puente.	The boat was under the bridge.
El barco pasó por debajo del puente.	The boat passed under the bridge.
El farol estaba delante de la casa.	The lamp-post was in front of the house.
Pasé por delante de la casa.	I passed (in front of) the house.

That is, when motion is implied the preposition " por " is used with the simple preposition.

Reir—to laugh

This verb (and the compound **sonreir**—to smile) is conjugated like pedir. Compare:

pedir	pido	pides	pide	pedimos	pedís	piden
	río	ríes	ríe	reímos	reís	ríen

	pida	pidas, etc.
	ría	rías, etc.

But notice:

	pidió	pidieron
	rió	rieron

	pidiendo
	riendo

Notice that in the case of **reir** the "i" of the ending is elided:

rió	not ri-ió
rieron	not ri-ieron
riendo	not ri-iendo

EXERCISES

(1) Answer the following questions in Spanish:

1. ¿ Quién escribió " el Quijote "? 2. ¿ En qué siglo vivió Cervantes? 3. ¿ Dónde está la Mancha? 4. ¿ Cómo podemos decir que Cervantes pintó un cuadro del hombre universal? 5. ¿ Cuál es, a su parecer, la novela más célebre de la literatura inglesa? 6. ¿ Qué quería hacer don Quijote? 7. ¿ Quién era Sancho Panza? 8. ¿ Cómo ayudaba Sancho a su amo? 9. ¿ Ha leído Vd. la historia de los molinos de viento? 10. ¿ Cómo se llama el caballo de don Quijote? 11. ¿ Tiene Sancho un caballo? 12. ¿ Cómo era Sancho Panza? 13. ¿ Conoce Vd. algún caballero andante de la literatura inglesa? 14. ¿ Cómo se llama una persona que sueña con ideales? 15. ¿ Qué nombre damos a una persona práctica?

(2) Replace the blanks by **sino** or **pero**.

1. Sancho no es idealista —— realista. 2. Sancho tiene un burro —— don Quijote tiene un caballo. 3. No tengo hambre —— sed. 4. Yo tengo hambre —— mi hermano tiene sed. 5. La chica no llora —— ríe.

(3) (*a*) Give the opposites of the following:

detrás de   más de   dentro de   después de   cerca de

(*b*) By means of short sentences distinguish between the following:

hacia, hacía   además de, más de   cabellos, caballos

(4) Put the following sentences into the negative:

1. Hazlo en seguida. 2. Pon el libro en la mesa. 3. Hablad más de prisa. 4. Sentaos. 5. Dime lo que hizo. 6. Vete. 7. Escríbelo con tinta. 8. Comed todo. 9. Dadme aquella novela. 10. Levántate.

(5) Complete the following sentences:

1. " El Quijote " es la —— de Cervantes. 2. Un pintor pinta ——. 3. Un novelista escribe ——. 4. Un rey vive en un ——. 5. Sancho era el —— de don Quijote. 6. Don Quijote creía que los molinos de viento eran ——. 7. Sancho está lleno de ——. 8. Un gigante no es débil, sino muy ——. 9. Don Quijote y Sancho Panza son los dos principales —— de la novela. 10. Un hombre que guarda cabras es un ——.

(6) Put into Spanish:

From many points of view the novelist Dickens can be compared with Cervantes. The former describes, like Cervantes, the men of his time, but also paints a picture of universal man. When we think of Dickens we cannot help recalling also such characters as schoolmasters, merchants, lawyers, thieves, and beggars who fill the pages of his books. Dickens too dreamed of an ideal world.

CHAPTER XXIV

LA ESPAÑA COMERCIAL

ESPAÑA es un país más agrícola que industrial pero, como ya hemos visto, florecen algunas industrias bastante importantes. Sin embargo, a pesar de sus riquezas naturales y sus abundantes yacimientos minerales, no se ha desarrollado la industria tanto como en otros países europeos debido en gran parte a la falta de comunicaciones adecuadas.

Gracias a la diversidad de clima todos los productos florecen en su suelo. Todo el mundo conoce, por ejemplo, las célebres naranjas valencianas pero ¿ cuántos se dan cuenta de que en Andalucía crecen dátiles, plátanos y hasta la caña de azúcar ? Valencia es también conocida por el cultivo del arroz, y por casi todas partes del país se cultiva el olivo.

Los vinos españoles tales como el de Málaga, de Jerez, de Valdepeñas y otros muchos gozan de fama universal y también se exportan no pocas uvas de mesa.

En Extremadura se da mucha importancia a la cría del ganado de cerda, y las dos Castillas producen cereales, vino, ganado vacuno y lanar. En Galicia y por toda la costa del Atlántico la pesca de la sardina y del atún constituye una de las principales industrias. El cultivo del maíz es también considerable.

En Vizcaya la industria metalúrgica está muy desarrollada y Bilbao, con sus fundiciones de hierro y sus minas de carbón, es una de las ciudades más industriales del país. Las renombradas minas de Río Tinto (no lejos de Huelva) dan cobre, cuya exportación es muy importante. En Almadén hay yacimientos de azogue.

Y no olvidemos una de las regiones más productoras de

MAPA AGRONÓMICO DE ESPAÑA

MAR CANTÁBRICO

FRANCIA

OCÉANO ATLÁNTICO

PORTUGAL

MAR MEDITERRÁNEO

REGIÓN de los PASTOS
id   de la VID
id   de los CEREALES
id   del NARANJO
id   del OLIVO
id   de la CAÑA
ZONAS de ALTITUD
ESTEPAS

toda la península—Cataluña que se distingue por sus grandes industrias textiles.

NOTES

Agrícola

Notice that this adjective has the one form for both the masculine and feminine.

la agricultura	agriculture
labrar	to plough
el labrador	ploughman, farmer
sembrar semilla	to sow seed
cosechar	to harvest
la cosecha	harvest
la vendimia	grape harvest

florecer

To flower.

la flor—flower

La naranja

Orange. In connection with this, it is interesting to note that the English was originally "a norange" and not "an orange."

el naranjo—orange tree

Similarly:

la manzana	apple	el manzano	apple tree
la cereza	cherry	el cerezo	cherry tree

El olivo

Olive tree.

la aceituna—olive (fruit)
el aceite   —(olive) oil

Exportación

The verb is **exportar.**
Similarly:

la importación   importar

Vino de Jerez

Sherry.
Famous wine produced in the district of Jerez de la Frontera in the province of Cadiz.

El ganado

Cattle.

la ganadería—ranch

ganado mayor (bueyes, caballos, vacas, mulas, etc.)
ganado menor (ovejas, cabras, etc.)
ganado de cerda (cerdos—pigs)

Note: el cerdo, el puerco (pig)

El carbón

" Coal " is, in Spanish, **la hulla** or **el carbón de piedra.**

In the domestic sense **carbón de piedra**, or simply **carbón, is** generally used.

> el carbón de leña—charcoal

Notice the distinction :

> la madera—wood
> la leña   —wood, fuel

> una casa de madera—a wooden house
> echar leña al fuego —to throw wood on the fire

El maíz

> el pan de maíz—maize bread

El cobre

Copper.

Note also :

> el hierro—iron   el acero—steel
> el oro   —gold   la plata—silver

GRAMMAR

Diminutive and Augmentative Suffixes

A distinctive feature of the Spanish language is the use of diminutive and augmentative suffixes. These suffixes should be used sparingly and with great caution. In fact, it is advisable to use only those cases which have been met with by experience in reading or conversation.

The following diminutive suffixes have occurred : -ecillo, -illo, -cito, -ito, -ico.

pan (loaf)	panecillo (roll)
cigarro (cigar)	cigarrillo (cigarette)
Carmen	Carmencita
pueblo (town)	pueblecito (village)
ventana (window)	ventanilla (carriage window)
burro (donkey)	borrico (little donkey)

And the following augmentatives : -on, -ote, -acho.

silla (chair)	sillón (arm-chair)
pico (peak, beak)	picacho (mountain peak)
cámara (chamber)	camarote (cabin)

If we compare " una taza pequeña " with " una tacita," it is obvious that the latter is neater, less cumbersome, and more euphonious.

Very often the form bearing the suffix has acquired a totally different meaning, as in the case of **cámara** (chamber) and **camarote** (cabin).

In addition to the idea of size, these suffixes often add further to the meaning. For example :

calle (street)	callejuela (small, narrow street)
papá (daddy)	papaíto (dear daddy)
flores (flowers)	florecitas (dainty little flowers)

These suffixes are found added to all parts of speech :

despacio (slowly)	despacito (very slowly)
poco (a little)	poquito (a tiny bit, ever so little)
cerca (near)	cerquita (just near)

Some words may add either a diminutive or augmentative suffix :

la cuchara (spoon)   la cucharita (tea-spoon)
el cucharón (ladle)

Other suffixes also exist in Spanish. We have met with one or two, such as :

un naranjal	orange grove
un olivar	olive grove
el zapatero	shoemaker
la panadería	baker's shop

Sólo

Distinguish between sólo (only) and solo (alone).

Siempre va solo (or) a solas—He always goes alone.

Tiene sólo (or) solamente diez pesetas.
He has only ten pesetas.

Notice also:

No es solamente hermosa, sino también inteligente.
She is not only beautiful, but also intelligent.

Aun, aún

Aún (with the accent) has a similar meaning to **todavía**. Even with this meaning it is sometimes found without accent when it precedes the verb.

Aun no ha venido.	He has not come yet.
No ha venido aún.	He has not come yet.
No ha venido todavía.	He has not come yet.

Aun (without accent) is used in the sense of **hasta**.

Aun la criada quería acompañarle.
Even the servant wished to go with him.

(or) Hasta la criada quería acompañarle.

Remember that **hasta** also means " as far as," " up to," " until."

Fue desde Madrid hasta Toledo.	He went from Madrid to Toledo.
Esperó hasta las doce.	He waited until twelve o'clock.

Ya

The usual meaning of **ya** is " already," but there are also a number of idiomatic uses.

Ya habían terminado.	They had already finished.
Ya no viven aquí.	They no longer live here.
Ya sabes lo que quiero decir.	You know quite well what I mean.
Ya caigo.	I understand now. (Now I tumble to it.)

Aquí, acá

Notice the distinction (not always observed) between these words.

Aquí está mi libro.	Here is my book.
Ven acá.	Come here (hither).

And similarly:

Allí está el vino.	The wine is over there.
Voy allá.	I am going there (thither).

The equivalent of the French *voici* and *voilà* (here is, there is) is expressed in Spanish by **he** (usually considered to be a corruption of **ve** (see)) used in conjunction with **aquí** and **allí**.

He aquí mi libro.	Here is my book.
He allí la iglesia.	There is the church.

The personal pronouns may also be appended to **he**:

Heme aquí.	Here I am.
Henos aquí.	Here we are.
Helos allí.	There they are.

Cuanto...tanto...

Notice particularly the Spanish equivalent of the English "the more...the more..."

> Cuanto más tiene, tanto más quiere.
> The more he has, the more he wants.

Según

Según (according to) may be used before either a noun or a verb.

> Según mi amigo, Anita no tiene dinero.
> According to my friend, Anita has no money.

> Según dice mi amigo.
> According to what my friend says.

Yacer

Connected with **el yacimiento** (mineral deposit) is the verb **yacer**—to lie. This verb is not often found except in the following cases: yace (third person singular, present indicative); yacía (third person singular, imperfect indicative). E.g.:

Aquí yace.   Here lies (on tombstones, for instance).

EXERCISES

(1) Answer the following questions in Spanish:

1. ¿ Es España un país agrícola o industrial? 2. ¿ Por qué no se ha desarrollado la industria tanto como en otros países europeos? 3. ¿ Se encuentran yacimientos minerales en España? 4. ¿ Dónde se cultiva el arroz? 5. ¿ Qué se extrae de la aceituna? 6. ¿ Cuál es el vino español más célebre? 7. ¿ Qué significa ganado lanar? ¿ ganado vacuno? 8. ¿ Dónde se cultiva el maíz? 9. ¿ Dónde están situadas las industrias metalúrgicas? 10. ¿ En qué parte de España se encuentran minas de cobre? 11. ¿ Dónde está Almadén? 12. ¿ Por qué se distingue Almadén? 13. ¿ Qué se produce en las llanuras de la meseta central? 14. ¿ Cómo se exportan sardinas? 15. ¿ De qué parte vienen las naranjas?

(2) Give the English equivalents.

1. Aquí yace don Paco. Que en paz descanse. 2. Ella no ha venido aún. 3. Ya no llueve. 4. Como ya hemos dicho. 5. Ven acá en seguida. 6. Cuánto más tiene, tanto más quiere. 7. Según el diario, el ladrón ha sido llevado a la cárcel. 8. Vendrá pasado mañana. 9. Basta decirlo una vez. 10. ¡ Qué chica tan hermosa !

(3) Give the verbs corresponding to the following nouns:

la flor   el criado   el producto   el yacimiento   la pintura

(4) Put the following verbs (in heavy type) into the preterite, imperfect, future, and future perfect tenses.

(Example: **Comemos** demasiado. Comimos; comíamos; comeremos; habremos comido.)

1. Los pescadores **vuelven** al puerto.   2. El guardia **dirige** la circulación.   3. **Nos sentamos** a la mesa.   4. **Siento** mucho no poder hacer eso.   5. El viajero **anda** hasta el muelle.

(5) Complete the following:

1. En Río Tinto hay importantes —— de cobre. 2. Muchas industrias florecen en Cataluña. Es una región muy ——.   3. Irlanda es un país casi completamente ——. 4. En las islas Canarias se cultivan muchos ——.   5. Los chinos y los japoneses comen mucho ——.   6. El trigo y el maíz son ——.   7. Bilbao se distingue por sus industrias ——.   8. En el sur del país de Gales hay importantes ——. 9. El mercurio se llama también ——.   10. El olivo da ——.

(6) Put into the polite imperative.

1. Dadme esos libros.   2. Come todas las frutas. 3. Hablad más despacio.   4. Escribe la carta.   5. ¡ Vete !

(7) Put into Spanish (using the polite form of the imperative).

1. Don't take it.   2. Go and have a wash.   3. Be so kind as to give it to me at once.   4. God help us !   5. Let's get up now.

(8) Put into Spanish:

Spain is a land of great variety and extreme climate. North of the Cantabrian mountains the climate is much rainier than in other parts, whilst in Málaga the climate resembles that of Africa on the other side of the straits.   All kinds of fruits are grown, from apples and pears to oranges and dates. Although for the most part an agricultural country, Spain has also many industrial centres, for example textile industries in Catalonia and iron foundries in the Basque provinces.   Even before the time of the Romans Spain was noted for her rich mineral deposits.

CHAPTER XXV

EN LA FRONTERA

Llegué al pueblo fronterizo de Puigcerdá a principios del mes de julio. Acababa de atravesar los Pirineos, estaba cansadísimo, tenía mucha hambre y mucha sed, y, lo que era peor, no llevaba suficiente dinero para pagar los derechos de aduana.

Como los carabineros no quisieron dejarme pasar, fui por consiguiente a ver al jefe de aduanas, el cual vivía en el centro del pueblo.

Este señor me recibió cordialmente y con mucha cortesía a pesar de lo sucio de mi persona, y, después de escuchar mi lamentable historia, me preguntó de dónde venía y a dónde iba. Le dije que pensaba ir a Barcelona, donde tenía amigos.

— ¿ Y cómo hará Vd. este viaje sin dinero ? preguntó el jefe.

— Iré a pie. Dormiré al aire libre. Eso no importa. Vd. ha de saber, señor, que lo importante es poder continuar el viaje.

Sin contestar el buen señor sacó su cartera, tomó un billete de cien pesetas y me lo dio.

— Aquí tiene Vd. lo suficiente para pagar los derechos de aduana y para el viaje.

Me maravillé de su generosidad, preguntándole cómo sabía que yo le devolvería el dinero.

— Veo que es Vd. hombre honrado. Sé que Vd. me devolverá este dinero.

— ¿ Y si Vd. se equivoca ?

— Entonces Dios me lo pagará. A Vd. le daría el dinero sin obligación ninguna pero, como Vd. ve, no soy rico.

Y este buen jefe de aduanas me ofreció luego la hospitalidad de su casa e hizo preparar una excelente comida.

Más tarde me acompañó hasta la carretera. Me acuerdo todavía de sus últimas palabras :

— ¡ Qué vuelva aquella dichosa edad en que los que en ella vivían ignoraban estas dos palabras de " tuyo " y " mío " ! Eran en aquella santa edad todas las cosas comunes.

Y me dio la mano, diciéndome : — Buen viaje, amigo mío. ¡ Vaya Vd. con Dios !

De este modo entré en una tierra desconocida, experimentando por primera vez la generosidad y caballerosidad de los españoles.

NOTES

Puigcerdá

A small town situated on the Franco-Spanish frontier, not far from the Republic of Andorra. An electric railway now runs from Toulouse to Barcelona, passing through Foix, Ripoll, and Vich.

A principios de

a principios de mayo—at the beginning of May.

Note also:

a mediados de mayo   in the middle of May
a fines de mayo   at the end of May

El derecho

Notice the two principal meanings of this word:

estudiar el derecho   —to study law
los derechos de aduana—customs dues

As an adjective **derecho** means " straight " or " right."

una línea derecha—a straight line
la mano derecha —the right hand

Note:

a la derecha—on the right (hand)
a la izquierda—on the left

Carabinero

el aduanero —customs officer
el carabinero—armed frontier guard

La cartera

Wallet.

Note:

la carta—letter   el cartero—postman
ministro sin cartera—minister without portfolio

Maravillarse

The noun is **la maravilla**—marvel.

Devolver

To return, in the sense of " to pay back." Do not confuse
with **volver**—to return, come back.

Suele volver a las once.
He usually returns at eleven.

No se olvide Vd. de devolverme el dinero.
Don't forget to pay me back the money.

Dichoso

The noun is la dicha—happiness.

>desdichado—unhappy

¡ Vaya Vd. con Dios !

A common expression of farewell in Spanish.

Note also :

>Buen viaje—bon voyage

GRAMMAR

Infinitive Constructions.   Uses of the Subjunctive

Normally the dependent infinitive construction is possible in Spanish only when the subject of the principal clause is the same as that of the subordinate clause.

Creo poder hacerlo.	I think I can do it.
But Creo que él puede hacerlo.	I think he can do it.

Such forms, therefore, as the English " I believe him able to do it " are not possible in Spanish.

Note the following constructions, however, which are permissible with certain verbs in Spanish.

>aconsejar—to advise

Le aconsejo hacerlo.	I advise him to do it.

>dejar—to let, allow

Déjeme Vd. hacerlo.	Let me do it.

>mandar—to order, command

Le mandó devolver el oro.	He ordered him to give back the gold.

The Spanish equivalent of " to have something done " is formed with **hacer** and the infinitive.

Hizo edificar la casa.	He had the house built.
Haré escribir la carta.	I will have the letter written.

With verbs of perception (seeing, hearing, etc.), the infinitive is used in Spanish.

Vio entrar a su amigo.	He saw his friend coming in.
Me oyó subir.	He heard me coming up.

In other cases where the subject of the principal clause is different from that of the subordinate clause, the infinitive construction cannot be used in Spanish.

I want to go.	Quiero ir.
But I want him to go.	Quiero que él vaya.

Whether the indicative or subjunctive mood is used in such sentences depends on the verb of the principal clause.

The indicative is used after verbs expressing belief (when positive) and certainty :

Estoy seguro de que vendrá.	I am sure he will come.
Creo que vendrá.	I believe he will come.

The subjunctive is used after verbs expressing a command, a wish :

Quiero que lo haga.	I wish him to do it.

After verbs expressing emotion :

Siento mucho que esté enfermo.	I am very sorry he is ill.
Es lástima que no pueda venir.	It is a pity he can't come.

After verbs of doubt (such as **dudar**), and after verbs of believing (such as **creer**), when the latter are negative and sometimes when interrogative if there is doubt in the speaker's mind :

Dudo que pueda hacerlo.	I doubt if he can do it.
No creo que venga hoy.	I don't believe he will come today.

¿ Cree Vd. que venga hoy?	Do you think he will come today? (The speaker believes not.)
¿ Cree Vd. que vendrá hoy?	Do you think he will come today? (The speaker thinks he will.)

After a relative, the antecedent of which is indefinite. Compare the two sentences:

¿ Conoce Vd. al caballero que habla español?
Do you know the gentleman who speaks Spanish?

¿ Conoce Vd. alguien que hable español?
Do you know anybody who speaks Spanish?

In the first case a definite person exists; in the second case the person addressed may or may not know someone who speaks Spanish.

After certain conjunctions in dependent clauses such as:

Déselo a su hermano cuando venga.
Give it to your brother when he comes.

No lo haré sin que él me ayude.
I shall not do it unless he helps me.

EXERCISES

(1) Answer the following questions in Spanish:

1. ¿ Cuándo llegó el viajero a la frontera? 2. ¿ A dónde iba? 3. ¿ Dónde está el pueblo de Puigcerdá? 4. ¿ Cuántas fronteras terrestres tiene España? 5. ¿ Cuánto dinero sacó el aduanero? 6. ¿ Qué le preguntó el viajero? 7. ¿ Cuántos kilómetros dista Puigcerdá de Barcelona? 8. ¿ Era rico el aduanero? 9. ¿ Qué aspecto tenía el viajero? 10. ¿ Qué hizo el aduanero después de darle el dinero? 11. ¿ En qué libro se encuentran las últimas palabras del jefe de aduanas? 12. ¿ Por qué se llama aquella edad " dichosa "? 13. ¿ Qué dijo el aduanero antes de despedirse del viajero? 14. ¿ Tiene Vd. intención de ir a España algún día? 15. ¿ Le gustaría a Vd. ir por tierra o por mar?

(2) Give the English equivalents.

1. Hizo escribir la carta. 2. Déjeme Vd. pasar. 3. Le aconsejo no hacer eso. 4. Cuando llegó a la estación, vio salir el tren. 5. Creo haberla visto antes.

(3) (a) Give verbs corresponding to the following nouns or adjectives:

el principio　el calor　cansado　la maravilla　el compañero

(3) (b) Give adjectives corresponding to the following nouns or verbs:

la generosidad　ignorar　la cortesía　la suciedad　lamentar

(4) Write short sentences to illustrate the use of the following:

1. volver, volver a, devolver. 2. oir, escuchar. 3. dar, dar a, dar con. 4. antes de, delante de. 5. Sino, pero.

(5) Give the English equivalents.

1. El señor está fumando un cigarrillo. 2. Siga Vd. esta callejuela. 3. He comprado dos sillones. 4. La viejecita me dio la carta. 5. Hable Vd. un poquito más de prisa. 6. El viajero echó el papel por la ventanilla. 7. Por esta parte se ven muchos olivares. 8. El borrico andaba despacito por la carretera. 9. Su madre le regaló un pañuelo rojo. 10. Los gitanos se alejaron del caserón.

(6) Put into Spanish:

For those who are not usually seasick the pleasantest way of travelling to Spain is undoubtedly by sea, from London, Southampton, or Liverpool to one of the Spanish ports. Other travellers may prefer, of course, to go overland via Paris or even by air. But what part of Spain do you want to go to? How long will you be able to spend in that country? My brother, who has lived in Spain for many years, says it is a pity you can't stay a year there, and then you could visit all parts of the country!

RECAPITULATION V

EXERCISES

(1) Put into Spanish:

1. Spain is a more mountainous country than you think.
2. If he comes, ask him if he intends to stay. 3. The pupil
had more than twenty mistakes. 4. How much does it cost
per kilo? 5. Wine is dearer in England than in Spain.
6. He didn't write plays but novels. 7. We passed the
theatre and took the first street on the right. 8. She was
laughing when I came in. 9. Give me a packet of cigarettes,
please. 10. The traveller walked from Madrid to Saragossa.
11. It is no longer raining. Let us go out. 12. Come here at
once! 13. The more he studies, the less he seems to know.
14. I shall have it sent to Madrid. 15. Did you hear her
come in? 16. The water could be seen slowly rising. 17. I
don't want him to do that. 18. When she comes, give her
this letter. 19. We advise you not to sell until next year.
20. It is better to be poor than wicked.

(2) Write short sentences in Spanish on each of the following topics:

1. Los ríos de España. 2. Andalucía—jardín de España.
3. La meseta central. 4. Cataluña. 5. Don Quijote.

(3) Put into Spanish:

Although it appears somewhat incredible, this story of the
customs officer in Puigcerdá is perfectly true. Unfortunately,
however, it is not possible to assure all travellers who cross the
Spanish frontier, that customs officers will be everywhere so
friendly and generous as our friend don Andrés. I am sorry
to say that poor don Andrés died during the Spanish Civil
War, but with him let us repeat: " May the day come when
the words ' mine ' and ' thine ' no longer exist." The
Golden Age of don Quixote existed in the mind of Cervantes.
Perhaps one day it will be a reality.

VOCABULARIES

THESE vocabularies are meant to be more than mere lists of words. The use of words which might present some difficulty is illustrated throughout by means of short phrases or sentences.

Generally speaking, the usages illustrated in the vocabulary are those which have occurred in the texts.

There are no separate lists of irregular or radical changing verbs. All irregular verb forms are given in full under the respective infinitive, listed alphabetically in the Spanish-English section.

Radical changing verbs are indicated in the Spanish-English section thus:

contar (ue) .	. .	of the type : contar—cuento
empezar (ie).	. .	of the type : empezar—empiezo
pedir (i)	. .	of the type : pedir—pido—pidió
morir (ue-u)	. .	of the type : morir—muero—murió
sentir (ie-i) .	. .	of the type : sentir—siento—sintió

Verbs of the type **conocer** which insert " z " before the " c " of the first person singular of the present indicative and throughout the present subjunctive, are indicated thus:

conocer (zc)—conozco—conozca

All nouns given in the vocabulary are preceded by the definite article. The definite article is bracketed in the following cases:

(el) inglés —where a word may be either a noun or an adjective. E.g. el inglés—the Englishman ; la nación inglesa—the English nation.

(la) España ⎱ names of countries with which the article is not
(el) Portugal ⎰ normally used.

Where the article is not bracketed, it is an indication that the article *is* normally used with the name of the country :

el Brasil, e.g. ir al Brasil—to go to Brazil

The following abbreviations are employed :

el agua (f)	.	Nouns which are of feminine gender, although preceded by the masculine article.
adj.	. .	adjective.
adv.	. .	adverb.
Imp.	. .	imperfect.
irr.	. .	irregular.
Fam. I.	. .	familiar imperative.
Fut.	. .	future indicative.
P.I.	. .	present indicative.
P.P.	. .	past participle.
Prep.	. .	preposition.
Pret.	. .	preterite.
Pr. P.	. .	present participle.
P.S.	. .	present subjunctive.

N.B.—The Spanish Alphabetical Order

As CH, LL, and Ñ are considered as separate letters and follow respectively C, L, and N, it is obvious that the alphabetical order differs from that of the English. Thus, in the following vocabulary, **collar** comes after **color** ; **charlar** comes after **cuyo** ; **puñal** comes after **punto.**

SPANISH–ENGLISH VOCABULARY

A

a, to, at, on, from, by
    aprender a leer—to learn *to* read
    ir a Madrid—to go *to* Madrid
    ir a pie—to go *on* foot
    estar a la puerta—to be *at* the door
    comprar algo a una persona—to buy something *from* a person
    hacerlo a mano—to do it *by* hand
abandonar, to abandon
el abanico, fan
la abeja, bee
abierto, open, opened
    la puerta está abierta—the door is open
    ¿ Quién ha abierto la puerta ?—Who has opened the door ?
el abogado, lawyer
el abril, April
abrir, to open. P.P. abierto
abundante, plentiful, abundant
abundar, to abound, be plentiful
el abuso, misuse, abuse
acá, here (hither). ¡ Ven acá ! —Come here !
acabar, to finish, complete
    acabar el trabajo—to finish the work
acabar de, to have just
    acabo de terminar—I have just finished

el aceite, oil
la aceituna, olive
aceptar, to accept
acercarse, to approach, draw near
    acercarse a la ciudad—to approach the town
acompañar, to accompany
aconsejar, to advise
    le aconsejo a Vd. volver a hacerlo—I advise you to do it again
acordarse (ue), to remember
    acordarse de algo—to remember something
acostarse(ue), to retire, go to bed
el actor, actor
acuerdo, estar de acuerdo con alguien—to be in agreement with someone
adecuado, adequate
adelante, forward, onwards
    de hoy en adelante—from today on
    ¡ adelante !—come in !
además, moreover ; besides
    además tiene mucho dinero—moreover, he has a lot of money
    además de esto—besides this
la administración, administration
admirar, to admire
admitir, to admit
adónde, whither. ¿ Adónde va Vd. ?—Where are you going to ?

la **aduana**, customs, customs office

el **aduanero**, customs officer

aéreo, aerial. La navegación aérea—aerial navigation

el **aerodromo**, aerodrome

el **aeroplano**, aeroplane

aficionado, fond of
ser aficionado al alpinismo —to be fond of mountain climbing
los aficionados al cine— film " fans "

afortunadamente, fortunately

afortunado, fortunate

las **afueras**, outskirts, suburbs

la **agencia**, agency

ágil, agile, nimble

agradable, pleasant, agreeable

agrícola, agricultural. Un país agrícola—an agricultural country

el **agua** (f), water

aguardar, to await, wait (for)

ahora, now

los **ahorros**, savings. Una caja de ahorros—savings bank

el **aire**, air. Al aire libre—in the open air

aislado, isolated

el **ajo**, garlic

alabar, to praise

alcanzar, to reach, attain

la **alcoba**, alcove, bedroom

la **aldea**, village

el **aldeano**, villager

alegre, glad, happy, merry

la **alegría**, merriment, joy

alejarse, to go away. Alejarse de la aldea—to go away from the village

(el) **alemán**, German

(la) **Alemania**, Germany

algo, something; somewhat
tener algo que decir—to have something to say
estar algo cansado—to be somewhat tired

el **algodón**, cotton

alguien, someone

alguno (algún), some, any, a few
algún día—some day
algunas vacas—a few cows

el **alma** (f), soul

almorzar (ue), to have lunch

el **almuerzo**, lunch

el **alpinismo**, mountaineering

el **alpinista**, mountaineer

alrededor, around. Sentados alrededor de la mesa—seated around the table

la **altitud**, altitude

alto, high, tall. En lo alto de la sierra—high up in the mountain

alumbrar, to light up, illuminate

allí, there

la **amabilidad**, friendliness, kindness

amable, friendly, kind. Es Vd. muy amable—it's very kind of you

amar, to love

(la) **América**, America

la **amiga**, friend

el **amigo**, friend

el **amo**, master, owner

el **anciano**, old man

(la) **Andalucía**, Andalusia

(el) **andaluz**, Andalusian

andante, un caballero andante —a knight *errant*

andar (irr.), to walk, go
Pret. anduve, anduviste,

anduvo, anduvimos, anduvisteis, anduvieron

andando el tiempo—as time went on

el andén, platform (railway)

el animal, animal

el anochecer, nightfall, dusk. Al anochecer—at nightfall

ansiosamente, anxiously

antes, before

¿ Por qué no vino Vd. antes?—Why didn't you come before?

antes de salir—before going out

la anticipación, anticipation

la antigüedad, antiquity

antiguo, old, ancient

el año, year

tener diez años de edad—to be ten years old

a los pocos años—after a few years

aprender, to learn. Aprender a escribir—to learn to write

apresurarse, to hasten. Apresurarse a contestar—to hasten to reply

aprovechar, to take advantage of, profit by

aprovechar la ocasión—to seize the opportunity

aquel, that (over there)

aquél, that one ; the former

aquí, here

(el) Aragón, Arragon

el árbol, tree

la aridez, aridness, barrenness

árido, arid, barren

el arquitecto, architect

la arquitectura, architecture

arrastrar, to drag, draw, pull

el buey arrastra el carro—the ox draws the cart

arriba, upstairs; at the top

las ventanas de arriba—the upstairs windows

el arriero, muleteer

arrojar, to throw, hurl

el arroyo, stream, rivulet

el arroz, rice

asar, to roast

el ascensor, lift, elevator

el asco, repugnance. Esto me da asco—this makes me feel sick

el asesinato, murder

el asiento, seat. Tome Vd. asiento—please sit down

el aspa (f), sail (of a windmill)

el aspecto, aspect, appearance. Hombre de aspecto sucio—a dirty-looking man

astuto, cunning

la atención, attention. Con atención—attentively

atentamente, attentively

atento, attentive

atestado, crowded. Un teatro atestado de gente—a theatre crowded with people

el Atlántico, Atlantic

atravesar (ie), to cross, traverse

atreverse, to dare. Atreverse a hacer algo—to dare to do something

el atún, tunny-fish

aun, even. Aun hoy día—even nowadays

aún, still, yet. No ha llegado aún—he hasn't arrived yet

el autobús, bus

avanzar, to advance. A una hora avanzada—at a late hour

la avenida, avenue
la aventura, adventure
(el) aventurero, adventurous;
adventurer
¡ay! alas!
ayer, yesterday
la ayuda, help, assistance
ayudar, to help. Me ayudó a
hacerlo—he helped me to do
it
el azogue, mercury, quicksilver
el azúcar, sugar
azul, blue

B

el bacalao, cod-fish
la bahía, bay
bailar, to dance
el baile, dance, ball
bajar, to lower; come down,
descend
bajar del tren—to get out
of the train
bajo, low, lower
la Baja California—Lower
California
hablar en voz baja—to
speak in a low voice
bajo (prep.), under. Bajo la
mesa—under the table
el balcón, balcony
Baleares, las Islas Baleares—
the Balearic Islands
el banco, seat, bench; bank
sentarse sobre un banco—
to sit down on a bench
el Banco de España—the
Bank of Spain
el bandido, bandit
el banquete, banquet
bañarse, to bathe, have a bath
el baño, bath. El cuarto de
baño—bathroom

l.s.—9*

el barbero, barber
la barca, boat, fishing boat
el barco, ship, boat. Barco
mercante—freighter
el barrio, quarter, district. El
barrio chino—the Chinese
quarter
bastante, enough, quite, fairly
tener bastante dinero—to
have enough money
no tener bastante dinero
para comprarlo—not to have
enough money to buy it
es bastante rico—he is
fairly rich
bastar, to suffice
basta mencionar esto—it
is enough to mention this
el bastón, cane, walking stick
la batalla, battle
el baúl, trunk (luggage)
beber, to drink
la belleza, beauty
bello, beautiful
la biblioteca, library
la bicicleta, bicycle. Ir en
bicicleta—to cycle
bien, well
el billete, ticket. Un billete de
ida y vuelta—a return ticket
blanco, white
la boda, marriage, wedding
la bolsa, purse; Stock Exchange
el bolsillo, pocket
bonito, pretty
bordo, ir a bordo—to go on
board (ship)
el borrico, donkey
el bosque, wood, copse
el boticario, chemist, pharma-
cist
el brasero, brazier
el Brasil, Brazil

(el) brasileño, Brazilian

el brazo, arm

Bretaña, la Gran, Great Britain

bueno (buen), good. Buenos dias—good morning

el buey, ox, bullock

el bullicio, bustle, confusion

el buque, ship. Buque de guerra—warship

el burro, donkey

la busca, search. En busca de aventuras—in search of adventures

buscar, to seek, look for. Buscar la verdad—to seek the truth

la butaca, arm-chair; stall seat (theatre)

C

el caballero, gentleman, knight. Caballero andante—knight errant

la caballerosidad, chivalry, gentlemanliness

el caballo, horse. Ir a caballo —to ride on horseback

los cabellos, hair. Tener los cabellos rubios—to have fair hair

caber (irr.), to fit, be able to be contained, hold

P.I. quepo, cabes, cabe, cabemos, cabéis, caben

Pret. cupe, cupiste, cupo, cupimos, cupisteis, cupieron

Fut. cabré, cabrás, cabrá, cabremos, cabréis, cabrán

P.S. quepa, quepas, quepa, quepamos, quepáis, quepan

¿ Cuántas personas caben en este cuarto ?—How many people does this room hold ?

la cabeza, head

el cabo, end; headland

al cabo de ocho días—at the end of a week

llevar a cabo—to carry out

al fin y al cabo—finally

el Cabo de Buena Esperanza—the Cape of Good Hope

la cabra, goat

el cabrero, goatherd

cada, each, every. Cada día— every day

la cadena, chain. Una cadena de oro—a gold chain

caer (irr.), to fall

P.I. caigo, caes, cae, caemos, caéis, caen

Pret. caí, caíste, cayó, caímos, caísteis, cayeron

P.S. caiga, caigas, caiga, caigamos, caigáis, caigan

P.P. caído. Pr. P. cayendo

Dejó caer el vaso—he dropped (let fall) the glass

¡ Ya caigo !—Now I understand (tumble to it) !

el café, café; coffee

Caín, Cain (Bible). Pasar las de Caín—to have an awful time

la caja, box. La cajita—little box

el cálculo—calculation, sum

la calefacción, heating. La calefacción central—central heating

el calendario, calendar

calentar (ie), to heat, warm

caliente, hot, warm. Agua caliente—hot (warm) water

el calor, heat
  tener calor—to be hot (person)
  hacer calor—to be hot (weather)
caluroso, hot.   Un día muy caluroso—a hot day
la calle, street
la callejuela, narrow street, alley
la cama, bed
el camarero, waiter
el camarote, cabin, berth
caminar, to walk, travel
el camino, way, road
el campanario, belfry
el campesino, peasant, countryman
el campo, country, countryside; field
el canal, canal.   El Canal de la Mancha—the English Channel
Canarias, las Islas Canarias—the Canary Islands
la canción, song
cansado, tired, weary.   Estar cansado—to be tired
cansar, to tire, weary
Cantábricos, los Montes Cantábricos—Cantabrian mountains
cantar, to sing
la caña, reed, cane.   La caña de azúcar—sugar cane
la capa, cloak, cape
la capital, capital (city)
el carabinero, frontier guard
la caravana, caravan (desert)
el carbón, coal
la cárcel, prison
cardar, to card (wool)
cargado, laden.   Cargado de mercancías—laden with merchandise

el cariño—affection, love
la carne, meat, flesh
el carnero, sheep, ram
la carnicería, butcher's shop
el carnicero, butcher
la carretera, main road, highway
el carro, cart
la carta, letter
la cartera, wallet, portfolio
la casa, house, home
  la casa de comercio—business house, firm
  la casa de correos—post office
  la casa de huéspedes—lodging house
  volver a casa—to return home
  estar en casa—to be at home
  en casa de un amigo—at a friend's
casarse, to get married
  Se casó con la princesa—he married the princess
el caserón, big, rambling house
casi, almost
el caso, case
  en este caso—in this case
  no hacer caso de alguien—not to take any notice of someone
(el) castellano, Castilian
(la) Castilla, Castile.   Castilla la Vieja (la Nueva)—Old (New) Castile
el castillo, castle
(el) catalán, Catalan
(la) Cataluña, Catalonia
(el) católico, catholic
el cazador, huntsman
célebre, famous, celebrated

los celos, jealousy
celoso, jealous
la cena, supper
cenar, to have supper
centellear, to twinkle
el céntimo, centime (100th part of the peseta)
central, central. La América central—Central America
el centro, centre
cerca, near. Cerca de la iglesia —near to the church
cerda, el ganado de, pigs, swine
el cerdo, hog, pig
los cereales, cereals
la cerilla, wax vesta
cerrar (ie), to close, shut
la cerveza, beer
el cielo, sky, heaven
cien, a hundred. Cien caballos —a hundred horses
la ciencia, science, knowledge
científico, scientific
ciento (cien), hundred. El 10 por ciento—10 per cent.
el cigarrillo, cigarette
cinco, five
cincuenta, fifty
el cine, cinema
la circulación, traffic, circulation. Dirigir la circulación— to direct the traffic
citar (se), to cite, quote; make an appointment
    citar un pasaje de Cervantes—to quote a passage from Cervantes
    los dos amigos se citaron para las once—the two friends arranged to meet at eleven o'clock
la ciudad, city, town
la civilización, civilisation

civilizador, civilising
la clase, class, kind
    la sala de clase—the classroom
    de todas clases—of all kinds
    en tercera clase—in third class
el clima, climate
el cobre, copper
la cocina, kitchen
el coche, cab, motor-car. Ir en coche—to go by car
coger, to seize, take
la colina, hill
colocar, to put, place
Colón, Cristóbal, Christopher Columbus
la colonia, colony
la colonización, colonisation
el colono, colonist
el color, colour
el collar, necklace. Un collar de perlas—a pearl necklace
la comarca, region, district
el combate, combat, fight
la comedia, comedy, play. Echar una comedia—to show a play
el comedor, dining-room
comenzar (ie), to commence, begin
comer, to eat, dine
comercial, commercial
el comercio, commerce, trade, business
    la casa de comercio— business house
los comestibles, eatables, foodstuffs
    la tienda de comestibles— store, grocery
la comida, meal, dinner

como, like, as

como su hermano—like his brother

no come tanto como yo—he doesn't eat as much as I do

cómo, how. ¿ Cómo está Vd. ? —How are you ?

la comodidad, comfort

el compañero, companion

la compañía, company. La compañía de navegación—steamship company

comparar, to compare

el compatriota, fellow country-man

completamente, completely

completo, complete. Por completo—completely

la compra, purchase. Ir de compras—to go shopping

el comprador, buyer

comprar, to buy

comprender, to understand; comprise

¿ Comprende Vd. esta teoría ?—Do you understand this theory ?

El libro comprende cuatro tomos—the book comprises four volumes

común, common, general. El sentido común—common sense

la comunicación, communication

con, with

concentrar, to concentrate

el concierto, concert

el conde, count (noble)

conducir (irr.), to lead, conduct

P.I. conduzco, conduces, conduce, conducimos, conducís, conducen

Pret. conduje, condujiste, condujo, condujimos, condujisteis, condujeron

P.S. conduzca, conduzcas, conduzca, conduzcamos, conduzcáis, conduzcan

El camino conduce al pueblo—the road leads to the village

Conducir al ciego—to lead the blind man

confrontar, to confront

confuso, confused

conmoverse (ue), to be disturbed, touched

conocer (zc), to know (be acquainted with). ¿ Conoce Vd. a mi amigo ?—Do you know my friend ?

conocido, known, famous. Un actor muy conocido—a well-known actor

el conocimiento, knowledge, acquaintance. Conocimientos científicos — scientific knowledge

la conquista, conquest

el conquistador, conqueror

conquistar, to conquer

la consecuencia, consequence, result. Como consecuencia de—as a result of

consentir (ie-i), to consent. Consentir en el matrimonio—to consent to the marriage

considerable, considerable, numerous

considerar, to consider

consiguiente, por, consequently, therefore

consolarse (ue), to console oneself, be consoled

constituir, to constitute

la **construcción**, construction, building. En construcción—under construction

construir, to construct, build

consultar, to consult

contar (ue), to count, tell, relate

contemplar, to contemplate, gaze upon

contestar, to answer. Contestar a una pregunta—to answer a question

el **continente**, continent, mainland

la **continuación**, continuation

continuar, to continue

contra, against

contrario, contrary. Al contrario—on the contrary

el **contraste**, contrast

la **conversación**, conversation

el **convidado**, guest

el **coñac**, cognac, brandy

la **copa**, wine glass

copiar, to copy

cordialmente, cordially

la **cordillera**, mountain chain, range

el **corral**, yard; corral (for cattle)

el **correo**, post, mail. Enviar por el correo—to send by post
la casa de correos—post office

la **corrida**, la corrida de toros—bull fight

la **cortesía**, courtesy

la **Coruña**, Corunna

la **cosa**, thing

la **costa**, coast

costanero, coastwise. Vapor costanero—coaster

costar (ue), to cost. Cuesta demasiado—it costs too much

costoso, dear, expensive, costly

crecer (zc), to grow, develop. Aquí crecen muchas rosas—many roses grow here

creer, to believe, think
¿ Lo cree Vd. ?—do you believe it ?
Creo que ha salido—I think he has gone out

la **cría**, breeding, raising (animals, etc.); young (of animals)
la cría de ganado—stock breeding
la cría de la pata—the young of the duck

la **criada**, maid servant

el **criado**, man servant

criar, to bring up, breed, raise

cristalino, crystalline, clear

(el) **cristiano**, Christian

criticar, to criticise

la **crueldad**, cruelty

el **cuaderno**, copy book

la **cuadra**, stable

el **cuadro**, picture

el **cual**, which, who

cuál, which ?

cuando, when. De vez en cuando—from time to time

cuándo, when ? ¿ Cuándo vendrá ?—When will he come ?

cuanto, en cuanto a su padre—as for his father

cuánto, how much, many ? ¿ Cuánto vale ? — How much does it cost ?

cuarenta, forty

el **cuarto**, room. El cuarto de baño—bathroom

cuarto, fourth

cuatro, four

(el) cubano, Cuban

cubierto, covered. La sierra está cubierta de nieve—the mountain range is covered with snow

cubrir, to cover. P.P. cubierto

la cuenta, account, bill. Darse cuenta de algo—to realise something, to take something into account

el cuento, story, tale. Decir un cuento—to tell a story

el cuerpo, body

el cuidado, care, worry.
    ¡ Cuidado !—Take care ! Look out !
    Pierda Vd. cuidado—don't worry

culminante, culminating

cultivar, to grow, cultivate. Cultivar patatas—to grow potatoes

el cultivo, cultivation

la cultura, culture

la cumbre, top, summit

el cumpleaños, birthday. El día de su cumpleaños—his birthday

la cuna, cradle, origin

el cura, parish priest

cuyo, whose, of which

CH

charlar, to talk, chat

la chica, girl

el chico, boy

la chimenea, chimney, funnel; fireplace

(el) chino, Chinese

el chocolate, chocolate

la chuleta, chop, cutlet. Una chuleta de ternera—a veal chop

D

la dama, lady

dar (irr.), to give
    P.I. doy, das, da, damos, dais, dan
    Pret. di, diste, dio, dimos, disteis, dieron
    P.S. dé, des, dé, demos, deis, den
    dar las gracias a alguien—to thank someone
    la ventana da al corral—the window overlooks the yard
    dar con alguien—to meet, come across someone
    dar la vuelta al mundo—to travel round the world
    dar un paseo—to go for a walk

el dátil, date (fruit)

de, of, from, as, in, by
    a principios de julio—at the beginning of July
    es de Madrid—he is from Madrid
    trabajar de criada—to work as a maid
    de este modo—in this way
    amado de todos—loved by all

debajo, under. Debajo del árbol—under the tree

deber, to owe; be obliged to, must
    Vd. no debe hacer eso—you must not do that
    ¿ Cuánto me debe Vd. ?—How much do you owe me ?

debe de estar muy enferma—she must be very ill
yo debería (debiera) salir —I ought to go out

debido, due, owing. Debido a la sequía—owing to the drought

débil, weak, feeble

decidirse, to decide. Decidirse a volver—to decide to return

decir (irr.), to say, tell
P.I. digo, dices, dice, decimos, decís, dicen
Pret. dije, dijiste, dijo, dijimos, dijisteis, dijeron
Fut. diré, dirás, dirá, diremos, diréis, dirán
P.S. diga, digas, diga, digamos, digáis, digan
P.P. dicho
Pr. P. diciendo
Fam. I., di
decir un cuento—to tell a story
es decir—that is to say
a decir verdad—to tell the truth, truth to tell
se dice que...—they say that...

dedicarse, to devote oneself
dedicarse al cultivo de naranjas—to go in for orange growing

el dedo, finger; toe
el dedo del pie—toe. El dedo de la mano—finger

dejar, to leave, let, allow
déjeme Vd. salir—let me go out
dejar la aldea—to leave the village
dejar caer—to drop (let fall)

delante, in front. Delante de la casa—in front of the house
pasar por delante de la casa—to pass the house

delicioso, delightful, delicious

demasiado (adj.), too much, many. Come demasiado pan —he eats too much bread

demasiado (adv.), too. Ser demasiado pobre para comprarlo —to be too poor to buy it

dentro, inside, within
meter dentro de la caja— to put inside the box
dentro de ocho días— within a week

el departamento, compartment (railway coach)

el dependiente, clerk, employee, shop assistant

el deporte, sport

el deportista, sportsman

el derecho, duty; law
estudiar el derecho—to study law
derechos de aduana— customs duties

derecho, right; straight
a la derecha—on the right (hand)
un camino derecho—a straight road

desaparecer (zc), to disappear

desarrollarse, to develop, unfold
la industria se ha desarrollado mucho en los últimos años—the industry has developed a great deal in the last few years

el desarrollo, development

desayunarse, to have breakfast

el desayuno, breakfast

descansar, to rest

el descanso, rest. Un día de descanso—a day of rest

desconocido, unknown

describir, to describe.　P.P. descrito

la descripción, description

descriptivo, descriptive

descrito, described

descubierto, discovered, uncovered

el descubrimiento, discovery

descubrir, to discover.　P.P. descubierto

desde, from, since

desde Madrid hasta Toledo—from Madrid to Toledo

desde las tres hasta las cinco—from three to five o'clock

desde entonces—since then, from that time on

desdeñoso, scornful

desear, to wish, desire. Desear comer—to want to eat

desembarcar, to disembark, land, go ashore

la desembocadura, mouth of a river

desembocar, to flow into the sea (of rivers)

El Ebro desemboca en el Mediterráneo—the Ebro flows into the Mediterranean

desempeñar, to carry out, fulfil desempeñar un papel—to play a part, rôle

desgraciadamente, unfortunately

el desierto, desert

despacio, slowly

el despacho, office, study

despedirse (i), to take leave, say good-bye. Despedirse de un amigo—to say good-bye to a friend

despejado, clear. Un cielo despejado—a cloudless sky

despertar (ie), to awaken. Despertar al niño—to awaken the child

despertarse (ie), to wake up. Despertarse a las siete—to wake up at seven

el despoblado, barren country, desert

despoblado, barren, depopulated, deserted

después, after, afterwards

¿ Qué hace Vd. después ?—What do you do afterwards ?

después de escribir la carta—after writing the letter

después del desayuno—after breakfast

detrás, behind. La silla está detrás de la mesa—the chair is behind the table

devolver (ue), to return, pay back. Devolver el dinero—to pay back the money

el día, day.　Buenos días—good morning

el diálogo, dialogue

diariamente, daily, every day

el diario, newspaper

diario, daily

dibujar, to draw, sketch

dicho, above mentioned. Volvió en dicho vapor—he returned by the above-mentioned steamer

dichoso, happy, blessed

diferente, different

difícil, difficult
la dificultad, difficulty
el dinero, money
Dios, God
directamente, directly, straight
dirigir, to direct. Dirigir la circulación — direct the traffic
dirigirse, to make one's way
el discípulo, pupil
la distancia, distance
distar, to be distant. Este pueblo dista cien kilómetros de Madrid—this village is a hundred kilometres from Madrid
distinguir, to distinguish, perceive. Distinguir la sierra lejana—to make out the distant mountain range
distinguirse, to be outstanding. Esta provincia se distingue por sus vinos—this province is famous for its wines
la diversidad, variety, diversity
la diversión, amusement, diversion
dividir, to divide
divisar, to see, perceive. Divisar algo a lo lejos—to make something out in the distance
doce, twelve
dócil, docile
el domingo, Sunday. La isla de Santo Domingo—Dominican Republic
don, doña, title used in Spanish with Christian names
    don Pedro. doña María
donde, where. La ciudad donde vive—the town where he lives

dónde, where? ¿ Dónde está?—Where is he? ¿ A dónde va Vd.?—Where are you going? ¿ De dónde viene Vd.?— Where are you coming from?
dormir (ue-u), to sleep. Dormir la siesta—to take the afternoon nap
dormirse (ue-u), to fall asleep. El viejo se durmió—the old man fell asleep
el dormitorio, bedroom
dos, two
la duda, doubt. Sin duda— without doubt
el dueño, master, owner
durante, during. Durante la semana—during the week
durar, to last
duro, hard (not soft)
el duro, five peseta coin equivalent to dollar at par

E

e, and. Españoles e ingleses— Spaniards and Englishmen
económico, economical, economic
echar, to throw, throw away. Echar una comedia, to put on, show a play
la edad, age
    tener diez años de edad— to be ten years old
    la edad de oro—the golden age
el edificio, building, edifice
el ejemplo, example. Por ejemplo—for example
elevado, high, elevated

la embarcación, boat, lifeboat, vessel

embarcarse, to embark, go aboard ship

embargo, sin, nevertheless

empezar (ie), to begin. Empezar a llover—to begin to rain

el empleado, employee

emplear, to employ, use

emprender, to undertake. Emprender la construcción de un ferrocarril—to undertake the building of a railway

en, in, at, to, into
estar en Madrid—to be *in* Madrid
estar en la escuela—to be *at* school
de ciudad en ciudad—from town *to* town
meter la mano en el bolsillo—to put one's hand *into* one's pocket

enamorado, in love. Estar enamorado—to be in love

encantador, enchanting, charming

encender (ie), to light, kindle. Encender un cigarrillo—to light a cigarette

encima, above. Encima de la puerta—above the door

encontrar (ue), to meet, encounter, find

el enemigo, enemy

enérgico, energetic

la enfermedad, illness

enfermo, ill. Estar enfermo—to be ill

engañarse, to be deceived

la enhorabuena, congratulation. Dar la enhorabuena a

alguien—to congratulate someone

enorme, enormous

la ensalada, salad, lettuce

enseñar, to show, teach. Enséñeme Vd. a escribir—teach me to write

entender (ie), to understand

entero, entire, whole

entonces, then. Desde entonces—from that time on

la entrada, entrance; entrance ticket
la entrada del palacio—the entrance to the palace
comprar dos entradas para la corrida—to buy two tickets for the bull-fight

entrar, to enter, go in, come in. Entrar en la casa—to enter the house

entre, between, amongst
entre el río y la montaña —between the river and the mountain
entre los pueblos de la América del Sur—amongst the peoples of South America

entregar, to hand, hand over, deliver

el entremés, entremets, side-dish

el entusiamo, enthusiasm

envuelto, wrapped. Envuelto en su capa—wrapped up in his cloak

el episodio, episode

la época, epoch, period

equivocarse, to be mistaken

errante, wandering, errant

(la) Escocia, Scotland

escoger, to choose

esconder, to hide

escribir, to write. P.P. escrito

el escritor, writer, author

escuchar, to listen. Escuchar la música—to listen to the music

el escudero, shield bearer, squire

la escuela, school. Ir a la escuela—to go to school

ese, that

ése, that one

eso, that. A eso de las tres— about three o'clock

el espacio, space, period, interval. Por espacio de cien años—for a period of a hundred years

la espada, sword

(la) España, Spain

(el) español, Spanish, Spaniard

especial, special

esperar, to wait; hope
  esperar a un amigo—to wait for a friend
  espero que sí—I hope so

la espina, thorn

la esquina, corner. La esquina de la calle—the corner of the street

el establecimiento, establishment

la estación, station; season
  la estación de ferrocarril — railway station
  el año tiene cuatro estaciones.—the year has four seasons

el estado, state. Los Estados Uuidos de Norteamérica— the United States

el estanco, shop where Government monopolies are sold; tobacconist's

estar, to be
  P.I. estoy, estás, está, estamos, estáis, están
  Pret. estuve, estuviste, estuvo, estuvimos, estuvisteis, estuvieron
  estar en Madrid—to be in Madrid
  estar cansado—to be tired
  estar trabajando—to be working
  estar para salir—to be about to go out

este, this

éste, this one, the latter

estimado, esteemed, dear. Estimado amigo — dear friend

estimar, to esteem, estimate

esto, this

estrecho, narrow

el estrecho, strait. El estrecho de Gibraltar—the straits of Gibraltar

la estrella, star

estrenarse, to show for the first time (theatre, etc.)
  la comedia se estrena esta noche—the play is being shown for the first time tonight

el estreno, première, first showing of a play, etc.

estupendo, stupendous, terrific, marvellous

estúpido, stupid

eterno, eternal

(la) Europa, Europe

(el) europeo, European

exactamente, exactly

la exactitud, exactitude, precision

exagerar, to exaggerate

examinar, to examine
la excelencia, excellence
excelente, excellent
la excepción, exception
la excursión, excursion, trip
existir, to exist
experimentar, to experience
el explorador, explorer
la exportación, export
exportar, to export
expresivo, expressive
extenderse (ie), to extend,
stretch. Este territorio se
extiende desde Méjico hasta
Chile—this territory stretches
from Mexico to Chile
la extensión, extent, stretch
extenso, extensive, far-reach-
ing
extraer (irr.) (see " traer "), to
extract. Se extrae mucho
aceite—a great deal of oil is
extracted
extranjero, foreign
el extranjero, foreigner ; foreign
land
los extranjeros—foreigners
ir al extranjero—to go
abroad
estar en el extranjero—to
be abroad
extraño, strange
extremo, extreme
el extremo, extreme, end, corner. De un extremo a otro
de la península—from one
end of the peninsula to the
other

F

la fábrica, factory
fabricar, to manufacture
fácil, easy

la facilidad, facility, ease
fácilmente, easily
la faja, strip, belt
la falda, skirt ; slope
una falda de seda—a silk
skirt
la falda de la montaña—
the slope of the mountain
la falta, lack, want ; fault
por falta de dinero—
through lack of money
no me hace falta—I don't
need it
una falta de gramática—
a grammar mistake
faltar, to lack, be wanting
me falta dinero—I am
short of money
la fama, fame, glory
la familia, family
famoso, famous
fantástico, fantastic
la farmacia, pharmacy, chemist's shop
el faro, lighthouse
el farol, street-lamp
el favor, favour. Haga el favor
de darme esa carta—please
give me that letter
la fe, faith, religion
el febrero, February
la fecha, date. ¿ Qué fecha es ?
—What date is it ?
feliz, happy
femenino, feminine
feo, ugly
férreo, pertaining to iron.
La vía férrea—railroad
el ferrocarril, railway
ferroviario, pertaining to railways. Una compañía
ferroviaria—a railway company

fértil, fertile
la fertilidad, fertility
la fibra, fibre
la figura, figure, face. El caballero de la Triste Figura —the Knight of the Sorrowful Countenance (Don Quixote)
fijo, fixed
filosóficamente, philosophically
filosófico, philosophical
el filósofo, philosopher
el fin, end
    por fin—finally
    a fines de diciembre—at the end of December
final, final
la finca, estate, property
fino, fine, delicate
físico, physical
la flor, flower
florecer (zc), to flower, flourish
fluvial, fluvial. Un puerto fluvial—a river port
la fonda, inn, refreshment room
la forma, form, shape
la fortuna, fortune. Probar fortuna—to seek one's fortune
(el) francés, French, Frenchman
(la) Francia, France
la frase, sentence
frecuentar, to frequent
fresco, cool, fresh
el fresco, coolness. Tomar el fresco—to enjoy the cool air
frío, cold
el frío, cold
    tener frío—to be cold
    hacer frio—to be cold (weather)
la frontera, frontier

fronterizo, frontier, border. Un pueblo fronterizo—a frontier village
la fruta, fruit. La naranja es una fruta muy jugosa—the orange is a very juicy fruit
el frutero, fruiterer
el fruto, fruit, produce. Los frutos de la tierra—the fruits of the earth
el fuego, fire
la fuente, well, fountain
fuera, outside, besides
    estar fuera de casa—to be away from home
    fuera de la finca heredó otras propiedades—besides the estate he inherited other property
fuerte, strong
fumar, to smoke. Fumar en pipa—to smoke a pipe
funcionar, to function, work. Esta máquina no funciona—this machine doesn't work
fundar, to found, establish
la fundición, foundry
furioso, furious, angry
el fútbol, football
    jugar al fútbol—to play at football
    un partido de fútbol—a football match

G

Gales, el País de Gales—Wales Nueva Gales del Sur—New South Wales
(la) Galicia, Galicia. Province of north-western Spain
(el) gallego, Galician
la galleta, biscuit
la gallina, hen

el **gallinero**, hen-run, poultry-yard

la **gana**, wish, desire
de mala gana—unwillingly
tener ganas de hacer algo —to want to do something

el **ganado**, cattle, stock
el ganado vacuno—cattle, cows
el ganado lanar—sheep
el ganado de cerda—swine, pigs

ganar, to earn, gain. Gana mucho dinero—he earns a lot of money

el **gas**, gas

gastar, to spend

los **gastos**, expenses

el **gato**, cat

general, general. Por lo general, por regla general—generally, as a rule

generalmente, generally

la **generosidad**, generosity

generoso, generous

la **gente**, people. Hay mucha gente—there are a lot of people

la **geografía**, geography. Una lección de geografía—a geography lesson

el **gerente**, manager

el **gesto**, gesture. Hacer gestos —to gesticulate

el **gigante**, giant

el **gitano**, gipsy

la **gloria**, glory

el **gobernador**, governor

gobernar (ie), to govern

el **gobierno**, government

el **golfo**, gulf, bay. El Golfo de Vizcaya—the Bay of Biscay

gordo, fat, stout

gozar, to enjoy. Este actor goza de fama universal—this actor enjoys universal fame

las **gracias**, thanks
Dar las gracias a alguien por algo—to thank someone for something
Gracias a Dios—thanks to God

grande (**gran**), great, big
una casa grande—a large house
un gran hombre—a great man
la Gran Bretaña—Great Britain

la **grasa**, fat, grease

la **gratitud**, gratitude

grato, pleasing. Un recuerdo grato—a pleasant memory

grave, serious, grave. Una enfermedad grave—a serious illness

gritar, to shout

el **grito**, shout, yell. Dar gritos—to shout out

grosero, uncouth, coarse

el **grupo**, group

guapo, handsome, smart, beautiful

guardar, to guard

el **guardia**, policeman

la **guerra**, war

la **guitarra**, guitar

gustar, to please
A mí no me gusta el té—I don't like tea
¿ Le gusta a Vd. leer ?— Do you like to read ?

el gusto, taste, pleasure
  Tendré mucho gusto en hacerlo—I shall be very glad to do it
    con mucho gusto—with pleasure

H

la Habana, Havana
haber (irr.), to have (auxiliary)
  P.I. he, has, ha, hemos, habéis, han
  Pret. hube, hubiste, hubo, hubimos, hubisteis, hubieron
  Fut. habré, habrás, habrá, habremos, habréis, habrán
  P.S. haya, hayas, haya, hayamos, hayáis, hayan
  He escrito la carta—I have written the letter
  Vd. ha de saber—you must know
había (from " haber "), there was, there were. Había dos caballos en el prado—there were two horses in the meadow
la habitación, room, apartment
el habitante, inhabitant
habitar, to live, dwell
el habla (f), speech. Países de habla española—Spanish-speaking countries
hablar, to speak, talk
  hablar con alguien—to talk to someone
  hablar de algo—to talk about something
  hablar español—to speak Spanish
  hablar el castellano—to speak Castilian

habrá (from " haber "), there will be. Habrá mucha gente—there will be a lot of people
hacer (irr.), to do, make
  P.I. hago, haces, hace, hacemos, hacéis, hacen
  Pret. hice, hiciste, hizo, hicimos, hicisteis, hicieron
  Fut. haré, harás, hará, haremos, haréis, harán
  P.S. haga, hagas, haga, hagamos, hagáis, hagan
  P.P. hecho
  Fam. I. haz
  ¿ Qué hace Vd. ?—What are you doing?
  hace mucho calor—it is very hot
  hacer preparar la comida—to have the meal prepared
  hace muchos años—many years ago
  hacer una pregunta—to ask a question
  hacerse médico—to become a doctor
hacia, towards. El chico caminaba hacia la aldea—the boy was walking towards the village
la hacienda, farm, plantation, estate
hallar, to find
el hambre (f), hunger. Tener hambre—to be hungry
hasta, until; as far as; even
  hasta medianoche—until midnight
  hasta la iglesia—as far as the church
  hasta el cura le conocía—even the priest knew him

hay, (from " haber "), there is, there are

no hay tinta—there is no ink

hay que escribir la carta—the letter must be written

he aquí, here is, behold. Heme aquí—here I am

hecho, done, made. Dicho y hecho—no sooner said than done

el hecho, deed, fact

heredar, to inherit

la hermana, sister

el hermano, brother

hermoso, beautiful

el hidalgo, noble, gentleman, knight

el hierro, iron

la hija, daughter

el hijito, little son

el hijo, son

hilar, to spin

la historia, story, history

histórico, historical

el hombre, man

honrado, honest, honourable

la hora, hour, time. ¿ Qué hora es ?—What time is it ?

la hortaliza, green vegetable

el hospital, hospital

la hospitalidad, hospitality

el hotel, hotel

hoy, today

huele (from "oler"), to smell. Huele a pescado—it smells of fish

la huerta, kitchen garden, cultivated land

el huésped, guest. La casa de huéspedes—lodging house

el huevo, egg

el humo, smoke

hundirse, to sink. El vapor se hundió—the steamer sank

I

(la) Iberia, Iberia

ibérico, Iberian

el ibero, Iberian

la idea, idea

el ideal, ideal

el idealista, idealist

el idioma, language

la iglesia, church

ignorante, ignorant

ignorar, to be ignorant of, not to know

iluminar, to illuminate, light

ilustrado, illustrated. Una revista ilustrada—an illustrated magazine

la imaginación, imagination

imaginario, imaginary

el imperio, empire

la importancia, importance

importante, important

importar, to matter, be of importance. Eso no importa—that does not matter

imposible, impossible. Es imposible escribir con este lápiz—it is impossible to write with this pencil

impropio, unsuitable. Un río impropio para la navegación—a river unsuitable for navigation

la impureza, impurity

el inca, Inca (of Peru)

el inconveniente, inconvenience, objection. Si Vd. no tiene inconveniente—if you have no objection independiente, independent

el indiano, former emigrant who has returned to his native Spain

indicar, to indicate, point out

Índico, Indian. El océano Índico—the Indian Ocean

la industria, industry

industrial, industrial

infantil, childish

el ingeniero, engineer

ingenioso, ingenious

(la) Inglaterra, England

(el) inglés, Englishman, English

inmediatamente, immediately

innumerable, innumerable

inocente, innocent

el insecto, insect

insistir, to insist. Insistir en hacerlo—to insist on doing it

el instrumento, instrument. Un instrumento de música—a musical instrument

la inteligencia, intelligence

inteligente, intelligent

la intención, intention. Tener intención de hacer algo— to intend to do something

interesante, interesting

interesar, to interest

el interior, interior, hinterland

interior, inside, interior. Ropa interior—underclothing

interminable, interminable

interrumpir, to interrupt

intrépido, intrepid

introducir (irr.) (see " conducir "), to introduce, insert. Introducir la llave en la cerradura—to insert the key in the lock

inútil, useless

la invención, invention

el invierno, winter

ir (irr.), to go

P.I. voy, vas, va, vamos, vais, van

Pret. fui, fuiste, fue, fuimos, fuisteis, fueron

P.S. vaya, vayas, vaya, vayamos, vayáis, vayan

Pr. P. yendo

Imp. iba, ibas, iba, íbamos, ibais, iban

Fam. I. ve

voy a acostarme—I am going to bed

vamos a ver—let us see

se fue en seguida—he went away at once

ir a pie—to walk, go on foot

ir en coche—to ride, go by car

(la) Irlanda, Ireland

la isla, island

el itinerario, itinerary

izquierdo, left. A la izquierda —on the left (hand)

J

jamás, ever, never

para siempre jamás—for ever and ever

no viene jamás—he never comes

el jamón, ham

el Japó, Japan

(el) japonés, Japanese

el jardín, flower garden

el jefe, chief, head. El jefe de estación—station master

Jerez—vino de Jerez—sherry

la jícara, special cup for drinking chocolate

el, la, joven, young man, young woman

joven, young

la joya, jewel

el joyero, jeweller

el juego, game, play

jugar (ue), to play. Jugar a los naipes—to play at cards

el julio, July

el junio, June

jurar, to swear

K

el kilo(gramo), kilogram

el kilómetro, kilometre

L

el labrador, farmer

el labriego, farm worker, labourer

el lado, side. Al lado de—at the side of

el ladrón, thief

el lago, lake

lamentable, lamentable

lamentar, to lament

la lámpara, lamp. Una lámpara de petróleo—a paraffin lamp

la lana, wool. Medias de lana—woollen stockings

lanar, pertaining to wool. El ganado lanar—sheep

lanzar, to throw, hurl

el lápiz, pencil

largo, long

la lata, tin. Una lata de sardinas—a tin of sardines

latino (adj.), Latin. La América latina — Latin America

el lavado, washing. El lavado de la lana—wool washing

lavar, to wash. Lavar la ropa —wash the clothes

lavarse, to have a wash, wash oneself

la lección, lesson

la leche, milk

leer, to read

legendario, legendary

la legumbre, vegetable

lejos, far, distant

    estar lejos de casa—to be far from home

    a lo lejos—in the distance

la lengua, tongue, language

lentamente, slowly

lento, slow

León, León (province of Spain)

la letra, letter (of the alphabet)

levantar, to lift. Levantar los ojos—to raise the eyes

levantarse, to get up, rise. Levantarse temprano—to get up early

la leyenda, legend

libre, free

    estar libre—to be free, at liberty

    al aire libre—in the open air

limitado, bounded, limited. Limitado por Portugal al oeste—bounded by Portugal in the west

la limosna, alms. Pedir limosna—to beg alms

el limpiabotas, boot-black

limpio, clean

la línea, line. Una línea recta—a straight line

Lisboa, Lisbon

la lista, list. La lista de platos—the menu

la literatura, literature

lo (que), that which, what. Eso es lo que me gusta—that's what I like

la locomotora, locomotive, engine

lograr, to succeed, achieve. Lograron alcanzar la cumbre—they succeeded in reaching the summit

la lotería, lottery, sweepstake

luego, then, presently. Hasta luego — good-bye for the present

lúgubre, gloomy

lujoso, luxurious

la luna, moon. Hay luna—it is moonlight

la luz, light

LL

llamar, to call. Llamar al camarero—to call the waiter

llamarse, to be called. ¿ Cómo se llama Vd. ?—What is your name ?

la llanura, plain, flat country

la llegada, arrival

llegar, to arrive. Llegar al pueblo—to reach the village

lleno, full. Lleno de agua—full of water

llevar, to carry, wear, take away, bear

llevar un vestido azul—to wear a blue dress

llevar carbón en un carro—to carry coal in a cart

¿ Quiere Vd. llevarme con Vd. ?—Will you take me with you ?

lleva quince días en Barcelona—he has been a fortnight in Barcelona

llevar a cabo—to carry out, accomplish

llorar, to cry, weep

llover (ue), to rain

la lluvia, rain

lluvioso, rainy. Un clima lluvioso—a rainy climate

M

la madera, wood. Una casa de madera—a wooden house

la madre, mother

el maestro, master. El maestro de escuela—schoolmaster

la obra maestra—masterpiece

Magallanes, Magellan. El estrecho de Magallanes — the straits of Magellan

magnífico, magnificent

el maíz, maize. El pan de maíz—maize bread

majestuoso, majestic

mal, badly

la maleta, suit case

malo (mal), bad

el pan es malo—the bread is bad

un mal negocio—a bad piece of business

maltratar, to ill-treat

la mamá, mummy, mother

la Mancha, province of Spain.
El canal de la Mancha—the
English Channel
manejar, to handle, manage.
Dos obreros pueden manejar
esta máquina—two workmen
can manage this machine
la mano, hand. Hacer algo a
mano—to do something by
hand
la mantequilla, butter
la manufactura, manufacture
la mañana, morning. Por la
mañana—in the morning
mañana, tomorrow. Mañana
por la mañana—tomorrow
morning
el mapa, map
la máquina, machine
el, la, mar, sea
el mar Mediterráneo—the
Mediterranean Sea
hacerse a la mar—to set
sail
la maravilla, marvel
maravillarse, to wonder, marvel. Maravillarse de algo—
to wonder at something
maravilloso, marvellous
la marcha, march. Ponerse en
marcha—to set off
marcharse, to go away
marearse, to be sea-sick
el marfil, ivory. La Costa del
Marfil—the Ivory Coast
el marinero, sailor
marítimo, maritime
(el) Marruecos, Morocco
más, more, most
¿ Quiere Vd. más?—Do
you want more?
más de cien pesetas—
more than a hundred pesetas

no tengo más que cinco—I
haven't more than five
más hermoso — more
beautiful
el más hermoso—the most
beautiful
el matador, killer
matar, to kill
la materia, material. La materia prima—raw materials
el matrimonio, marriage, matri-
mony ; married couple
el mayo, May
mayor, greater, greatest; older,
eldest
la mayor parte—the lar-
gest part
mi hermano mayor—my
elder brother
el mecánico, mechanic, engineer
mecánico, mechanical
la medianoche, midnight
el médico, doctor
el medio, middle ; way, means.
En medio de la plaza—in
the middle of the square
medio, half. Una media hora—
half an hour
el Mediterráneo, Mediterranean
(el) Méjico, Mexico
mejor, better, best
su mejor amigo—his best
friend
este lápiz es mejor que el
mío—this pencil is a better
one than mine
la melancolía, melancholy,
gloom
melancólicamente, gloomily
melancólico, gloomy, melancholy
el melón, melon

mencionar, to mention

el mendigo, beggar

menor, smaller, smallest; younger, youngest
no tengo la menor duda—I have not the slightest doubt
es menor que su hermana—she is younger than her sister

menos, less, least
menos de diez—less than ten
por lo menos—at least
no puedo menos de admirarla—I cannot help admiring her

la mente, mind

el mercado, market

la mercancía, merchandise

mercante, mercantile. Un vapor mercante—freighter

merced, vuestra, your Honour. (Contracted to Vd.)

el mercurio, mercury

el merino, merino (sheep)

el mes, month

la mesa, table

la meseta, table-land, plateau

el mesón, inn

metalúrgico, metallurgical

meter, to put. Meter cerillas en una caja—to put matches into a box

el metro, metre. Cien metros encima del nivel de mar—a hundred metres above sea-level

el miedo, fear. Tener miedo a alguien—to be frightened of someone

el miembro, member

mientras (que), whilst

mil, a thousand
mil libros—a thousand books
miles de libros—thousands of books

el millonario, millionaire

la mina, mine. Una mina de cobre—a copper mine

el mineral, mineral. Un país rico en minerales—a country rich in minerals

mineral, mineral. El aceite mineral—mineral oil

el minuto, minute. Esperar cinco minutos—to wait five minutes

mirar, to look at, consider

la misa, Mass. Oir misa—to hear Mass

mismo, same, self, very
el mismo día—the same day
yo mismo—I myself
ahora mismo—this very minute

misterioso, mysterious

moderno, modern

el modo, way, means. De este modo—in this way

molestar, to disturb

el molino, mill. El molino de viento—windmill

la moneda, coin. Una moneda de plata—a silver coin

montado, mounted. Montado en un burro—mounted on a donkey

la montaña, mountain

el montañés, mountaineer, mountain dweller

montañoso, mountainous

el **monte,** mountain ; forest

el monte más alto de España—the highest mountain in Spain

el cazador se fue al monte —the huntsman went off into the woods

moreno, dark complexioned, brown

morir (ue-u), to die.   P.P. muerto

morirse (ue-u), to be dying

morisco, Moorish

el **moro,** Moor

la **mosca,** fly (insect)

el **mostrador,** counter (for display)

mostrar (ue), to show

la **moza,** girl

el **mozo,** boy, lad ;   porter ; waiter

mucho, much, many

mucho dinero—a lot of money

trabajar mucho—to work a great deal (hard)

el **muelle,** quay, wharf ; spring

descargar un vapor en el muelle — to discharge a steamer on the quay

el muelle de un reloj—the spring of a watch

la **muerte,** death

muerto, dead

mugriento, grimy, dirty

la **mujer,** woman ; wife

la **mula,** mule

el **mundo,** world.   Todo el mundo—everybody

municipal, municipal

el **museo,** museum.   El museo de pinturas—art gallery

la **música,** music

el **músico,** musician

muy, very

N

nacer (zc), to be born ; to rise (of rivers)

nació en España—he was born in Spain

el Ebro nace en los Montes Cantábricos—the Ebro rises in the Cantabrian mountains

el **nacimiento,** birth

la **nación,** nation

nacional, national

la **nacionalidad,** nationality

nada, nothing.   No tengo nada —I have nothing

nadar, to swim

nadie, nobody.   No ha venido nadie—nobody has come

el **naipe,** playing card.   Jugar a los naipes—to play cards

la **naranja,** orange

natal, native.   La tierra natal —native land

el **natural,** native.   Un natural de Galicia—a native of Galicia

natural, natural

naturalmente, naturally

navegable, navigable

la **navegación,** navigation

el **navegante,** navigator

navegar, to navigate, sail

necesitar, to need.   No lo necesito—I don't need it

el **negociante,** business-man

negro, black

nevar (ie), to snow

ni, nor. No tengo ni pluma ni tinta—I have neither pen nor ink

la niebla, mist, fog

la nieve, snow

ninguno (ningún), no, none. No tiene ningún dinero—he has no money at all

la niña, little girl, child

el niño, little boy, child

el nivel, level. Mil metros sobre el nivel del mar—a thousand metres above sea-level

no, no, not

el noble, noble, nobleman

noble, noble

la noche, night
por la noche—at night
de noche—by night
buenas noches—good night

nombrar, to name

el nombre, name

el norte, north

(el) norteamericano, North American

(la) Noruega, Norway

(el) noruego, Norwegian

la nostalgia, homesickness

la noticia, piece of news. Noticias de casa—news from home

la novela, novel

el novelista, novelist

la novia, sweetheart, fiancée

el novio, fiancé, suitor

la nube, cloud

nueve, nine

nuevo, new

el número, number

numeroso, numerous

nunca, never. No trabaja nunca—he never works

O

o, or

el obispo, bishop

la obligación, obligation

la obra, work (of art, literature, etc.). Una obra maestra—masterpiece

el obrero, workman

obtener (irr.), to obtain. (Conjugated like " tener ")

la ocasión, occasion, opportunity. Aprovechar la ocasión —to take advantage of the opportunity

occidental, western

el océano, ocean

ochenta, eighty

ocho, eight

el oeste, west

oficial, official

la oficina, office

ofrecer (zc), to offer

oir (irr.), to hear
P.I. oigo, oyes, oye, oímos, oís, oyen
Pret. oí, oíste, oyó, oímos, oísteis, oyeron
P.S. oiga, oigas, oiga, oigamos, oigáis, oigan
P.P. oído
Pr. P. oyendo
Fam. I. oye
oir misa—to hear Mass
le oyó entrar—he heard him come in

oler (ue), to smell. (Before the diphthong ue this verb takes " h ")
P.I. huelo, hueles, huele, olemos, oléis, huelen
P.S. huela, huelas, huela, olamos, oláis, huelan
oler a ajo—to smell of garlic

el olivar, olive grov
el olivo, olive tree
olvidar, to forget
once, eleven
la operación, operation
operar, to operate, work
el operario, workman, operative
lo opuesto, opposite. Lo opuesto de " negro " es " blanco "—the opposite of " black " is " white "
orgullosamente, proudly
oriental, eastern
el origen, origen
la orilla, bank, shore. A orillas del río—on the banks of the river
la oscuridad, darkness, obscurity
oscuro, dark, obscure
otro, other, another. Tráigame otro vaso de vino—bring me another glass of wine

P

la paciencia, patience
paciente, patient
el Pacífico, Pacific (ocean)
el padre, father
pagar, to pay. Pagar diez pesetas por el libro—to pay ten pesetas for the book
el país, country (political)
el paisaje, countryside, landscape
la palabra, word
el palacio, palace
pálido, pale. Ponerse pálido—to turn pale
el palote, pothook (writing)
el pan, bread
la panadería, baker's shop

el panadero, baker
el panecillo, roll (bread)
el panorama, panorama
el pañuelo, handkerchief
el papá, father, daddy
el papel, paper. Desempeñar un papel—to play a part
el paquete, parcel, packet
para, for, in order to
    comemos para vivir—we eat to live
    este libro es para usted—this book is for you
    salir para Madrid—to set out for Madrid
    hablar para sí—to talk to oneself
parecer (zc), to seem, appear
    a mi parecer—in my opinion
    ¿ Qué le parece ?—What do you think about it ?
    parece estar contento—he appears to be content
parecerse (zc), to resemble. Se parece mucho a su hermano—he is very like his brother
parecido, similar. Es un animal muy parecido al tigre—it is an animal very similar to the tiger
la parra, vine
la parte, part
    por todas partes—everywhere
    en parte—partly
    por otra parte—on the other hand
particular, private
el pasado, past
pasado, past. Pasado mañana—the day after tomorrow
el pasajero, passenger (by sea)

pasar, to pass, spend
    pasar la noche en el campo —to spend the night in the country
    páseme Vd. el pan—pass the bread
    pasar por la ciudad—to pass through the town
    pasar las de Caín—to have an awful time

pasearse, to take a walk, ride

el paseo, walk, ride; avenue
    dar un paseo en coche—to go for a ride in a car
    dar un paseo—to go for a walk
    el Paseo de Colón—Columbus Avenue

el pastor, shepherd

el patio, courtyard

la patria, native land

la pava, turkey-hen. Pelar la pava—to pay court to a lady (literally, " to pluck the turkey ")

la paz, peace

pedir (i), to ask for
    pedir limosna—to beg alms
    no me pidió nada—he asked me for nothing

peinar, to comb

pelar, to pluck. Pelar la pava —to pay court to a lady. (See " pava ")

la película, film

el peligro, danger

la pelota, ball, pelota. Jugar a la pelota—to play ball, pelota

la pena, trouble, sorrow. No vale la pena—it's not worth the trouble

penetrar, to penetrate

la península, peninsula

pensar (ie), to think; intend
    ¿ Qué piensa Vd. de esto? —What do you think of this?
    pensar en algo—to think of something
    Pienso ir a Madrid—I intend to go to Madsid

peor, worse, worst
    la peor ciudad del mundo —the worst city in the world
    de mal en peor—from bad to worse

pequeño, small, little

perder (ie), to lose

perezoso, lazy

la perfección, perfection

el periódico, newspaper

permanecer (zc), to remain, stay

pero, but

la persona, person

el personaje, character (in a play, book, etc.)

la perspectiva, perspective, view

pertenecer (zc), to belong. El libro me pertenece—the book belongs to me

pesar, a pesar de sus dificultades—in spite of his difficulties

la pesca, fishing

el pescado, fish (as a commodity)

el pescador, fisherman

pescar, to fish

la peseta, peseta. Spanish coin worth about 10*d.* at par

el peso, weight; Spanish-American dollar

el petróleo, petroleum, paraffin

el **picacho**, mountain peak

el **pico**, beak; peak
   el pico de un pájaro—a bird's beak
   el pico de Aneto—mountain peak in the Pyrenees

el **pie**, foot.
   ir a pie—to go on foot
   estar de pie—to be standing

la **pieza**, room; play
   la casa tiene diez piezas—the house has ten rooms
   una pieza de teatro—a play

pintar, to paint

el **pintor**, painter

la **pintura**, painting

pique, irse a pique—to sink.
   El barco se fue a pique—the ship sank

el **piso**, storey, floor, flat. El piso bajo—ground floor

el **pitillo**, cigarette

la **pizarra**, blackboard

la **plata**, silver. El Río de la Plata—River Plate

el **plátano**, banana

el **plato**, dish, course; plate
   un plato de sopa—a plate of soup
   una comida de seis platos—a six-course meal

la **playa**, beach, shore

la **plaza**, square, place
   la plaza del mercado—market place
   la plaza de toros—bullring

la **pluma**, pen; feather

la **población**, population; town

pobre, poor

la **pobreza**, poverty

poco, little, few
   hace pocos días—a few days ago
   un poco de pan—a little bread
   hablar poco—to speak little (seldom)

poder (irr.), to be able
   P.I. puedo, puedes, puede, podemos, podéis, pueden
   Fut. podré, podrás, podrá, podremos, podréis, podrán
   Pret. pude, pudiste, pudo, pudimos, pudisteis, pudieron
   P.S. pueda, puedas, pueda, podamos, podáis, puedan
   Pr. P. pudiendo
   no puedo hacerlo—I cannot do it
   no podría hacerlo—I couldn't do it
   ¿Puede Vd. venir mañana?—Can you come tomorrow?
   no puedo menos de decirlo—I cannot help saying so

político, political

polvoriento, dusty

poner (irr.), to put, place
   P.I. pongo, pones, pone, ponemos, ponéis, ponen
   Fut. pondré, pondrás, pondrá, pondremos, pondréis, pondrán
   Pret. puse, pusiste, puso, pusimos, pusisteis, pusieron
   P.S. ponga, pongas, ponga, pongamos, pongáis, pongan
   P.P. puesto
   Fam. I. pon
   poner el dinero sobre la mesa—to put the money on the table

el sol se pone—the sun is setting

ponerse un traje—to put on a dress

ponerse pálido—to turn pale

ponerse en marcha—to set off

por, for, through, along, in, on, by

por eso—*for* that reason

pasar por la ciudad—to pass *through* the town

pasar por la calle—to go *along* the street

por la tarde—*in* the afternoon

Una novela escrita por Cervantes—a novel written *by* Cervantes

por fin—finally

por supuesto—of course

porque, because

por qué, why?

(el) portugués, Portuguese

el porvenir, future

posible, possible. Es posible que venga—it is possible he may come

los postres, dessert

práctico, practical

el prado, meadow

preciso, necessary. No es preciso enviarlo en seguida—it is not necessary to send it immediately

preferir (ie-i), to prefer. Prefiero hacerlo ahora—I prefer to do it now

la pregunta, question. Hacer una pregunta—to ask a question

preguntar, to ask, enquire. Preguntar por alguien—to enquire about someone

preparar, to prepare

prestar, to lend

pretencioso, pretentious

la prima, cousin

prima, la materia, raw material

primero (primer), first

el primer día—the first day

por primera vez—the first time

primero (adv.), at first, firstly

primitivo, primitive

el primo, cousin

principal, main, principal

principiar, to begin. Principiar a comer—to begin to eat

el principio, beginning. A principios de enero—at the beginning of January

la prisa, haste

tener prisa—to be in a hurry

de prisa—quickly

probar (ue), to try, taste. Probar fortuna—to seek one's fortune, try one's luck

procedente, procedente de—proceeding from, deriving from

proceder, to proceed, come from. La lana procede del carnero—wool comes from the sheep

el procedimiento, process

la producción, production

producir (irr.) (see "conducir"), to produce

el producto, product, produce

productor, productive. Un país productor — a productive country el **profesor**, teacher

prohibir, to prohibit. Se prohíbe fumar—no smoking

la **propiedad**, property, possession, estate

el **propietario**, proprietor, landlord, owner

la **proporción**, proportion

proteger, to protect

protestar, to protest

la **provincia**, province

próximo, next. La semana próxima—next week

público, public. Vender en pública subasta—to sell by auction

el **pueblecito**, small village

el **pueblo**, village; people, nation. El pueblo mejicano—the Mexican people

la **puerta**, door

el **puerto**, port, harbour

pues, for, well, then, so. Hasta mañana pues—until tomorrow then, so until tomorrow

el **punto**, point, dot

desde este punto de vista—from this point of view

punto y coma—semicolon (i.e. dot and comma)

el **puñal**, dagger

el **puro**, cigar. Fumar un puro—to smoke a cigar

puro, pure. Agua pura—pure water

Q

que, that, which, what, who, whom, than

el lápiz que está sobre la mesa—the pencil that is on the table

el señor que ha venido—the gentleman who has come

la señora que he visto—the lady (whom) I have seen

lo que me gusta—what I like

es mayor que yo—he is older than I

qué, what, what a, how (interrogative and exclamatory)

¿ Qué vio Vd. ?—What did you see ?

¡ Qué día !—What a day !

¿ Qué tal ?—How goes it ?

quedar, to rest, remain. ¿ Cuánto dinero le queda a Vd. ?—How much money have you left ?

quedarse, to remain. Se quedó en la ciudad—he remained in the town

quejarse, to complain. Se queja de todo—he complains of everything

querer (irr.), to love, like, want

P.I. quiero, quieres, quiere, queremos, queréis, quieren

Fut. querré, querrás, querrá, querremos, querréis, querrán

Pret. quise, quisiste, quiso, quisimos, quisisteis, quisieron

P.S. quiera, quieras, quiera, queramos, queráis, quieran

Fam. I. quiere

Quiere a su madre—he loves his mother

No quiero hacerlo—I don't want to do it

¿ Qué quiere decir esto ?—What does this mean ?

querido, dear, beloved

el queso, cheese

quien, who, whom

　el señor quien vino—the gentleman who came

　la amiga a quien vi—the friend whom I saw

quién, who, whom (interrogative)

　¿ Quién vino ? — Who came?

　¿ A quién ha visto Vd. ?— Whom did you see ?

　¿ De quién es este lápiz ?— Whose is this pencil ?

quieto, quiet, peaceful

la quietud, peace, quietude

don Quijote, don Quixote

quince, fifteen

quinto, fifth

quizá(s), perhaps. Quizá (or) quizás vendrá mañana—perhaps he will come to-morrow

R

radiar, to broadcast

la radio, radio, wireless

rápidamente, rapidly

rápido, rapid, swift

el rato, while, interval. Esperar un rato—to wait a short while

la raza, race, breed. La raza humana—the human race

la razón, right, reason. Tener razón—to be right. No tener razón—to be wrong

el realista, realist

recibir, to receive

recordar (ue), to recall, remember

recorrer, to travel over. Recorrer el país—to travel all over the country

el recreo, recreation. El patio de recreo—playground

el recuerdo, memory, souvenir. Recuerdos a su señora—remember me to your wife

la red, net, luggage rack

regalar, to give, present. Me regaló un reloj—he presented me with a watch

el regalo, gift

la región, region, district

la regla, rule, ruler. Por regla general—as a general rule

regresar, to return

el regreso, return

el reino, kingdom

reir (i), to laugh. Reirse de alguien—to laugh at someone

la reja, grating, barred window

relacionado, related, connected. Relacionado con—connected with

el reloj, clock, watch

　un reloj de bolsillo—pocket watch

　un reloj de pared—wall clock

el remedio, remedy. No hay remedio—it can't be helped

el rendimiento, yield

renombrado, famous, renowned

repetir (i), to repeat

la representación, representation, showing, play, performance

representar, to represent, show

la república, republic

reservar, to reserve, book

resistir, to resist. Resistir a la tentación—to resist temptation

el respecto, con respecto a esto —with respect to this

el restaurant, restaurant

retirado, retired

retirar, to retire, withdraw, take out. Retirar la mosca del vaso —to take the fly out of the glass

retirarse, to retire, retreat

el retraso, delay. El tren trae diez minutos de retraso—the train is ten minutes late

la reunión, reunion, gathering, meeting

reunirse, to gather, assemble

el rey, king

la ría, estuary

rico, rich

el río, river

la riqueza, wealth

rodeado, surrounded. Rodeado de colinas—surrounded by hills

rojo, red

(el) romano, Roman

romper, to break. P.P. roto— broken

Se ha roto el brazo—he has broken his arm

la ropa, clothes, clothing

la rosa, rose

roto, broken

el ruido, noise

ruidosamente, noisily

la ruina, ruin

el rumbo, course, direction, route. Con rumbo a Buenos Aires—bound for Buenos Aires

(el) ruso, Russian

S

el sábado, Saturday. Viene los sábados—he comes on Saturdays

saber (irr.), to know, know how, be able

P.I sé, sabes, sabe, sabemos, sabéis, saben

Fut. sabré, sabrás, sabrá, sabremos, sabréis, sabrán

Pret. supe, supiste, supo, supimos, supisteis, supieron

P.S. sepa, sepas, sepa, sepamos, sepáis, sepan

No sé qué hacer—I don't know what to do

¿ Sabe Vd. nadar ?—Do you know how to swim ?

el sabio, wise man

sabio, wise, learned

sabroso, tasty, enjoyable, delicious

sacar, to take out, pull out. Sacar un billete—to get a ticket

el sacerdote, priest

la sala, drawing-room. La sala de clase—classroom

la salchicha, sausage

la salida, way out, exit, departure

salir (irr.), to come out, go out, leave

P.I. salgo, sales, sale, salimos, salís, salen

Fut. saldré, saldrás, saldrá, saldremos, saldréis, saldrán

P.S. salga, salgas, salga, salgamos, salgáis, salgan

Fam. I. sal

¿ A qué hora sale el tren ? —What time does the train leave ?

Salir para España—to set out for Spain

Salir del comedor—to leave the dining-room

saltar, to jump, leap

la salud, health. ¡ Salud !—Good health !

saludar, to greet, salute

salvar, to save

san. (See "santo")

la sangre, blood

Santo (San), Saint

San Pedro—Saint Peter

Santo Domingo—Dominican Republic

santo (adj.), holy. La Semana Santa—Holy Week

la sardina, sardine

seco, dry

la sed, thirst. Tener sed—to be thirsty

la seda, silk

seguida, en seguida—at once, immediately

seguir (i), to follow, go on

Sígame Vd.—follow me

seguir un camino—to follow a road

seguir hablando—to go on talking

según, according to. Según el diario—according to the newspaper

el segundo, second. Dos minutos cincuenta segundos—two minutes fifty seconds

segundo, second. La segunda vez—the second time

seguro, sure, certain. Estoy seguro de que vendrá—I am sure he will come

el sello, seal, postage stamp

la semana, week

semejante, similar, like. Dos cosas semejantes—two similar things

sencillo, easy, simple

sentado, seated. Estar sentado—to be seated

sentarse (ie), to sit down. ¡ Siéntese Vd. !—Sit down !

el sentido, sense, feeling

los cinco sentidos—the five senses

el sentido común—common sense

sentir (ie, i), to feel; be sorry, regret

Se siente enfermo—he feels ill

Siento mucho haber dicho eso—I am very sorry I said that

el señor, gentleman ; Mr. Muy señor mío—Dear Sir (as in letters)

la señora, lady, wife ; Mrs.

la señorita, young lady ; Miss

el señorito, young man ; Master

separar, to separate

el se(p)tiembre, September

ser (irr.), to be

P.I. soy, eres, es, somos, sois, son

Pret. fui, fuiste, fue, fuimos, fuisteis, fueron

Imp. era, eras, era, éramos, erais, eran

P.S. sea, seas, sea, seamos, seáis, sean

Fam. I. sé

Son molinos de viento—they are windmills

Es de Vd.—it is yours

Son las once—it is eleven o'clock

el sereno, night-watchman

sereno, clear, fine

el servicio, service. Un buen servicio de autobuses—a good bus service

el servidor, servant. S.S.S. (su seguro servidor) — Yours faithfully (literally, Your faithful servant)

servir (i), to serve
servir la sopa—to serve the soup
No sirve para nada—it is of no use for anything
Sírvase Vd. darme la carta —please give me the letter

sesenta, sixty

setenta, seventy

Sevilla, Seville

si, if, whether
Me preguntó si vendría— he asked me whether I would come
Si viene, se lo daré—if he comes I shall give it to him

sí, yes

sí, oneself, himself, etc. Hablar para sí—to talk to oneself

siempre, always

la sierra, mountain chain

la siesta, siesta, nap. Dormir la siesta—to take an afternoon nap

siete, seven

el siglo, century

significar, to signify, mean

siguiente, following. Al día siguiente—on the following day

silbar, to whistle

la silla, chair

el sillón, arm-chair

simpático, affable, pleasant, charming

sin, without
No se marche Vd. sin mí— don't go away without me
salir sin hablar—to go out without speaking
sin embargo—nevertheless

sinfónico, symphonic, symphony

sino, but (after negative). No está cansado sino enfermo —he isn't tired but ill

la situación, situation, position

situado, situated

sobre, on, over
El libro está sobre la mesa —the book is on the table
sobre todo—above all, especially

sobre todo. (See "sobre")

la sociedad, society

el socio, member, partner

el sol, sun
Hace sol—it is sunny
El sol sale—the sun rises
El sol se pone—the sun sets
tomar el sol—to enjoy the sunshine

solamente, only

el soldado, soldier

la soledad, solitude

solemne, solemn

soler (ue), to be wont to, accustomed to. (This verb is found only in the present indicative and the imperfect indicative.) Suele llegar a las ocho—he usually arrives at eight

solitario, solitary, lonely

sólo, only

    sólo cien pesetas—only a hundred pesetas

    no sólo... sino también... not only... but also...

solo, alone

    Viene siempre solo—he always comes alone

    café solo—black coffee (coffee alone)

la soltera, spinster

el soltero, bachelor

el sombrero, hat

el son, sound. Al son de la música—at the sound of the music

sonreir (i), to smile

el soñador, dreamer

soñar (ue), to dream. Soñar con la felicidad—to dream of happiness

la sopa, soup

sorprender, to surprise, take by surprise. Nos sorprendió la noche—night overtook us

la sorpresa, surprise

la subasta, auction. Vender en pública subasta—to sell by auction

subir, to rise, climb, get in

    subir a un árbol—to climb a tree

    subir al tren—to get in the train

    El agua sube—the water is rising

súbitamente, suddenly

el submarino, submarine

la suciedad, dirt

sucio, dirty

la sucursal, branch (of a business)

(la) Sudamérica, South America

(el) sudamericano, South American

el suelo, ground, soil, floor

    echar por el suelo—to throw on the ground (floor)

    un suelo muy fértil—very fertile soil (land)

el sueño, dream ; sleep.

    tener sueño—to be sleepy.

    El sueño de una noche de verano — "A Midsummer Night's Dream"

la suerte, luck, fortune. Tener suerte—to be lucky

suficiente, sufficient

supuesto, por, of course

el sur, south. La América del Sur—South America

surcar, to plough, furrow

T

el tabaco, tobacco

la taberna, tavern, inn

el Tajo, River Tagus

tal, such

    tal hombre—such a man

    ¿ Qué tal ?—How goes it ?

también, also

tampoco, either, neither. A mí no me gusta tampoco—I don't like it either

tan, so, such, as

    tan difícil—so difficult

    tan inútil como costoso— as useless as it is costly

    un niño tan perezoso— such a lazy child

tanto, so much, so many, as much, as many

    No tiene tanto dinero como yo—he hasn't as much money as I have tantas cosas—so many things

por lo tanto—therefore

tardar, to delay. Tardar en venir—to be late in coming

la tarde, afternoon, evening

por la tarde—in the afternoon, evening

buenas tardes—good afternoon, evening

tarde, late. Llegar tarde—to arrive late

la tarea, task

la tarjeta, card. Una tarjeta postal—post card

la taza, cup

el té, tea (also found without accent—el te)

el teatro, theatre

tejer, to weave

los tejidos, textiles, woven fabrics

el telar, loom

telefonear, to telephone

el teléfono, telephone. Llamar por teléfono—to ring up

la temperatura, temperature

la tempestad, storm, tempest

templado, mild, temperate

temprano, soon, early. Llegar temprano—to arrive early

el tendero, shopkeeper

tener (irr.), to have, possess

P.I. tengo, tienes, tiene, tenemos, tenéis, tienen

Fut. tendré, tendrás, tendrá, tendremos, tendréis, tendrán

Pret. tuve, tuviste, tuvo, tuvimos, tuvisteis, tuvieron

P.S. tenga, tengas, tenga, tengamos, tengáis, tengan

Fam. I. ten

tener sed—to be thirsty

tener hambre—to be hungry

tener que salir—to have to go out

tener diez años—to be ten years old

tener sueño—to be sleepy

tener ganas de hacer algo—to want to do something

tener razón—to be right

no tener razón—to be wrong

la tentación, temptation

teñir (i), to dye

tercero (tercer), third. El tercer día—the third day

terminar, to terminate, end

la ternera, veal. Una chuleta de ternera—a veal chop

la terraza, terrace

terrestre, pertaining to the land. Comunicaciones terrestres—land communications

terrible, terrible

el territorio, territory

la tertulia, gathering of friends, meeting, party

textil, textile. Las industrias textiles—textile industries

la tía, aunt

el tiempo, time; weather

hace poco tiempo—a short time ago

Hace buen tiempo—it is fine (weather)

andando el tiempo—as time went on

la tienda, shop

la tierra, earth, land

la tinta, ink

el tinte, dye

el tío, uncle

el **tipo,** type

la **tiza,** chalk

tocar, to touch; play (musical instruments). Tocar el piano —to play the piano

todavía, still, yet. No ha venido todavía—he hasn't come yet

todo, all, every; everything
  todos los días—every day
  todo el mundo—everybody
  todo lo que ve—everything he sees

tomar, to take
  tomar asiento—to take a seat
  tomar el fresco—to enjoy the cool air
  tomar refrescos—to take refreshment

el **torero,** bull-fighter

el **torno de hilar,** spinning-wheel

el **toro,** bull

la **torre,** tower

total, total, complete

la **totalidad,** total, whole. La totalidad de la tripulación —the whole of the crew

trabajador, hardworking

trabajar, to work

el **trabajo,** work

la **tradición,** tradition

tradicional, traditional

la **traducción,** translation

traducir (irr.) (see "conducir"), to translate. Traducir al castellano—to translate into Castilian

traer (irr.), to bring, carry
  P.I. traigo, traes, trae, traemos, traéis, traen

  Pret. traje, trajiste, trajo, trajimos, trajisteis, trajeron
  P.S. traiga, traigas, traiga, traigamos, traigáis, traigan
  Pr. P. trayendo
  P.P. traído
  Tráigame Vd. otro vaso— bring me another glass

el **traje,** suit, dress, costume

la **tranquilidad,** tranquillity, peace

tranquilo, tranquil, peaceful

el **transatlántico,** liner

el **transeunte,** passer-by, pedestrian

el **tránsito,** traffic, transit

el **transporte,** transport

el **tranvía,** tram-car

trasladar, to move, transfer

trasnochar, to stay the night; sit up all night

tratar, to treat, consider, try
  Me trata de amigo—he treats me as a friend
  tratar de nadar—to try to swim

tratarse, to be a question of. ¿ De qué se trata?—What is it about?

la **travesía,** crossing, sea passage

tremendo, tremendous, terrific. Hace un calor tremendo— it's terribly hot

el **tren,** train

el **trigo,** wheat

la **tripulación,** crew (ship)

triste, sad

tristemente, sadly

la **tristeza,** sadness

el **turista,** tourist

U

u, or. Siete u ocho—seven or eight

últimamente, finally

último, final, last. Por último —finally

el ultramar, overseas. Países de ultramar—countries overseas

ultramarino, overseas. Posesiones ultramarinas—overseas possessions

los ultramarinos, foodstuffs from overseas. La tienda de ultramarinos—grocery store

únicamente, solely, only

único, sole, only. Un hijo único—an only child

unido, united. Los Estados Unidos—the United States

unir, to unite, link

universal, universal

el Uruguay, Uruguay

usar, to use, wear
    usar gafas—to wear glasses
    ropa usada—worn clothing

útil, useful

utópico, Utopian

la uva, grape

V

la vaca, cow

vacuno, pertaining to cows. El ganado vacuno—cattle

(el) valenciano, Valencian

valer (irr.), to be worth
    P.I. valgo, vales, vale, valemos, valéis, valen

Fut. valdré, valdrás, valdrá, valdremos, valdréis, valdrán

P.S. valga, valgas, valga, valgamos, valgáis, valgan
    ¿Cuánto vale esto?— What's the price of this?
    No vale la pena de hacerlo —it's not worth doing
    No vale nada—it's worthless
    Más vale tarde que nunca— better late than never

el valle, valley

el vapor, steamer, steamship

la variedad, variety

varios, various, several. Varios días—several days

(el) vasco, Basque

vascongado, Basque. Las Provincias Vascongadas— the Basque Provinces

el vascuence, Basque language

el vaso, glass. Un vaso de leche—a glass of milk

vasto, vast

la vecindad, vicinity, neighbourhood

el vecino, neighbour

la vegetación, vegetation

vegetal (adj.), vegetable. El aceite vegetal—vegetable oil

veinte, twenty

la velocidad, speed

vencer, to conquer, overcome

vender, to sell

venir (irr.), to come
    P.I. vengo, vienes, viene, venimos, venís, vienen
    Fut. vendré, vendrás, vendrá, vendremos, vendréis, vendrán

Pret. vine, viniste, vino, vinimos, vinisteis, vinieron

P.S. venga, vengas, venga, vengamos, vengáis, vengan

Pr. P. viniendo

Venga Vd. a verme—come and see me

la venta, sale; inn

la venta pública—public sale

pasar la noche en la venta —to spend the night at the inn

la ventana, window

la ventanilla, window (carriage)

ver (irr.), to see

P.I. veo, ves, ve, vemos, veis, ven

Pret. vi, viste, vio, vimos, visteis, vieron

P.S. vea, veas, vea, veamos, veáis, vean

P.P. visto

Imp. veía, veías, veía, veíamos, veíais, veían

Vamos a ver—let's see

No tiene nada que ver con eso—it's nothing to do with that

el verano, summer

la verdad, truth

decir la verdad—to speak the truth

Vd. vendrá mañana ¿ verdad?—You will come tomorrow, won't you?

verdaderamente, really, truthfully

verdadero, true, real

verde, green

verificarse, to take place

¿ A qué hora se verificará la boda?—What time will the wedding take place?

el vestido, dress. Un vestido azul—a blue dress

vestido, dressed. Vestido de verde—dressed in green

vestir (i), to dress. Vestir una muñeca—to dress a doll

vestirse (i), to dress, get dressed. Vestirse de negro—to dress in black

la vez, time, occasion

Una vez—once. Dos veces—twice

Algunas veces — sometimes. A veces—sometimes

Tres veces cuatro son doce —three times four is twelve

Muchas veces—often

Por primera vez—for the first time

la vía, way. La vía férrea—the railway

el viajante, commercial traveller

viajar, to travel

el viaje, journey

el viajero, traveller, passenger

la víctima, victim

la vida, lif

el vidrio, glass. Una botella de vidrio—a glass bottle

la vieja, old woman

el viejo, old man

viejo, old

el viento, wind. Un molino de viento—windmill

el vigilante, watchman

vigorosamente, vigorously

el vino wine. El vino de Jerez —sherry

la viña, vineyard

violento, violent

la virtud, virtue

la visita, visit, call

visitar, to visit

la vista, view

una hermosa vista — a beautiful view

hasta la vista—au revoir

desde este punto de vista —from this point of view

visto, seen

vivir, to live

Vive en América—he lives in America

Ya no vive—he is no longer living

Vizcaya, Biscay. El Golfo de Vizcaya—the Bay of Biscay

vociferar, to shout aloud

volar (ue), to fly

volver (ue), to return, turn, come back

P.P. vuelto

No ha vuelto todavía—he has not returned yet

volver a escribir la carta— to write the letter again

la voz, voice

el vuelo, flight

la vuelta, turn, return, walk

dar la vuelta al mundo— to go round the world

un billete de ida y vuelta— a return ticket

dar una vuelta por la calle—to go for a stroll in the street

vuelto, returned. (See "volver")

Y

y, and

ya, already, yet; now; soon

ya no—no longer

ya veremos—now we shall see, we shall soon see

ya hemos dicho—we have already said

ya caigo—now I understand

ya no llueve—it's no longer raining

yacer (zc), to lie

P.I. first person singular yazco (or yazgo or yago)

Aquí yace—here lies (inscription on tombstones)

el yacimiento, deposit. Un yacimiento de cobre—a deposit of copper

Z

zambullirse, to dive, plunge. Zambullirse en el agua—to dive into the water

la zapatería, shoemaker's shop

el zapatero, shoemaker

el zapato, shoe

ENGLISH–SPANISH VOCABULARY

A

a, an, un, una

    once a week—una vez por semana

    five pesetas a bottle—cinco pesetas la botella

to be able, poder; saber (to know how to)

    Can you swim ?—¿ Sabe Vd. nadar ?

about, to talk about something —hablar de algo

    about thirty—cerca de treinta

    at about eleven o'clock—a eso de las once

abroad, to go abroad—ir al extranjero

    to live abroad—vivir en el extranjero

to accompany, acompañar

account, on account of the cold —a causa del frío

to admit, admitir

to advise, aconsejar

aerodrome, el aerodromo

affectionate, cariñoso

Africa, (el) África

after, después

    after supper—después de la cena

    after writing the letter—después de escribir la carta

afternoon, la tarde

    in the afternoon—por la tarde

    good afternoon—buenas tardes

afterwards, después, luego

again, otra vez

    to do something again—volver a hacer algo

age, la edad. To be ten years old—tener diez años de edad

ago, two years ago—hace dos años

agricultural, agrícola

air, el aire

    by air—por aeroplano

    air line—línea aérea

all, todo

almost, casi

alms, to beg alms—pedir limosna

along, por ; a lo largo de

already, ya

also, también

although, aunque

always, siempre

America, (la) América

and, y, e

Andalusia, (la) Andalucía

animal, el animal

another, otro

answer, la contestación, la respuesta ; la solución

to answer, contestar, responder

any, alguno, algunos

anywhere, por cualquier parte

to appear (seem), parecer

apple, la manzana

Arab, el árabe

architect, el arquitecto

Argentine, la República Argentina

to arrive, llegar

as, como

    as well—también

    as rich as he—tan rico como él

    as many friends as he—tantos amigos como él

to ask, preguntar; pedir (to ask for). To ask a question—hacer una pregunta

to fall asleep, dormirse

to assure, asegurar

at, en, a

    at school—en la escuela

    at home—en casa

    at the door—a la puerta

Atlantic, el (océano) Atlántico

attention, la atención

    to pay attention—prestar atención

    not to pay any attention to (to take no notice of)—no hacer caso de

attentively, atentamente, con atención

aunt, la tía

avenue, la avenida, la alameda, el paseo

to await, esperar, aguardar

to awake, despertar; despertarse

awful, to have an awful time—pasar las de Caín

B

bad, malo

balcony, el balcón

bandit, el bandido

bank, la orilla (of a river); el banco (finance). On the banks of the river—a orillas del río

barber, el barbero

basket, la cesta

Basque Provinces, las Provincias Vascongadas

to bathe, bañarse

battle, la batalla

battlefield, el campo de batalla

bay, la bahía

to be, ser; estar

beach, la playa

beautiful, hermoso, lindo, bello

because, porque. Because of the cold—a causa del frío

bed, la cama. To go to bed—acostarse

before, antes; delante

    before three o'clock—antes de las tres

    before going out—antes de salir

    before (in front of) the church—delante de la iglesia

beggar, el mendigo

to begin, empezar, principiar, comenzar. To begin to eat—empezar a comer

beginning, el principio. At the beginning of June—a principios de junio

behind, detrás. Behind the table—detrás de la mesa

to believe, creer

better, mejor. Better late than never—más vale tarde que nunca

big, grande

birthday, el cumpleaños

biscuit, la galleta

bishop, el obispo

black, negro. Dressed in black—vestido de negro
blue, azul
boarding house, la casa de huéspedes
book, el libro
border (frontier), la frontera
to be born, nacer
both, ambos, los dos. Ambos (los dos) hermanos—both brothers
bottle, la botella
box, la caja
branch (business), la sucursal
Brazil, el Brasil
bread, el pan
breakfast, el desayuno. To have breakfast—desayunarse
to bring, traer
brother, el hermano
to build, construir, edificar
bull-fight, la corrida de toros. To go to a bull-fight—ir a los toros
bus, el autobús
business house, la casa de comercio
business man, el negociante
but, pero; sino
butter, la mantequilla
to buy, comprar. To buy something from someone—comprar algo a alguien

C

café, el café
to call, llamar. To be called—llamarse
can. (See " to be able ")
canal, el canal
cantabrian, cantábrico

car, el automóvil, el coche (motor-car); el tranvía (tram-car)
caravan, la caravana
to card (wool), cardar
carefully, cuidadosamente
cargo steamer, el vapor mercante
to carry, llevar
carter, el carretero
Catalonia, (la) Cataluña
cathedral, la catedral
catholic, (el) católico
central, central
centre, el centro
century, el siglo
certain, cierto. To be certain—estar seguro
character (in a play, book, etc.), el personaje
charming, encantador
cheese, el queso
chemist, el boticario
child, el niño, la niña
Christian, (el) cristiano
church, la iglesia
cigarette, el cigarrillo, el pitillo
cinema, el cine
city, la ciudad
civil, civil
class, la clase. In third class—en tercera clase
climate, el clima
cloak, la capa
to close, cerrar
coast, la costa
coffee, el café
cold, el frío; frío (adj.). To be cold—tener frío (persons), hacer frío (weather)
colonisation, la colonización
colony, la colonia
colour, el color

coloured, a coloured handker-chief—un pañuelo de color
to comb, peinar. To comb one's hair—peinarse
to come, venir
to come in—entrar
to come back—volver, re-gresar
to come with—acompañar
comedy, la comedia
commercial, comercial
to compare, comparar
compartment, el departamento
to conquer, conquistar
to continue, continuar, seguir
contrast, el contraste
cool, fresco. To enjoy the cool air—tomar el fresco
corner, el extremo; la esquina (street corner); el rincón (of a room)
to cost, costar
to count, contar
country, el país (nation); el campo (countryside)
countryman, el campesino, el aldeano; el compatriota
of course, por supuesto, natural-mente
cousin, el primo, la prima
covered, cubierto
cow, la vaca
to cross, atravesar, cruzar
cup, la taza
customs officer, el aduanero
to go cycling, dar un paseo en bicicleta

D

to dance, bailar
date, la fecha. What is the date? ¿ Qué fecha es ?

date (fruit), el dátil
daughter, la hija
day, el día
day after tomorrow—pasado mañana
day before yesterday—anteayer
a great deal, mucho
dear, querido (beloved); caro, costoso (costly)
to depart, salir, partir, mar-charse
deposit (mineral), el yacimiento
to describe, describir
desert, el desierto, el despoblado
to develop, desarrollarse
to die, morir. To be dying—morirse
different, diferente, distinto; varios (several)
dining-room, el comedor
dinner, la comida. To have dinner—comer
dirt, la suciedad
dirty, sucio
to discover, descubrir
in the distance, a lo lejos
distant, lejos, lejano
divided by, dividido por
to do, hacer
doctor, el médico
donkey, el burro
don Quixote, don Quijote
door, la puerta
to draw (sketch), dibujar
to dream, soñar
dream, el sueño
to dress, vestir; vestirse
dressed in, vestido de
to drink, beber
to drop, dejar caer
dry, seco

during, durante
dusty, polvoriento
dye, el tinte

E

early, temprano
to eat, comer
egg, el huevo
eight, ocho
either, o, u ; tampoco. I haven't
  it either — no lo tengo
  tampoco
eleven, once
to employ, emplear
England, (la) Inglaterra
Englishman, el inglés
to enjoy, gozar
enough, bastante
to enter, entrar
episode, el episodio
especially, especialmente,
  sobre todo
to establish, establecer, fundar
even, aun, hasta
evening, la tarde
    in the evening—por la
    tarde
    good evening—buenas
    tardes
ever, jamás
every, cada
everybody, todo el mundo
everything, todo
everywhere, por todas partes
to exaggerate, exagerar
for example, por ejemplo
excellent, excelente
except for, excepto, fuera de, a
  excepción de
to exist, existir
expenses, los gastos
extreme, extremo

F

face, la cara
factory, la fábrica
to fall, caer
to fall asleep, dormirse
fame, la fama
family, la familia
far, lejos. As far as—hasta
farm, la granja, la finca
farmer, el labrador
father, el padre
fertility, la fertilidad
few, pocos. A few—algunos
fibre, la fibra
field, el campo, el prado
fifteen, quince
fifth, quinto
to fill, llenar
film, la película
to find, hallar, encontrar
fine (weather), it is fine—hace
  buen tiempo
to finish, acabar, terminar
firm, la casa comercial, la
  compañía
first, primero
firstly, primero
fish, el pescado (commodity) ;
  el pez (individual fish)
fishing boat, la barca de pesca
five, cinco
fluently, corrientemente
fly (insect), la mosca
to follow, seguir
following, siguiente. On the following day—al día siguiente
fond of, to be fond of—ser
  aficionado a
    I am fond of oranges—me
    gustan las naranjas
    She is fond of her sister—
    quiere mucho a su hermana
foot, el pie. On foot—a pie

football, el fútbol

for, para, por; porque

This is for me—esto es para mí

to buy it for ten pesetas—comprarlo por diez pesetas

He won't go more quickly, for he's tired—no quiere andar más de prisa porque está cansado

foreigner, el extranjero

to forget, olvidar

former, aquél, el primero

to found, fundar

foundry, la fundición

four, cuatro

France, (la) Francia

freighter, el barco mercante

frequented, frecuentado

friend, el amigo, la amiga

friendly, amable, simpático

to be frightened, tener miedo; temer. To be frightened of someone—tener miedo a alguien

from, de, desde

from Madrid to Toledo—desde Madrid hasta Toledo

from time to time—de vez en cuando

frontier, la frontera

fruit, la fruta; el fruto

to eat fruit—comer frutas

the fruits of the earth—los frutos de la tierra

full of, lleno de

furious, furioso

G

Galician, (el) gallego

game (pastime), el juego

garden, el jardín (flowers); la huerta (vegetables)

generally, generalmente, por regla general

generous, generoso

gentleman, el señor, el caballero

to get, obtener, conseguir

to get into the train—subir al tren

to get out of the car—bajar del coche

to get up—levantarse

to get to Madrid—llegar a Madrid

gipsy, el gitano

girl, la niña, la muchacha

to give, dar, regalar

glass (drinking), el vaso

to go, ir

to go out—salir

to go in—entrar

to go for a walk—dar un paseo

to go for a ride—dar un paseo en coche, en bicicleta, etc.

to go away—marcharse, irse

to go to bed—acostarse

goat, la cabra

goat-herd, el cabrero

God, Dios

golden, de oro

good, bueno

grandfather, el abuelo

grape, la uva

grease, la grasa

great, grande, ilustre

Great Britain, la Gran Bretaña

greatly, mucho

to grow, crecer; cultivar

guest, el convidado

guitar, la guitarra

H

half, half an hour—media hora;
half-past one—la una y
media
hand, la mano
handkerchief, el pañuelo
harbour, el puerto
hard, duro (not soft); difícil.
To work hard—trabajar
mucho
hat, el sombrero
to have, tener (to possess);
haber (auxiliary)
to have to—tener que
to have a glass of milk—
tomar un vaso de leche
head, la cabeza
to hear, oir
to help, ayudar. I can't help
doing it—no puedo menos de
hacerlo
hen, la gallina
here, aquí; acá (hither)
historical, histórico
to hold, caber (to be able to be
contained). This box holds
fifty matches — cincuenta
cerillas caben en esta cajita
home, at home—en casa. To
go home—volver a casa
hospital, el hospital
hot, caliente, caluroso
a hot day—un día caluroso
hot water—agua caliente
to be hot—tener calor
(persons), hacer calor (weather)
hotel, el hotel
hour, la hora
house, la casa
how, cómo
How are you?—¿ Cómo
está Vd. ?

How much?—¿ Cuánto?
How many?—¿ Cuántos?
however, sin embargo; pero
hundred, ciento. A hundred
books—cien libros
to be hungry, tener hambre
husband, el marido, el esposo

I

ideal, el ideal
if, si
ill, enfermo
imagination, la imaginación
important, importante
impossible, imposible
in, en, dentro de, de, por
in the country—en el campo
in the morning—por la
mañana
at two in the afternoon—a
las dos de la tarde
the largest house in the
village—la casa más grande
de la aldea
dressed in black—vestido
de negro
in five days—dentro de
cinco días
incredible, increíble
independent, independiente
industrial, industrial
industry, la industria
inn, la venta, el mesón
innumerable, innumerable
insect, el insecto
intelligence, la inteligencia
intelligent, inteligente
to intend, pensar; tener intención de
into, en
Ireland, (la) Irlanda
iron, el hierro

J

James, Jaime
job, el empleo, la colocación (situation)
journey, el viaje
July, el julio
June, el junio
to have just, acabar de. I have just finished—acabo de terminar

K

kilo, el kilo (gramo)
kind (adj.), amable, simpático. Be so kind as to...—haga Vd. el favor de...
kind (sort), la clase. Of all kinds—de todas clases
king, el rey
kingdom, el reino
kitchen, la cocina
kitchen-garden, la huerta
to know, saber; conocer (to be acquainted with). To know how to do something—saber hacer algo

L

lad, el mozo, el muchacho
laden with, cargado de
lady, la señora, la dama
lake, el lago
lamp, la lámpara. Street lamp—el farol
land, la tierra; el país
to land, desembarcar
language, el idioma, la lengua
large, grande
last, último
    at last—por fin
    last night—anoche

late, tarde. To be ten minutes late—traer diez minutos de retraso
Latin (adj.), latino
to laugh, reir. To laugh at someone—reirse de alguien
lawyer, el abogado
to learn, aprender
to leave, dejar, abandonar; salir, partir
left, izquierdo. On the left—a la izquierda
less, menos
letter, la carta
life, la vida
light, la luz
to light, encender; alumbrar
like, como. Like (similar to)—parecido a
to like, gustar
    He likes onions—le gustan las cebollas
    I don't like smoking—no me gusta fumar
liner, el transatlántico
to link, unir
to listen, escuchar
little, pequeño
little boy, el niño, el chico, el muchacho
to live, vivir; habitar (to dwell)
London, Londres
long, largo
    a long time—mucho tiempo
    How long have you been in Madrid?—¿Cuánto tiempo lleva Vd. en Madrid?
no longer, ya no. They no longer live in Paris—ya no viven en París
to lose, perder

a lot, mucho. There were a lot of people—había mucha gente

to be in love, estar enamorado

lover, el amante, el novio, la novia

lunch, el almuerzo

to have lunch, almorzar

M

magazine, la revista

magnificent, magnífico

man, el hombre

manager, el gerente

to manufacture, fabricar

many, muchos

map, el mapa

March (month), el marzo

maritime, marítimo

market, el mercado

market place, la plaza del mercado

to get married, casarse. To marry someone—casarse con alguien

master, el maestro, el amo

match, la cerilla (wax vesta); el fósforo (wooden match)

May, el mayo

meal, la comida

meat, la carne

Mediterranean, el Mediterráneo

to meet, encontrar. To come across—dar con

melon, el melón

merchandise, las mercancías

merchant, el comerciante

Mexican, (el) mejicano

Mexico, (el) Méjico

midnight, la medianoche

millionaire, el millonario

mind, la mente

not to mind, if you don't mind

—si Vd. no tiene inconveniente

mineral (adj.), mineral

minus, menos

mistake, el error, la falta. To be mistaken—equivocarse

modern, moderno

money, el dinero

month, el mes

Moor (Arab), el moro

more, más

morning, la mañana

in the morning—por la mañana

tomorrow morning—mañana por la mañana

most, el más, lo más. Most of these apples—la mayor parte de estas manzanas

mostly, generalmente, en gran parte

mother, la madre

mountain, la montaña, el monte

mountainous, montañoso

much, much

music, la música

must, to have to—tener que, haber de, deber. He must be ill—debe de estar enfermo (supposition, not obligation)

mysterious, misterioso

N

name, el nombre

to be named, llamarse

narrow, estrecho

nation, la nación

native, el natural

native land, la patria

naturally, naturalmente

navigable, navegable

near, cerca. Near to the house —cerca de la casa

nearly, casi

neither...nor...,ni...ni... He has neither money nor friends—no tiene ni dinero ni amigos

never, nunca

new, nuevo

newspaper, el periódico, el diario

next, próximo. Next week—la semana próxima, la semana que viene

night, la noche. Good night—buenas noches

nine, nueve

nineteen, diez y nueve, diecinueve

no, no; ninguno

He has no money—no tiene dinero

no hope—ninguna esperanza

nobody, nadie

noon, el mediodía. It is noon—son las doce

north, el norte

North Sea, el mar del Norte

north-west, el noroeste

not, no

noted, ilustre, famoso, renombrado. To be noted for—distinguirse por

nothing, nada

novel (book), la novela

novelist, el novelista

now, ahora

nowadays, hoy día, en la actualidad

O

occasion, la ocasión. On many occasions—en muchas ocasiones

o'clock, it is three o'clock—son las tres

of, de

office, la oficina, el despacho

often, frecuentemente, amenudo, muchas veces

oil, el aceite

old, viejo. To be eighty years old—tener ochenta años de edad

older, mayor

old man, el viejo, el anciano

old woman, la vieja, la anciana

on, sobre, en

on Sunday—el domingo

on the seventh of May—el siete de mayo

once, una vez

at once, en seguida, inmediatamente

one, uno, una

onion, la cebolla

only, solamente, sólo

open, opened, abierto

to open, abrir; abrirse. The door opened—la puerta se abrió

or, o, u

orange, la naranja

other, otro

ought, I ought to go—yo debería (debiera) ir

over, sobre, encima. Over the door—encima de la puerta

overland, por tierra

overlook, the window overlooks the garden—la ventana da al jardín

overseas, el ultramar. Countries overseas — países de ultramar

ox, el buey

P

packet, el paquete
page (book), la página
to paint, pintar
painting, la pintura
pale, pálido. To turn pale—ponerse pálido
parents, los padres
Paris, París
part, la parte. For the most part — principalmente, en gran parte
partner, el socio
to pass, pasar. To pass the school—pasar por delante de la escuela
passenger, el pasajero (by sea), el viajero
past, el pasado. It is half-past ten—son las diez y media
patient, paciente. To be very patient — tener mucha paciencia
to pay, pagar. To pay no attention to—no hacer caso de
pear, la pera
peasant, el campesino, el aldeano
pelota, el juego de pelota
pen, la pluma
pencil, el lápiz
peninsula, la península
people, la gente; el pueblo (nation)
per, three pesetas per kilo—a tres pesetas el kilo
perfectly, perfectamente
perhaps, quizá(s), tal vez
period, la época
peseta, la peseta
picture, el cuadro

pig, el cerdo, el puerco
it is a pity, es lástima
place, el sitio, el lugar
plain, la llanura
plate, el plato
plateau, la meseta
platform (railway), el andén
to play, jugar; tocar (musical instruments)
play (theatre), la pieza, la comedia, la representación
pleasant, agradable
please, por favor. Please give me the book—hágame Vd. el favor de darme el libro, sírvase Vd. darme el libro
pleased, I am pleased to receive your letters—tengo mucho gusto en recibir sus cartas
plus, ten plus four is fourteen—diez y cuatro son catorce
point of view, el punto de vista. From this point of view—desde este punto de vista
policeman, el guardia
poor, pobre
port (harbour), el puerto
possible, posible
to prefer, preferir
to prepare, preparar
at present, ahora, actualmente, hoy día
to preserve, conservar
pretty, bonito
price, el precio. What is the price?—¿Cuánto vale?
priest, el sacerdote
process, el procedimiento
to produce, producir
to protect, proteger
to protest, protestar
province, la provincia

pupil, el alumno, la alumna
to purchase, comprar
to put, poner, meter (to put into)
    to put on one's jacket—ponerse la chaqueta
    to put on a play—echar una comedia
    to put to sea—hacerse a la mar
Pyrenees, los Pirineos

Q

quarter (district), el barrio
quay, el muelle
question, la pregunta; el problema (problem). To ask a question — hacer una pregunta
quickly, de prisa, rápidamente

R

by rail, por ferrocarril
railway, el ferrocarril
to rain, llover
rain, la lluvia
rainy, lluvioso
rapid, rápido
to reach, alcanzar, llegar a
to read, leer
real, verdadero
to realise, darse cuenta. To realise his mistake—darse cuenta de su error
reality, la realidad
really, verdaderamente, de veras
to recall, recordar, acordarse. To recall something—acordarse de algo, recordar algo

to receive, recibir
reconquest, la reconquista
reign, el reinado
to remember, acordarse. Do you remember his name? —¿ Se acuerda Vd. de su nombre ?
to remove (take away), quitar
to repeat, repetir
representation, la representación
representative, el representante
to resemble, parecerse. He resembles his mother — se parece a su madre
restaurant, el restaurant(e)
to return, volver, regresar; devolver (to pay back)
return, el regreso
rich, rico
to be right, tener razón
right, derecho. On the right hand—a la derecha
to ring up, llamar por teléfono
to rise, subir (go up) ; levantarse (get up) ; salir (of the sun)
river, el río
road, el camino, la carretera
Roman, (el) romano
room, el cuarto, la habitación. There is no room for us here—no cabemos aquí

S

sadly, tristemente
to sail, navegar. To set sail—hacerse a la mar
sailor, el marinero
same, mismo
Saragossa, Zaragoza
sardine, la sardina
to say, decir
school, la escuela

sea, el (la) mar. By sea—por mar

seaport, el puerto de mar

to be sea-sick, marearse

seated, sentado

to see, ver

to seek, buscar

to seem, parecer

to sell, vender

to send, enviar, mandar

to separate, separar

serenade, la serenata

serious, grave, serio

seriousness, lo serio

servant, el criado, la criada

service, el servicio

to set (of the sun), ponerse

to set sail, hacerse a la mar

several, unos, algunos, varios

Seville, Sevilla

sharp (time), en punto ; at ten o'clock sharp—a las diez en punto

sheep, la oveja, el carnero

shepherd, el pastor

ship, el barco, el vapor (steamer), la embarcación

shop, la tienda

to go shopping, ir de compras

side, el lado

siesta, la siesta ; to take the siesta—dormir la siesta

silently, silenciosamente

simple, sencillo, fácil

since, desde ; porque (because) ; visto que (seeing that)

sister, la hermana

to sit down, sentarse

situation, la situación

sky, el cielo

to sleep, dormir. To fall asleep —dormirse

to be sleepy, tener sueño

slowly, despacio, lentamente

small, pequeño

to snow, nevar

snow, la nieve

so many, tantos

soil, el suelo

some, unos, algunos

sometimes, algunas veces, a veces

somewhat, algo, un poco

son, el hijo

soon, pronto, dentro de poco. As soon as possible— cuanto antes, tan pronto como posible

to be sorry, sentir. I am very sorry—lo siento mucho

soup, la sopa

south, el sur, el sud. South America—la América del Sur

Sovereigns, Catholic, los reyes católicos

Spain, (la) España

Spaniard, el español

Spanish, español

to speak, hablar

to spend, pasar (time) ; gastar (money)

to spin, hilar

in spite of, a pesar de

sport, el deporte

square (place), la plaza

stamp (postage), el sello (de correo)

star, la estrella

to start, empezar, principiar (to begin) ; salir, ponerse en camino (to set out)

state, el estado. The United States—los Estados Unidos de Norteamérica

station, la estación (de ferrocarril)

to stay, permanecer, quedarse

steamer, el vapor

still (yet), todavía, aún

story, el cuento, la historia

stout, gordo

straits, el estrecho

street, la calle

street lamp, el farol

to stretch, extenderse

strong, fuerte

to study, estudiar

suburbs, las afueras

to succeed, lograr (to be successful)

such, tal; tan
    such a man—tal hombre
    such a hot day—un día tan caluroso

sum, el cálculo

summer, el verano

summit, la cumbre

sun, el sol

to be sunny, hacer sol

supper, la cena. To have supper—cenar

sure, seguro. To be sure, certain—estar seguro

to swim, nadar

T

to take, tomar; llevar (to lead)
    to take a walk—dar un paseo
    to take out—sacar, retirar

to talk, hablar, charlar

tea, el té

to teach, enseñar

teacher, el maestro de escuela, el profesor

to tell, decir

ten, diez

terribly, it is terribly hot—hace un calor tremendo

territory, el territorio

textile (adj.), textil

textiles, los tejidos

than, que, de
    he has more than I have—tiene más que yo
    he has more than twenty—tiene más de veinte

to thank, dar las gracias

thanks, gracias. Thank you very much—muchas gracias

that, que; eso, ese, ése; aquello, aquel, aquél

theatre, el teatro

then, entonces, después, luego (afterwards); pues (so)

there, allí

there is, are, hay
    there was, were—había
    there will be—habrá

thief, el ladrón

thing, la cosa

to think, pensar. To think of something—pensar en algo

third, tercero

to be thirsty, tener sed

this, esto; este; éste

thousand, mil

through, por

throughout, throughout the land—por todo el país

to throw, echar, arrojar, lanzar

ticket, el billete

time, el tiempo; la hora; la época
    a long time ago—hace mucho tiempo
    What time is it?—¿Qué hora es?
    to have an awful time—pasar las de Caín

as time went on—andando el tiempo

times, two times four—dos veces cuatro

tin, la lata. Tinned sardines —sardinas en lata

to, a, en, hasta (as far as)
    to go to Madrid—ir a Madrid
    from town to town—de ciudad en ciudad

tobacconist's, el estanco

today, hoy; hoy día (nowadays)

tomorrow, mañana. Tomorrow morning—mañana por la mañana

too, demasiado; también (also). Too tired to work—demasiado cansado para trabajar

tourist, el turista

town, la ciudad, la población

trade, el comercio

tradition, la tradición

traditional, tradicional

train, el tren

tram-car, el tranvía

to travel, viajar. To travel by air—viajar por aeroplano

traveller, el viajero; el viajante (commercial traveller)

trip, la excursión, el paseo

true, verdadero. It is true that...—es verdad que...

truth, la verdad

to try, tratar. To try to write —tratar de escribir

twelve, doce

twenty, veinte

twice, dos veces

to twinkle, centellear

two, dos

U

ugly, feo

umbrella, el paraguas

uncle, el tío

under, bajo, debajo. Under the table—debajo de la mesa

undoubtedly, sin duda

unfortunate, desgraciado, desafortunado

unfortunately, desgraciadamente, desafortunadamente

to unite, unir

united, unido

United States, los Estados Unidos de Norteamérica

universal, universal

university, la universidad

until, hasta

upstairs, arriba

up to, up to ten o'clock—hasta las diez

usually, generalmente, por regla general. He usually dines here—suele comer aquí

V

variety, la variedad

various (several), varios

vast, vasto

vegetable, la legumbre, la hortaliza

very, muy. To be very cold—tener mucho frío

vessel (ship), la embarcación, el barco

via, por. Ir por Irún—to go via Irún

village, la aldea, el lugar, el pueblecito

to visit, visitar

voice, la voz

volume (book), el tomo

W

to wait, esperar, aguardar

waiter, el camarero, el mozo

waiting-room, la sala de espera

to walk, andar, caminar, ir a pie. To go for a walk—dar un paseo

walk, el paseo, la vuelta. To go for a stroll—dar una vuelta

to want, querer, desear

war, la guerra

warm, caliente, caluroso

un día caluroso—a warm day

agua caliente — warm water

to be warm—tener calor (persons), hacer calor (weather)

to wash, lavar

to have a wash—lavarse

watchman, el vigilante, el sereno

water, el agua (f)

way, el camino; el modo (manner)

de este modo—in this way

weak, débil

to wear, llevar

weather, el tiempo

it is fine weather—hace buen tiempo

to weave, tejer

Wednesday, el miércoles

week, la semana

well, bien

as well—también

wharf, el muelle

what, qué; lo que

when, cuando, ¿ cuándo?

the day when he came—el día en que vino

where, donde, ¿ dónde?

whereas, mientras que

whether, si

which, que; ¿ qué? ¿ cuál?

whilst, mientras (que)

whilst he was speaking— mientras (que) hablaba

white, blanco

who, que, quien, ¿ quién?

whole, todo

whom, que, ¿ a quién?

whose, cuyo, ¿ de quién?

why, ¿ por qué?

wicked, malo

window, la ventana, la ventanilla (carriage)

wine, el vino

wise, sabio

to wish, desear, querer

with, con

without, sin

woman, la mujer

old woman—la vieja

wool, la lana

woollen, de lana

word, la palabra

to work, trabajar

work, el trabajo; la obra (writing, painting, etc.)

workman, el obrero, el operario

world, el mundo

wrapped in, envuelto en

to write, escribir

to be wrong, no tener razón; equivocarse (to be mistaken)

Y

yard, el corral; el patio (court-yard)

yarn (textiles), la hilaza

year, el año

yes, sí
yesterday, ayer
    the day before yesterday—
   anteayer
yet, todavía, aún

young, joven
young man, el joven
young woman, la joven
youth, el joven (young man);
    la juventud (adolescence)